"Rediscovering God's Grand St
form of discourse for conveyir
man is a rare modern example
amateur scholar. Amateur in the sense of lover and scholar
who lives comfortably and discerningly among books and ideas. If you, too, love
the same and are looking for help in understanding how the world's understanding of itself got to where it is today—and why God has been and always will be
central to that understanding—this book will be a boon companion."

—**Daniel Taylor**, Author of *Death Comes for the Deconstructionist and Do We Not Bleed?*

Rediscovering God's Grand Story

Rediscovering God's Grand Story

In a Fragmented World of Pieces and Parts

James M. Roseman

RESOURCE *Publications* · Eugene, Oregon

REDISCOVERING GOD'S GRAND STORY
In a Fragmented World of Pieces and Parts

Resource Publications
An Imprint of Wipf and Stock Publishers
199 W. 8th Ave., Suite 3
Eugene, OR 97401

www.wipfandstock.com

PAPERBACK ISBN: 978-1-5326-1798-0
HARDCOVER ISBN: 978-1-4982-4313-1
EBOOK ISBN: 978-1-4982-4312-4

Manufactured in the U.S.A.   SEPTEMBER 12, 2017

To
my wife Janet,
my father and mother, Warren and Dean,
and my whole family,
with special dedication to my brother Rick and niece Nicki

We tell stories because we desire a world with a story.

SIR MICHAEL EDWARDS

As far back as there have been human beings, there have been stories. From the bard weaving word magic around the fire, to the troubadour singing in the great hall, to the celluloid myths of the grand Hollywood mythmakers, nothing is more human than stories and storytelling. And no stories are more resonant than those that tap the deepest reservoirs of what it is to be human. But one theme is almost universal—the picture of life as a journey.

"Midway on our life's journey I found myself in a dark wood." So begins Dante's famous metaphysical adventure story, *Divine Comedy* . . . Life is a journey, a voyage, a quest, a pilgrimage, a personal odyssey, and we're all . . . between the beginning and the end of it.

OS GUINNESS, *LONG JOURNEY HOME*

The younger son gathered all he had and traveled to a distant country, and there he squandered his property in dissolute living. When he had spent everything, a severe famine took place throughout that country, and he began to be in need. . . . But when he came to himself he said, "How many of my father's hired hands have bread enough and to spare, but here I am dying of hunger! I will get up and go to my father, and I will say to him, 'Father, I have sinned against heaven and before you; I am no longer worthy to be called your son; treat me like one of your hired hands.'" So he set off and went to his father. But while he was still far off, his father saw him and was filled with compassion; he ran and put his arms around him and kissed him. Then the son said to him, "Father, I have sinned against heaven and before you; I am no longer worthy to be called your son." But the father said to his slaves, "Quickly, bring out a robe—the best one—and put it on him; put a ring on his finger and sandals on his feet. And get the fatted calf and kill it, and let us eat and celebrate; for this son of mine was dead and is alive again; he was lost and is found!" And they began to celebrate.

LUKE 11:13–25, NRSV

Contents

A Personal Note

UNLIKE MOST PEOPLE WHO write books like this one, I am not a professional academic. In my professional life, I am a businessperson. I spent the first ten years of my career as a banker, and for the last thirty years I have been in management and information technology consulting, working with and for global companies. I am now an independent consultant. But before my business career, my formal college and graduate school training was in religion, philosophy, theology, and psychology, with designs on an academic career. It was during that time I fell in love with learning and became preoccupied with the big questions of life, an outgrowth of my newfound Christian faith. My faith and this preoccupation became my avocation and have remained so ever since.

I am an elder at Highland Park Presbyterian Church in Dallas, a fellow and board member of the Lewis Tolkien Society for the Renewal of the Common Tradition in Dallas, and cofounder and former chairman of the board of the past HPPC Murray and Jeanne Johnson Theologian in Residence Institute in Dallas. I teach regularly at my church and at the Lewis Tolkien Society and occasionally lecture on topics in this book and others of interest, including "God and Human Work" and "God and Human Flourishing."

The question may arise, why would I write such a book as this? Aren't there plenty of professional academics who could do this so much better? That's fair. But if you are familiar with academic works, you will quickly notice that this book doesn't fit the normal mold. Today's academy is given primarily to advancing the knowledge base of the guild. Most scholarly works are written by scholars for scholars, not for public consumption (though they are available if one wants to pick them up and read them, as I tend to do). This book doesn't tap new springs to fill the scholarly reservoirs, but it does draw from those reservoirs to open them up to a wider world of nonacademics. I wrote this book partly because its breadth is not something today's academy encourages. The modern academy, like all modern life, is specialization focused. And this book is not that. On the other side of the coin, for most nonacademics, religious and nonreligious, many of the Disciplines brought together in this work are only ivory tower matters, properly left to the academy. We live in a cultural moment not given to reflection on deep things. Where familiarity with the Disciplines exists, even in the siloed academy, all too often the passive assumption is that they are unrelated—particularly science, the liberal arts, and religion.

So while the scholars who encounter this book may be disappointed it's too broad, the popular audience may be disappointed it's too deep. I wrote it precisely for this reason.

This book is written to three broad audiences: religiously skeptical non-believers; inquirers who have not yet believed or fully-believed but are open to the prospect (in particular to Christianity); and to Christians and others interested in understanding the Christian story. To skeptics or doubters of all things transcendent, especially God and the Christian story in particular, it offers a fresh way to look at and hopefully overcome old doubts. To inquirers, it will enable, I hope, a much broader way to understand this age-old story as God's Grand Story. To Christians, it is not parochial or a polemic for a particular denominational point of view, but rather is written to Christians of all stripes, Catholic, Orthodox, and Protestant. It does, however, take a traditional theologically orthodox point of view. In these ways, it is similar in breadth and orientation to the idea of "mere" Christianity that C. S. Lewis adopts in his book by that title. Its value for Christians, I hope, will encourage a step back and reflection on just how extraordinary the story they live in really is. Overall it should be a wider and deeper view on the Christian story than is typically found in a single short book. Its character is semi-academic, with detailed notes and references to support scholarly credibility and to enable further exploration, if desired. Having said that, however, I should hasten to say, as Lewis does in the preface of *Mere Christianity*, that despite my use and reference to many different scholarly disciplines and works, in so many ways that will be obvious to those who should know, "I [am] out of my depth in such waters: more in need of help myself than able to help others." Like Lewis, "I am a very ordinary layman of [a particular Presbyterian] denomination, not especially 'high,' nor especially 'low,' nor especially anything else."[1]

1. Lewis, *Mere Christianity*, vi.

Acknowledgments

THERE IS NOTHING GROUNDBREAKING or genuinely new in this book. However, I expect that some aspects of what is touched upon will be new to some and perhaps to many readers. What I believe might be a somewhat new experience for some readers when reading a book about God is the combination of intellectual history; science; philosophical, literary, mythical, and poetic reflections; and biblical storytelling, all brought together in a short essay. This combination is conscious and deliberate.

While this book is not groundbreaking in the scholarly or academic sense, because it is not the habit of most people to read deeply in the disciplines just mentioned and even less commonly across them, I anticipate that the particular approach I have taken to create a broad narrative across a range of scholarly disciplines to talk about the story of God offers a way of seeing age-old things in a new way. This is my goal at least, targeted primarily to astute readers who are not professional interdisciplinary scholars. My goal, therefore, is to be something of an intermediary. Anyone who chooses can access the many different sources I cite and explore the various dimensions of what I address—indeed far deeper and more fully than I do here. Less easily can one see the impact of ideas across the disciplines. Therefore, I bring together something of philosophy, the sciences, and the liberal arts to help us see a whole amid the parts. Though it may be hard to see today, as Oxford Senior Research Fellow Michael Ward says, "In Christ, poetry and philosophy have met together. Meaning and truth have kissed."[1]

Of course, to do this I am indebted to many different scholars and artists—so many I couldn't begin to list them all. But I will mention some

---

1. Ward, "How Lewis Lit the Way."

of those I have relied on most heavily and some whose counsel I have asked for and graciously received.

You will see quickly that I most prominently rely on C. S. Lewis, T. S. Eliot, and N. T Wright—Lewis in his three different roles as Oxford and Cambridge professor of Medieval & Renaissance Literature, Christian apologist, and fantasy author; Eliot for his poem *Four Quartets*; and Wright for a host of his scholarly and popular books and articles, cited throughout Appendix 2. I also rely on J. R. R. Tolkien in his relation to his friend C. S. Lewis and on G. K. Chesterton, who significantly influenced both. I also rely heavily on many Lewis scholars, including Humphrey Carpenter, Michael Ward, and Alister McGrath.

The philosophers and writers on philosophy I most rely on include Plato, Aristotle, St. Augustine, St. Thomas Aquinas, St. Bonaventure, Friedrich Nietzsche, Alasdair MacIntyre, William P. Alston, Charles Taylor (especially his book *A Secular Age*), Alvin Plantinga (particularly his book *Where the Conflict Really Lies*), Nicholas Wolterstorff (especially his book *Art in Action*), and David Bentley Hart (especially his book *The Experience of God*). Others I cite and rely on include Peter Kreeft, Roger Scruton, C. Stephen Evans, and James K. A. Smith. Those whom I have consulted as personal friends, who read and commented on different versions of the manuscript as I worked on this project, and whose insights and work I value enormously include William J. Abraham, Robert Prevost, and David K. Naugle (especially his book *Worldview: The History of a Concept*).

The scientists I cite or rely on include especially Stephen Hawking, Leonard Mlodinow, Michio Kaku, Stephen M. Barr, Francis Collins, and polymath Blaise Pascal.

The historians, intellectual historians, and those writing intellectual history I rely heavily on include especially Charles Taylor, Louis Dupré, Will and Ariel Durant, Michael Grant, Edward Grant, Thomas Cahill, Allan Bloom, James Turner, George Marsden, Mark A. Noll, Paul Johnson, Jaroslav Pelikan, Richard A. Muller, Alister McGrath, Craig M. Gay, and personal friend Michael Walker.

The sociologists, sociologists of knowledge, and anthropological historians I rely most on include Peter L Berger, Robert Bellah, Christian Smith, and Rodney Stark.

The literature, poetry, and myth scholars I rely most on include Lewis, Tolkien, Eliot, Thomas Howard, Joseph Campbell, Louise Cowan, and Daniel Taylor (who graciously read this manuscript and counseled me).

The biblical scholars and theologians I rely on the most include N. T. Wright, John H. Walton, St. Augustine, Hans Urs von Balthasar, Kevin J. Vanhoozer, Eugene H. Peterson, and James A. Patrick.

In addition, I want to thank my longtime friend Dr. Gareth Icenogle for urging me to write a book. And a special thank you goes to Jonathan L. Schindler, my invaluable copyeditor.

Beyond the scholars and artists I rely on so heavily for this book, those I rely on in even more important ways are my family. Most especially, the love of my life and wife, Janet, who read and endured my scribbles with great insight, even though this kind of thing is not her favorite reading material. I am especially grateful to my skeptic brother Rick, with whom I'm very close and have had wonderful and ongoing conversations on these matters for more than forty years, and his youngest daughter, my always-exploring niece Nicki. And I am grateful to my other brother, Bob, with whom I commiserate in our common faith, and to everyone else in my very large family. But I am preeminently grateful to my ninety-plus-year-old mom and to my dad, who bequeathed to me his inquisitive life (and who died way too young). My parents, by their marriage and actions, taught me what love is, the ultimate source of this book.

Whatever is of value in this book is due to those listed above and to many more. Whatever errors, misinterpretations, or mistakes remain are wholly and completely my own.

Introduction

"WHY WAS IT VIRTUALLY impossible not to believe in God in, say, 1500 in our Western society, while in 2000 many of us find this not only easy, but even inescapable?" Charles Taylor asks in his *A Secular Age*.[1] Of course, belief in God has not gone away, but in our day, we default to unbelief rather than to belief. Yet for many today who do still believe in God, as illustrated in the recent sociological studies *Soul Searching: The Religious and Spiritual Lives of American Teenagers* and *Souls in Transition: The Religious and Spiritual Lives of Emerging Adults*,[2] faith is a bit like a cafeteria buffet; what in the case of the teenagers Christian Smith and Melinda Lundquist Denton call "moralistic therapeutic deism." Many today tend no longer to believe in God, and for many who do, their belief is shallow. Of course, there are still many in between, believers whose theology is robust, makes good sense to them, and enables them to live in a narrative that is intelligible, has a point, and gives meaning to their lives. But whereas in the Western world of 1500 there was a common metanarrative sourced in God, one which gave meaning not only to people's individual lives but to the whole world and all of reality, today there are only discrete and fragmented stories.

This book is about rediscovering God's Grand Story, *the* story that encompasses the whole of creation and every human story. It is the overarching story that makes sense of the world and the way we experience and live in it. It is a rediscovery in two senses. First, I contend, it is a rediscovery for all of humanity because we are all a part of this story, the actual grand story of which all the signals of transcendence we encounter are an echo and all the world's great myths and religions are pale or distorted reflections.

1. Taylor, *A Secular Age*, 25.
2. See Smith and Denton, *Soul Searching*, and Smith and Snell, *Souls in Transition*.

Secondly, it is a rediscovery for the West, whose own legacy is this story but which we have in many ways discarded. It is God's Grand Story in that it encompasses the individual stories we each inhabit and the whole story of human history and the history of the world. This essay contends that though we all do in truth live in this Grand Story, in today's modern Western world the prevailing cultural predilection has become that there is no God and no grand story. This default bias is because we went on a long imaginative and intellectual journey that closed the world in such a way as to make us skeptical of God and of all things transcendent. We are left now only with small, discrete stories. Yet even within this default tendency, we still experience divine transcendence, what can be called echoes of the voice of God. The result is a kind of cognitive confusion and dissonance.

I originally titled the book "And the end of all our exploring . . . ," taken from T. S. Eliot's self-reflective poem *Four Quartets*. This phrase suggests that we in the West embarked on a long journey to the modern world and lost our way in the process. And yet, at "the end of all our exploring," we can "arrive where we started and know the place for the first time." In his great poem *The Rime of the Ancient Mariner*, Samuel Taylor Coleridge, writing in 1798, just as the journey to the modern world began in earnest in the wake of the Enlightenment, tells a similar story of how Western humanity launched upon a great journey of exploration, got caught in a great fog, and were led through it to safety by the Albatross (a symbol of the human soul and of Christ), only to become annoyed by it. We shot to kill it, but rather than merely dying, it lives on as a great and haunting weight around the neck.

The picture of a great voyage to modernity captures the conundrum of our cultural moment. Despite all the extraordinary discoveries of the modern world on the one hand, on the other hand we often find ourselves left with persisting, deep longings in the human soul that cannot be satisfied by what we've found in all our exploring. We became a skeptical lot, but the longings won't go away. How do we account for this dilemma? Is there a resolution? Might it be that, as Eliot wrote, at "the end of all our exploring," we can "arrive where we started and know the place for the first time"?

God's Grand Story is most commonly understood, as it should be, as the story of God's redemption of his people and the whole of creation. Yet it is also a way of seeing and interpreting the world that yields the best explanation. An explanation that not only makes intellectual sense of the world but also makes sense of the transcendent mysteries, the echoes of the voice of God. Because the whole of creation is a story written and told by God, it is impossible for signs of his authorship not to be present in and throughout it. Creation itself is the glaring one, along with the persisting unexplainable echoes of his presence. God's Grand Story is found in his story of redemption, and through it we find the best lens to make sense of the world, know our place and purpose in it, and satisfaction to our souls.

We rediscover this story in two parts: the first is "Resolving Modernity's Dilemma: Doubt & The Persisting Echoes of God," and the second is "The Nightingale of the Heart & the Poetry of God."

Much has been written and spoken about this topic in sermons, in popular works, and in scholarly ones. For many Christians the answer to why we don't recognize the persistent transcendent voices that call out in our hearts and in the thirsts of our souls is simple. It is human idolatry and sin, as St. Paul notes in Romans 1:20–21: "Ever since the creation of the world his eternal power and divine nature, invisible though they are, have been understood and seen through the things he has made. So they are without excuse; for though they knew God, they did not honor him as God or give thanks to him, but they became futile in their thinking, and their senseless minds were darkened. Claiming to be wise, they became fools; and they exchanged the glory of the immortal God for images resembling a mortal human being or birds or four-footed animals or reptiles" (NRSV).

While I, too, subscribe to this diagnosis as the root condition of us all, I am convinced that in the West we have complicated things and made them worse, and with great irony. The West is largely a product of the Judeo-Christian story, which is the source of the simple diagnosis. But the gauntlet of the passage to modernity that began in in the West in the late Renaissance and birthed a new world in the wake of the eighteenth-century Enlightenment changed everything. This passage has given us much, but it largely closed off the world to true transcendence, and yet we still live with deep echoes of it. This has compounded our problem, and its historical and philosophical complexity is hard to understand. Many philosophers, sociologists, and intellectual historians have sought to describe it and understand it. But unless they work in the academy, most people never see these expositions.

This conundrum of modernity in the West is intellectually important, existentially important, and spiritually important. This essay is intended to address each of these three dimensions.

In chapter 1, "Passages & Echoes," we look briefly at what passages and echoes are. The point here is that to begin to reckon with modernity and its default skepticism of all things transcendent, we must acknowledge how subtle some passages we go through are and how profoundly they affect us. The passage to modernity is like the slow, gradual change in the water temperature when a frog is placed in a cool pan of water and the heat is turned up. Eventually the frog boils to death. The death, for purposes of this illustration, is belief in God in the default consciousness of modern man that resulted from the passage from the premodern to the modern world. To use a different image, despite the change in the default consciousness, all along the way as we walk through modern life, we still persistently encounter echoes of the voice of God, bellowing like an Albatross, but we increasingly find it difficult to interpret them *as* God's voice. For a those unfamiliar I provide an expanded cursory context of the passage to modernity in the Western intellectual tradition, along with recommended resources, in Appendix 1.

In chapter 2, "Backcloth," we explore the assumptions of modernity that make us default to a world without God. We come to realize that what we think is just "the way things are" and common sense is really a particular set of glasses we wear when interpreting reality, glasses that have blind spots, born of the new metaphors and intellectual traditions of modernity.

In chapter 3, "Myth & the Prospects of a Whole," we explore how even the modern story that "what is real is only what can be proven by scientific methods" is a form of myth. I contend that all peoples in all times live in and through a kind of "myth"—not myth in the sense of an untrue legend, but myth in the sense of interpretive narrative. We see that we are all myth-makers ("mythopoetic," as J. R. R. Tolkien says). This human characteristic is itself an echo of the voice of God and has something big to tell us about reality, that our own small myths reflect that the world we all live in and our own human stories are part of a grand myth written not by us but by God. The prospect of a whole is God's Grand Story.

In chapter 4, we conclude Part 1 with "Reweaving the Tapestry: Finding the Whole in the Parts." One of the unique challenges modernity has when addressing some of the biggest questions and making sense of the most profound mysteries of reality is its prevailing cultural practice of being so analytical. To find the whole amid the parts is far less a scientific enterprise than an imaginative one. But this is not to say imagin*ary*, that is, made up or untrue. Rather, it is best illustrated in the way poetry works. The details and images of our own storied lives are, as in poems, the concrete realities of our lives, yet they echo a transcendent drama. The concreteness of creation and the specifics of world and human history have real meaning, yet that meaning is anchored beyond the mere concrete reality in God. Just as the concrete images and words of poems serve as *looking glasses*, so too do the concrete details of this world and our own stories serve as looking glasses to detect God's Grand Story of this world. The parts make up a whole, and the whole is the story of God that encompasses our personal stories.

In Part 2, "The Nightingale of the Heart & the Poetry of God," we turn to the Judeo-Christian story. We explore this story in two chapters and an appendix (Appendix 2).

For most, especially in the West, the Judeo-Christian story is familiar and straightforward—so much so, especially in our postmodern moment, that we conceive of it as just one among many other discrete, culturally formed stories from which to choose, and in doing so, we miss its full, universal scope. So we begin in chapter 5 with "The Grand Story—in the Artist's Hand," first looking at an example of how nature itself witnesses to a grand story through art as an expression of a language and vocabulary of the heart, and second by looking at a particular artist and work of art, T. S. Eliot's *Four Quartets*. Then in chapter 6, "Rediscovering the Grand Story—As a Whole," we look anew at the old familiar story, but in a simple, even childlike and poetic way to avoid getting caught in the weeds of modernist analysis, yet expounding on this in its full historical narrative form in Appendix 2 that summarizes the biblical story.

This essay tells why the story and promise of Christianity is so hard to hear today but won't go away. It is because the story and promise of Christianity is the love story of God. It is the concrete story of the world in which the echoes of the voice of God come together in symphony. It is the story of the distant longing from beyond the Grey Mountain, the call from the home that is our true home. It is the kind of water of which Jesus spoke to the woman at the well, which when drunk we never thirst again.

> And the end of all our exploring
> Will be to arrive where we started
> And know the place for the first time.[3]

---

3. Eliot, *Four Quartets*, 59.

PART 1

Resolving Modernity's Dilemma
Doubt & the Persisting Echoes of God

Day after day, day after day,

We stuck, nor breath nor motion;

As idle as a painted ship

Upon a painted ocean.

Water, water, every where,

And all the boards did shrink;

Water, water, every where,

Nor any drop to drink.

SAMUEL TAYLOR COLERIDGE,

THE RIME OF THE ANCIENT MARINER

LIKE FERDINAND MAGELLAN'S GREAT voyage in pursuit of new passages to new worlds, since the seventeenth and eighteenth centuries the Western intellectual tradition has sailed far and wide and discovered many wonderful things. But just as Magellan faced great risk navigating the treacherous waters around Cape Horn, the tumultuous intellectual waters of the modern West presented great risks too. How would we find our way?

Samuel Taylor Coleridge captures the picture well in his poem *The Rime of the Ancient Mariner.* Having been guided through the treacherous waters and early-modern fog by the Albatross (the soul), the captains of the new world became annoyed by the bird. In hubris, they killed it and hung it as a trophy around the neck, believing it a good thing that they had killed it. By the mid-twentieth century, the ship of modernism stalled. It is now adrift in a postmodern sea, bobbing like a cork with no soul to guide it.[1]

> At length did cross an Albatross,
> Through the fog it came;
> As it had been a Christian soul, We hailed it in God's name. . . .
> "God save thee, ancient Mariner!
> From the fiends that plague thee thus!—
> Why look'st thou so?"—With my cross-bow
> I shot the ALBATROSS.[2]

In a huge ocean of uncharted intellectual waters, the winds no longer fill the sails. Down in the ship's modern navigation room we plot new courses with greater and greater confidence; at chow in the galley we constantly ruminate over whether what we say is anything but self-talk. Up on deck we stare blankly across the horizon, adrift on the still waters, no land in sight. "Water, water every where, . . . Nor any drop to drink," wrote Coleridge in the late eighteenth century near the formal end of the Enlightenment project. Coleridge's poems, and those of his close friend William Wordsworth, mark the birth of Romanticism in English poetry that was a reaction to the ideas that became prevalent during the Enlightenment. The Romantic movement and this best known of Coleridge's poems highlight a blindness that occurs when secondary things are made primary. The voyage to the modern world discovered great things and filled us with hubris only to leave us thirsty.

As the Western ship of progress sailed forward into the unknown, led by its intellectual captains, the modern world became disenchanted and sanitized of the transcendent and the soul became mere neurology. In the postmodern world, everything is either nothingness or anything we want it to be. As with

---

1. For references that address this reality, see Lewis, *The Abolition of Man,* and a fictionalized version of the same story, *That Hideous Strength*; a detailed intellectual history by Dupré, *Passage to Modernity*; Marsden, *Twilight of the American Enlightenment*; and Jenson, "How the World Lost Its Story."

2. Coleridge, *Poems,* 24.

Coleridge's captain, having killed the soul, we carry an Albatross around our necks. But for some reason the bird won't completely die. Try as we might to empty everything of transcendence, we remain captivated and enchanted by unexplainable wonders of the world and perplexed by the persistent desires of our deepest longings that won't go away. Echoes of the voice of God continue to reverberate,[3] but in today's modern Western world we are inclined to ignore them altogether or to hear them as merely white noise. Our culture of doubt surrounded by echoes of God leaves us with cognitive dissonance.

In the introduction, I began with Charles Taylor's profound question: "Why was it virtually impossible not to believe in God in, say, 1500 in our Western society, while in 2000 many of us find this not only easy, but even inescapable?" Though belief in God still remains prominent among many in the West, particularly in America,[4] Taylor goes on to say that in the secular age, the conditions of belief have changed. In our modern age the conditions default to unbelief, whereas in the premodern world the conditions defaulted to belief. In the modern world, we're inclined not to believe whereas in the old world virtually everyone was inclined to believe. In modern conditions, skepticism is easy, yet we must still confront the perplexities of the persisting echoes of God. Belief is hard in these conditions, even if warranted in virtue of being a properly basic belief[5] (i.e., not arrived at through a rigorous intellectual exercise, which is most believers), because believers must struggle to make sense of their belief. Whether skeptic or believer, Taylor's question remains important. If there is a Grand Story written by God, the skeptic must overcome today's prevailing conditions of unbelief, and the believer must live in these conditions and avoid becoming either a practical atheist[6] or a moralistic therapeutic deist.[7]

3. Examples of these echoes are described in a sociological study as "signals of transcendence," in Berger, *Rumor of Angels,* and in philosophical terms as "natural signs," in Evans, *Natural Signs and Knowledge of God.*

4. See Pew, "Belief in God." *Pew Research Center: Religion in Public Life,* online at pewforum.org/religious-landscape-study/belief-in-god. It should be noted that despite the shift to a default to unbelief in the West, in what has been recently termed the "Global South," not only is belief in God prevalent, but the embrace of the Christian faith is exploding. For a record of this phenomenon, see Noll, *From Every Tribe and Nation.*

5. See Plantinga, *Warranted Christian Belief* or *Knowledge and Christian Belief;* and Wolterstorff, *Reason within the Bounds of Religion.*

6. This term has been around for a while. It basically means living as if God doesn't exist, even though one professes to believe in God. Though not focused on the term, an excellent exposition of the idea is Gay, *Way of the Modern World.*

7. Smith and Denton, *Soul Searching,* 162–70. A summary of Moralistic Therapeutic Deism is God exists, orders the world, and watches over human life on earth; God wants people to be good and fair to each other; the central goal of life is to be happy and to feel good about oneself; God does not need to be particularly involved in one's life

In a review comment on Taylor's book, the *London Review of Books* makes clear that Taylor is not suggesting "the modern age is not an age without religion; instead, secularization heralds a move from a society where belief in God is unchallenged and indeed, unproblematic, to one in which it is understood to be one option among others."[8] The difference between the premodern world and the modern is the way we experience the world, what Wilfred McClay, reviewing Taylor's book, says is our "prelogical, prelinguistic apparatus."[9] Unlike the traditional, straight-line subtraction argument for secularization, Taylor argues that the West didn't simply become secular once God was removed by natural science (e.g., as Marx, Freud, Weber, and Durkheim suggest) and everyone was set free to live in a world of neutral facts in their native states, in effect as naturalists (e.g., as Hobbes, Hume, Goethe, and Rousseau suggest). No, it's not a *subtraction* thesis but a *replacement* thesis. The new world was invented but not easily, not quickly, and not obviously. The conditions of lived experience changed over a long time and in subtle ways, replacing one way of experiencing the world with another one—from a world where everything had a purpose and a meaning given it by its transcendent order found in God, in which order our identity and meaning resides and where our ultimate fulfillment is found only in God; to a world of random purposelessness and facticity,[10] an infinite array of individualized choices through which we accumulate experiences, identities, and existential moments of meaning and where the best hope of a fulfilling human life comes from maximized capacities and minimalized constraints to do as we please.

The great journey from the old, premodern world to the new, modern one has enabled great insight and the understanding of many things and has given rise to new ways to harness the power of the world to provide relief from the physical burdens of life. But with this new insight came a new kind of blindness, an inability to interpret the persisting mysteries in the world—which mysteries are wrapped in the age-old question about a reality transcendent to the physical reality and whether we can know anything about it. In this kind of world, when confronted with those who continue to

---

except when God is needed to resolve a problem; and good people go to heaven when they die (162–63).

8. See "Secular Age."

9. McClay, "Uncomfortable Belief."

10. "Facticity" is used here intentionally to cover the variety of historical and contemporary meanings: e.g., facts and factuality as found in positivism; of that which cannot be explained; or existent only in an idea; or Martin Heidegger's idea of "thrownness" of existence; or the existentialist idea of the background against which freedom operates; or Continental philosophy's use to describe the impossibility of determining any ground for existence.

believe, if not actually at least culturally, as modernists we treat that belief as an irrational relic of the past, to be dismissed as if it is premodern and thus without intellectual credibility, or as postmodernists we tacitly give an "okay" nod to such belief but only as cultural identity monikers or for personal therapeutic purposes and meaning-making, not as something real that we must contend with.

With today's cultural predisposition that the present is always superior to the past, we readily dismiss the possibility that in the course of the journey to the modern world, there are things we discarded that can make better sense of the world than how we see it today. With a bit of historical perspective, we can see that even today the same phenomena that gave rise to earlier ways of seeing the world have not gone away but have merely been pushed into the background. We can uncover fundamental ways of seeing that offer a fuller, more robust explanation of the persisting echoes.

We cannot, as the old saying goes, put the old-world genie back in the new-world bottle, nor would anyone truly want to. But not ceasing to explore, we can "at the end of all our exploring arrive where we started and know the place for the first time." To do so, we must become attuned to key losses incurred in the passage to the new world and overcome our prejudice against the old world. We must reckon with the fact that on our long journey of discovery, we shrank, flattened, and splintered the world into fragments so that we no longer see things whole. We reduced the meaning of reason and closed the world to nature only and eliminated all things transcendent.

Like the captain with the Albatross, though we may declare with Nietzsche, "God is dead, and we killed him," we find that God doesn't die so easily or completely. Despite our new intellectual prowess, we remain thirsty. The echoes still ring out, and we sympathize with the character Knight in Ingmar Bergman's cinematic classic *The Seventh Seal* as he intones, "Why can't I kill God within me? Why does he live on in this painful and humiliating way even though I curse him and want to tear him out of my heart? Why, in spite of everything, is he a baffling reality that I can't shake off?"[11] Like the Romantics, deep in our souls we seem just to know that there is more than our abstract rationalism and science can deliver, but we cannot see it. The journey to the new world left us stricken with intellectual macular degeneration. We see only pieces and parts. We need a more robust explanatory model. In hopes of satisfying of our souls, we must begin to see things whole.

Part 1 addresses the intellectual inadequacies of the modern outlook that have led to skepticism of all things transcendent and why theism, particularly Christian theism and the Christian story, and discarded elements

11. Kreeft, *Heaven*, 52–53.

of the premodern outlook provide a much better way to make sense of the world. In chapter 1 we will look at key "passages" that occurred over a long time from the premodern to the modern world that led to a culture of doubt and yet how persisting echoes of transcendence leave us unsatisfied with our doubt. (For a broader context on the passage to the modern world, I provide brief expanded comments on the premodern Western intellectual tradition in appendix 1.) In chapter 2, we will consider our "backcloth," those rarely talked about background assumptions about reality—what Wifred McClay calls the prelogical, prelinguistic apparatus—that cause us to experience the world the way we do and that today lead us to conclude that belief in transcendence and God is irrational. Through five examples, we see that not only is this conclusion untrue but also that buried in our backcloth are unasked questions and answers that reflect the story of the world as God's story. In chapter 3 we will come to see that it is erroneous to think that only the premodern world experienced reality through myths but that all cultures in all times do—indeed, each one of us does—and that, as we recognize this, we will see the possibility that the world we all live in, including nature itself, is a kind of myth written by God himself. This will position us to see things whole. Since we live today in such an analytical world of pieces and parts, in chapter 4 we will begin to reweave the tapestry of reality to find the whole amid the parts.

Now to the passages from the premodern to the modern world, thought to be humanity's great march out of a cave of shadows, and the echoes of the voice of God that leave us perplexed.

1

Passages & Echoes

I WAS STANDING IN a galley of the Lufthansa 747 watching the little airplane icon on the screen chart the arc of our path directly over Istanbul, the old see of the Eastern Roman Empire, as I called my wife, Janet, from the air phone. Having spent just one night on a bare mattress on the floor of our new home after eight hard weeks in a hotel in Philadelphia, I was back on a plane for fourteen hours. When she heard my voice, Janet immediately burst into tears and continued to cry while directing the movers not to drop the glass dining tabletop. She missed me and I missed her. I had left her with a big mess of house moving work to get through on her own. I felt deep regret. I arrived back in Philly ten days later, and after another week at the hotel, I caught another flight back home—home for Christmas. Exhausted and yet invigorated with the prospect of home and to try and get my head right for Christmas, I got out my laptop and started to write my annual Christmas reflection.

Hallowed Terminal

The wheels roll rapidly down the corridor.
Clicking sounds echo off the polished pageantry of the contrived comfort.
They fade, drowning in a sea of flesh and fancy—people running, walking, waiting, talking.
Many moods meld in a modern maze of mice and men:
> the trip to bountiful
> the trip to kin

7

the trip to heaven
the trip to zen
the trip to begin again, and
the trip just begins again.

In the hallowed hall, jet-ways beckon as if wormholes weaving worlds apart.

Like God's voice it's hard to hear, the clarity of departure noise is muffled, almost silenced by the clatter of the crowd.

Listen, listen—that's the key to hear the voice meant for me.

Dreams aplenty await the ears of those who sift the sounds.

Eyes widen and weep, arms open and reach, hearts leap and lay 'lorn in the coming and going.

Passenger, purser, captain, crew
Pager, chauffeur, waiter, wife

—to each the other is a dream in wonderland, their longing for home, to be together again.

O Hallowed Terminal, be my beginning and my end. Alpha and omega be, doorway to my dreams and my gateway home. Be my place of beginning and to begin again.

Relax, my heart, and listen lest the cacophony of Christmas crowd make me miss my flight.

It's not much of a poem but it captures my sentiments that Christmas—and, I imagine, the sentiments of many wandering through airports across the world, especially in the frenetic United States at Christmastime. And the scene does capture a bit of the contemporary human situation, especially (with great irony) in the West. The airport at Christmastime is a kind of world we experience. The focus of the travelers is almost exclusively horizontal, keeping track of their kids, making sure they have their bags, checking their boarding passes, looking at the flight screens and gates, and moving from one to another to make sure they catch their flight. At the same time, there is another reality operating in, through, and around them all the time, glimpses of which they see in signs and signals and voices echoing in the background—a kind of transcendent world, always there yet unnoticed without intense concentration. Like the muffled, muted sounds of departure announcements amid the cacophonous noise of the airport at Christmastime, in the real world transcendent echoes persist all around, perplexities grand and mysterious, simple and profound. Amid the sounds bouncing all around, having traversed through passages to a modern culture of doubt, distracted by the hustle and bustle of life today, we dismiss them.

Yet despite our horizontal focus the echoes of transcendence persist, if only as background noise. Hearing them, even if only faintly, creates modernity's dilemma born of cognitive confusion and dissonance. Our present way of experiencing the world cannot account for what our modern conditions of unbelief say should no longer be there but still is.

Unceasing in our exploration, we will now explore key passages from the premodern to the modern world and perhaps discover doubts about our doubtfulness that will prepare us to hear the echoes of transcendence and understand why our great voyage leaves us thirsty despite there being water all around.

PASSAGES: THE PAST AS PROLOGUE

What are passages? Some are long, narrow spaces that connect one place to another or that people or things move through. Others are passages from one place or state of being to another.

The first kind we're usually very aware of, such as when we experience the narrowing, almost claustrophobic feelings when walking through the crevasses of the slot canyons in Utah or driving through the majestic box canyon in Ouray, Colorado. Or we see this kind illustrated when Lucy steps through the armoire in C. S. Lewis's *The Lion, the Witch and the Wardrobe* and like the mirror Lewis Carroll's Alice goes through in *Through the Looking-Glass*. These passages we are fully aware of. So too when Magellan navigates Cape Horn and the Captain navigates the fog in Coleridge's poem. Such passages can break open to new vistas and whole new worlds. We have seen many of these as we moved from the premodern to the modern world, as reflected in the Age of Discovery, the time of extensive European overseas exploration between the fifteenth and eighteenth centuries, and in the Scientific Revolution. Such narrow passages are not always and only fortunate. They can also lead to deep, dark caverns in which one can become trapped, lost, or imprisoned, closed off to greater realities. We have seen both new vistas and imprisonment in the narrow, exploratory passages to the modern world.

The other passages, where we move from "one place or state of being to another," are often much subtler—changes that occur *to us* or *within us,* often unawares. As we go through them, they change the way we experience and live in the world. This notion of passage is intrinsically metaphorical—like rites of passage from childhood to adulthood. We may mark them, as with a Bar Mitzvah, but the actual passage from one state of being to another is elusive. As we travel through them, for example, like changes in the state of being, living, or seeing and interpreting the world we live in, they are frequently subtle and unnoticeable until the passage has occurred and we look back.

This is the kind of passage that marks the transition from the classical to the medieval to the modern world. Without a historical perspective, it is easy to assume that where we've arrived now simply must be the most advanced and the wisest age and that all past periods by comparison are naive or childish. This is a particularly entrenched habit of mind today, especially about the ancient past. The prevailing modern view of the premodern world is that it was naive, simpleminded, and just ignorant. A common but debilitating practice issuing from the modern and postmodern narratives is a rejection of the past. The modern habit "adores today, worships tomorrow, disavows yesterday, and loathes antiquity."[1] This limits self-understanding and masks unjustified prejudice. We cannot understand our own moment and prejudices unless we understand some key historical, intellectual, and cultural events—*passages*—that occurred over a long time and see the consequences that contribute to today's conditions of unbelief and unwarranted skepticism.

Today we imagine that the modern world began when it passed from the age of faith to the age of reason. We believe erroneously that the age of reason began when the Renaissance returned to the classical period and came into its fullness with the rise of science and the Enlightenment. With little consideration otherwise, we believe erroneously that a natural casualty of the rise of reason and science is the loss of transcendent reality and therefore that faith and religion must be irrational.

To disabuse ourselves of the view that the premodern world was naive, simpleminded, and ignorant, whereas the modern world is sophisticated, learned, and rational, we must look back. We must see the past as prologue. As we do, we will be able to see that the loss of transcendence that occurred in the voyage to the modern world both is unnecessary and leaves us with less explanatory power and that faith and reason are not in conflict.

The Western world we currently know grew out of the soil of the ancient classical philosophical and Judeo-Christian religious traditions. To understand ourselves today, we need a sense of the past and previous passages from one age to another. This sense allows us to see how dramatic the passage to the modern world has affected us. As Craig Gay cautions, "Simply returning to the classical . . . orthodoxies of the eighteenth, nineteenth, or early twentieth centuries" is not sufficient. "We . . . need to follow the . . . tradition back to the onset of modernity, and perhaps back even further, to

1. Oden, *After Modernity*, 43.

recover . . . resources adequate to the task."[2] The age of reason did not begin with the Renaissance, the Scientific Revolution, and the Enlightenment. Reason and rationality did not emerge in the West *only after* discarding the primitive superstitions of religion and overcoming the authoritarianism of the church. Reason and rationality have deep roots and extend far wider than just to science, empirical proof, and rationalism. Reason and rationality are fundamental parts of the human enterprise. But they did become more sophisticated, especially in the West, with the emergence of the Greek and Roman cultures. The roots of Western rationality are found in this ancient classical world. Christianity didn't simply jump into the historical story, nor did it emerge simply because the Roman emperor Constantine legalized it in the fourth century. It was born into the ancient classical world, and Christian thinkers took the great intellectual culture of the Greco-Roman world and transformed it in the light of the gospel. They formed an integrated, coherent intellectual and cultural outlook that is the foundation of Western civilization. Christianity and the church were not power-hungry authoritarian inhibitors to rational progress and science. The science so prized today grew from and in the soil of Christianity. (See appendix 1 for an additional short explanation of this history and for further references.)

The passages from the ancient classical world to the medieval world laid the foundation for how we conceive civilization, and the foundations of what we think of as reason and rationality were laid during these periods. Such passages don't occur quickly but slow and subtly, as did the passage to modernity. In and through each such passage we experience a change in the state of being—in the way we live and experience the world.

Our relative unconsciousness of these subtler kinds of passages is due to the slowness of them over time, like the frog who starts in a cool pot of water, is left to its own sense of comfort in the gradually heating water, and winds up boiling to death. In another sense, as in the great modern voyage since the Enlightenment, the increased velocity of the changes contributes to our unawareness of the passage.

For example, notice how, though the intellectual, social, and technological world was dramatically changing in the eighteenth and nineteenth centuries, the world of daily life and the common outlook remained significantly unaffected for a long time. The subtlety hides our awareness of the change until something awakens us to it. In the late nineteenth and all during the twentieth century, and especially now in the twenty-first century, the velocity of change has accelerated. When the velocity of change accelerates and the order of magnitude is big, cataclysmic eruptions in our

2. Gay, *Way of the Modern World*, 266.

worldview may occur that we take notice of if only with a sense of vertigo. High-velocity changes are hugely disruptive and disorienting. Consider the Guns of August that began World War I in 1914 and how the whole world changed around this time.

Before WWI, there was an extraordinary culture-wide sense of optimism—the notion of unceasing progress forward and the betterment of man was in the water everywhere. Political, economic, and technological progress had ostensibly shown unwavering signs of positive progress forward during the 19th century. With this came a strong and building sense of power, how the new ideas of the science and the Enlightenment were being deployed to control nature and set up systems for the common good. Despite problems that resulted from industrialization, we believed we could apply science to social problems through politics, such as when Marx criticized labor as capital and he designed a social "system" to solve for this using Hegel's idea of the dialectic. The optimism of constant progress, systems and models carried into the 20th century with a high spirit—until 1914. Suddenly, everything changed immediately. This is poignantly noticed in art, in virtually all forms but particularly notably in poetry, as reflected in T. S. Eliot's The Waste Land and William B. Yeats' The Second Coming. Just after the war in 1921, Yeats expresses the disequilibrium everyone felt, the sense that everything is going faster and faster, chaos has been loosed upon the world, and everything is spinning out of control. The world cannot hold together. "The best lack all conviction, while the worst/Are full of passionate intensity."[3]

This I refer to as the Downton Abbey Effect. The TV series Downton Abbey opens in the year 1912 with the sinking of the unsinkable Titanic. It is a portent, a symbol of how the world is changing. The extraordinary optimism of Southampton, and the whole world at the time, gives way to chaos in the cold North Atlantic waters 375 miles south of Newfoundland. This event is only the beginning.

Before long the docile dream of life as it had been known begins to break apart. Not all the change is bad. Indeed, most today are deeply sympathetic toward and attracted to many of the changes in the drama. But there's sympathy for the Earl of Grantham, too. The ground is shifting under his feet, and he can't make sense of it. The high order of magnitude and increasing speed of the change is disorienting. Everyone watching notices this.

As the velocity of change in our day increases—for example, the rapid pace of technological and social change—though everyone reacts to it, it is often hard to a make sense of the import of the changes.

3. Yeats, The Poems, "The Second Coming," 187.

Consider, for example, the difference between social changes, like recent changes in marriage laws, and intellectual changes and the changes that led to the default inclination of a culture to believe in God or not. We definitely noticed the changes in marital laws, but the velocity of the change itself caught almost everyone off guard. How could the change have happened so fast?[4] But the change in the default position on belief in God was much subtler and less noticeable because it was slower in coming and tied more with the shift in the prevailing intellectual climate and the prevailing metaphor of nature and the cosmos (i.e., alive, integrally organic, hierarchical, and geocentric versus largely inanimate, law driven, mechanical, and heliocentric—we'll come back to this in chapter 2). The starkness of this change is not immediate, as with the rapid change in marital laws, but it is arresting when compared between epochs, as reflected in the opening question posed by Charles Taylor.

The effects of these passages are sometimes subtle acclimation like frogs in a pot and at other times jarring like a shift in tectonic plates. In both cases, we are left with feelings of vertigo and disequilibrium when we look back on the passage.

For over three hundred years now the Western world has been traversing a variety of high-impact passages of the kind that are moving from one way of being, living, and seeing and interpreting the world to another. Many of them have been subtle, with long gestation periods as far as the broad culture is concerned, and largely unnoticed until public intellectual, social, and political crises erupt.[5] The residual effect has formed the modernist interpretive model, or backcloth, resulting in a narrowing and closing of the cultural mind-set to all things transcendent.

Some interpret these passages as progress, some as the loss of the soul. Our perspective is largely determined by the passages themselves, our awareness of them, and how we interpret their importance. But even if they are deemed the common good of modern progress, these passages have left us in a dilemma. As in Coleridge's poem of the captain and the Albatross, the soul still cries out.

4. In August 2005 60 percent of the US populace believed marriage between same-sex couples to be wrong, whereas in May 2015 it was the reverse: 60 percent believed it to be right. See Gallup, "Marriage."

5. Consider, for example, the changes in the intellectual landscape of America in the 1950s that preceded the 1960s and '70s social revolution, as described in Marsden, *Twilight of the American Enlightenment*, 43–95.

ECHOES OF THE VOICE OF GOD

Now, just a few comments about the persisting echoes. Echoes are interesting things. If you look in the dictionary, there are typically three specific meanings. In the first and most dominant sense an echo conjures the image of a reverberating sound in a canyon whose source and origination are not immediately clear. In this sense echoes are phenomena, things that we encounter, can observe, and even can research and study to analyze and discover where they come from, most often resolving their mystery. In a second sense an echo is a sound that was once prominent but is increasingly diminishing amid competing sounds. In this sense echoes are hard to hear without greater and greater concentration. We often mean by this sense that echoes are all around us all the time but are the remnants of sounds that now make up part of the "white noise" of everyday life—sounds that few but specialists pay attention to, and when the specialists do pay attention, it is to break the sounds apart and analyze them in their pieces and parts. In a third sense an echo is something like a persistent still, small voice, something that when we hear it, it rings loud and clear, but only as an internal resonance at a profound and deep level. An echo of this sort means something that strikes a chord deep inside—like a word spoken just to us, a kind of discourse or disclosure. Or, perhaps more apt but more elusive, this sense of an echo is like a distant longing or desire that, upon encountering the source, finds its true satisfaction, its place of rest. Each definition of an echo captures a sense of a presence among us, and around us, reverberating in our surroundings and within us, yet at the same time it is sourced beyond us.

As at the airport at Christmastime, in everyday life we encounter a host of these echoes, some like the mere bouncing sounds within a narrow canyon, others faint remnants of things we recognize but have a hard time making sense of without intense concentration. Some are like latent memories from a bygone era that still resonate but we hardly know why. Some are what might be called natural signs of transcendence, such as the sense of cosmic wonder spurred in us by the world, especially the beauty we encounter in and through it; nature's order and predictability; a deep sense of responsibility (that we are responders to something) and of an innate human dignity; and a persistent sense that something is wrong with the way things are and yet that hope springs eternal.[6] These might be called anchors of the human story, the constant fodder of the arts and literature. Others might be termed hauntings, mysterious yet routine encounters beyond the veil that are just taken for granted, such as human play, humor,

---

6. And, of course, there are the persisting questions of "being" that were so much a focus in the premodern world, which we'll turn to again in chapter 2.

music, the resonance with true otherness seemingly present in the human body (particularly faces), romance, and the sheer story-ness and adventure of life.[7] Embedded in each of these mysteries are the questions *what* and *why*. Through these and others there seems a deep echo of longing, like the longing for "home," a beckoning echoed in our longing for the comfort and satisfaction of our own home when we've been away. But more than this, it is a transcendent longing from a far-off place, as depicted in the following exchange between sisters Psyche and Orual in C. S. Lewis's novel *Till We Have Faces*.

At a meeting of the two sisters, Psyche shares a deeply held secret with her sister Orual, one that not only reflects Psyche's longing but captures Orual's own longings as well—indeed a universal longing of the human soul.[8]

> "I've always—at least, ever since I can remember—had a kind of longing for death."
>
> "Ah, Psyche," I said, "have I made you so little happy as that?"
>
> "No, no, no," she said. "You don't understand. Not that kind of longing. It was when I was happiest that I longed most. It was on happy days when we were up there on the hills, the three of us, with the wind and the sunshine . . . where you couldn't see Glome or the palace. Do you remember? The colour and the smell, and the looking across the Grey Mountain in the distance? And because it was so beautiful, it set me longing, always longing. Somewhere else there must be more of it. Everything seemed to be saying, Psyche come! But I couldn't (not yet) come and I didn't know where I was to come to. It almost hurt me. I felt like a bird in a cage when the other birds of its kind are flying home."[9]

If only momentarily or occasionally, almost everyone experiences this sense of longing, a kind of beckoning from a voice we have not yet fully heard to a place we have not yet fully known, yet with a clear sense that somewhere there is a true home—a home of which our longing for home at Christmastime is an echo. The persistent mysteries, the big questions, and our deep sense of longing are signposts along the journey, signals of

---

7. For an exploration of some of these, see Evans, *Natural Signs and Knowledge of God*; Berger, *Rumor of Angels*; Bellah, *Religion in Human Evolution*, and comments and critiques on this work in Reno and McClay, *Religion and the Social Sciences*; Scruton, *Soul of the World* and *Face of God*; Esolen, "Humor on the Move"; Begbie, *Resounding Truth*; Webb, *Divine Voice*.

8. See Arnell, "On Beauty, Justice, and the Sublime," 25.

9. Lewis, *Till We Have Faces*, 74. (Thanks to Peter Kreeft for this reference in his *Heaven: The Heart's Deepest Longing*.)

transcendence, echoes heard in the language and vocabulary of the human heart.

These I call echoes of the voice of God. When we stop and really reflect on them, we see how truly unexplainable they are apart from God—from the most pedestrian kind to the most haunting. The passages we go through don't make transcendent echoes suddenly appear or disappear. These echoes reverberate all around us all the time. Yet though they are constant, their source *as* the voice of God often eludes us, especially these days. We easily brush them off like momentary cold shivers in the middle of summertime. We may admit that in times past the persistent echoes were called the voice of God. We may say that in the past the echoes seemed louder, more prominent, or at least more easily recognized. But in our time, we explain them away. We easily dismiss them as relics of a bygone era, naive remnants of a less mature time. Yet these echoes remain, if only in the background, as unasked questions and as themes in our stories, art, literature, movies, and even our politics, science, and economics. They are still there, but for us "mature moderns," they are absorbed as cultural white noise.

But on occasion, if allowed, when staring out of a quiet cabin window into the dark twinkling sky on a sleepless night over the Adriatic, we can still be awakened to the resonant longing deep within us: the call home from beyond the Grey Mountain.

Having gone through the passage from the premodern to the modern way of seeing and interpreting the world, our new way of living inhibits us from hearing the persistent echoes as the voice of God. The subtleties of the passage to modernity give the illusion of enlightenment with little notice to how this passage has imprisoned us in a new cave of shadows. This reality is hidden in the modern backcloth.

2

Backcloth

WHAT IS MEANT BY the term *backcloth*? It was coined by C. S. Lewis in his last book, *The Discarded Image* (1964). The backcloth is a largely unconscious milieu that affects the way we see and interpret our world—for Lewis's purposes, particularly the arts. Here's how he describes it:

> In every period the Model of the Universe which is accepted by the great thinkers helps to provide what we may call a backcloth for the arts. But this backcloth is highly selective. It takes over from the total Model only what is intelligible to a layman and only what makes some appeal to imagination and emotion. Thus our own backcloth contains plenty of Freud and little of Einstein. . . . [And] the backcloth [doesn't] always respond very quickly to great changes in the scientific and philosophical level.
>
> Furthermore, and apart from actual omissions in the backcloth version of the Model, there will usually be a difference of another kind. We may call it a difference of status. The great masters do not take any Model quite so seriously as the rest of us. They know that it is, after all, only a model, possibly replaceable.
>
> The business of the natural philosopher is to construct theories which will "save appearances." . . . A scientific theory must "save" or "preserve" the appearances, the phenomena, it deals with, in the sense of getting them all in, doing justice to them.[1]

Lewis is best known as a Christian apologist and a fantasy writer, but his day job was as a professor, initially of philosophy and later of English at Magdalen College, Oxford, and from 1954 onward as Chair and Professor of Medieval and Renaissance Literature at Magdalen College, Cambridge

1. Lewis, *Discarded Image*, 14.

University.[2] It is in his role at Cambridge that he wrote *The Discarded Image*. In it he explains how necessary it is to understand the overall "model" of the premodern Medieval and Renaissance literary writers to interpret their work. By model he means their prevailing Aristotelian and Ptolemaic cosmological outlook compared to the later modern Newtonian and Einsteinian outlooks. His notion of "backcloth" is related not to the scientist's use of model but to the layman's[3] incorporation of the model as a worldview lens to interpret his world. That is, the layman's outlook is not precise but is the background of his day-to-day imaginative outlook. It takes a long time for changes in a given model to take effect in the culture at large. Further, he explains, the great scientists recognize that their models are constructs, used for a specific purpose. The models scientists develop provide a frame into which to fit what has been discovered. The goal of the model is to allow the scientist to "save appearances," Lewis says, by which he means that the model is chosen in the belief that it can hold or accommodate all that has been discovered within the scope. The models are always metaphorical, images. Today we more commonly call them "theoretical models." If a theoretical model cannot hold enough of the pieces, the model is changed; the *image* is changed. But because the layman does not use the model for scientific purposes, he is shaken when the model changes. But he doesn't accept the change fast. Once accepted, though, the new model becomes his lived experience. It becomes his broad interpretive frame of reference, even though the new model is still just a model.

The average businessperson sees this notion at work every day, and all managers know how hard it is to get a handle on and change once it becomes "lived experience." We see the idea expressed regularly in business when we talk about business models, operating models, process models, and so on. And in the world of business, particularly consulting (the field I'm in), we observe the change effect of such models in new business or operating models, organizational change models, disruptive trends, and so on. Because the world of commerce and business has been in a state of dramatic change for a long time, especially since the First Industrial Revolution (c. 1760–1820), through the Second Industrial Revolution (c. 1870–1920), and since then the Scientific and Information Technology & Telecommunications Revolutions (mid twentieth century through today), it has largely constructed its own mental model and measured its success against change-as-such. Today we even chart the change cycles on graphs and correlate them with other

2. For an excellent recent biography of Lewis, see McGrath, *C. S. Lewis—A Life*, particularly "Part 2: Oxford" and "Part 4: Cambridge."

3. My use of traditional gender language in this essay is for ease of reading and is not intended as patriarchal.

cycles such as the grief cycle, the technology hype cycle, the innovation cycle, and the organization and process change management cycles.

But the order of magnitude of the change Lewis describes in *The Discarded Image* is far more fundamental. It's a shift in the core mental model associated with the prevailing cosmological metaphor used by the culture at large to interpret the world. Lewis charts the shift from the premodern, heavily alive, and organic Aristotelian/Ptolemaic earth-centered cosmological model to the modern Baconian/Newtonian "law-driven," "mechanical," Copernican sun-centered cosmological model. What Lewis shows is how much the prevailing cosmological model affects the lived experience of culture, as exemplified particularly in the art and literature of the culture. The lived-experience nature of the prevailing model shows how deeply embedded the model becomes. It affects the total cultural outlook. This is why it takes so long for a new model to be accepted, even well after the scientific theory has changed.

Notice Lewis's comment about how such models are recognized as models by the "great masters" who develop them but how, once they are absorbed in broader culture, they no longer are recognized as-models. Once the model is absorbed into the culture at large, it is no longer functioning as a model. It is perceived simply as "the way things are." As Robert Holyer comments on Lewis's observation, the "scientific metaphors more easily become fossilized: we quite quickly forget that they are metaphors and assume they are literal."[4]

I use the example of how the prevailing cosmological model affects the lived-experience of culture to show how constructs designed for a specific narrow focus, like scientific models, can and do wind up forming and shaping a culture's lens for interpreting reality as a whole. And how once absorbed into the culture's backcloth, how easily we come to assume our interpretive lens is simply "the way things are." This is where we are today, but not just with the change in the cosmological model. There were so many philosophical changes as we moved through the Enlightenment passage into the modern world that the prevailing modernist cultural outlook came to hold that if something cannot be proven by the modern scientific methodology, it simply doesn't exist. This is the prevailing intellectual model of modernity. The question is, does this model allow us to fit all the pieces of what we know into it? But just as with a change in the cosmological model, the modernist scientific model of how we know what can be known and therefore what actually exists is largely settled. It is our lived experience. We don't see it as a model, nor do we think of it as one. It sits in the background as self-evident. We don't talk about it. We just assume it.

4. Holyer, "Lewis on the Epistemic Significance of Imagination," 220.

CHANGE IN THE PREVAILING IMAGE OF REALITY: OPEN- TO CLOSED-WORLD STRUCTURE

Even though the Western tradition is built on and pervaded by the Judeo-Christian story, many have now convinced themselves this story is not only not true but also harmful for the world. The contention is that this story, and all religion of real transcendence, is irrational. Resulting from many factors but especially indebted to the Enlightenment, a new image and way of interpreting reality, a new model, developed. This new model changes the overall picture of reality—what Charles Taylor calls a shift from an "open world structure" to a "closed world structure."[5]

Open World Structure	Closed World Structure
Theory of being: All of nature is because of Being-as-Such. It *borrows* its being from Being-as-Such.	Theory of being: Material reality simply *is* reality. There is nothing beyond nature, no metaphysical.
Being-as-Such is metaphysical, beyond the physical. This is what true transcendence is.	Existence *just is*; there is no source or reason why. There is nothing transcendent to material reality.
Being-as-Such is God.	The universe or multiverse is what there is, nothing more.
In Judeo-Christian terms, God is the to-be verb: "I Am."	There is no Being-as-Such, no God.

5. Taylor, *A Secular Age*, 3, 30. Taylor defines a "closed world structure" (CWS) as "[t]he force of secularist spin" that restricts "our grasp of things which are not recognized as such." The structure aspect of a world structure is the same, Taylor says, as what "[Ludwig] Wittgenstein calls a 'picture,' a background to our thinking, within whose terms it is carried on, but which is often largely unformulated, and to which we can frequently . . . imagine no alternative" (*A Secular Age*, 549, 551). What I am saying here is that today the default background world structure (picture) is a closed world structure, and the premodern default background world picture was an open world structure. As Taylor makes clear in his retracing of the story of secularization, the CWS is not fundamentally more rational than the open world structure. To suggest otherwise is a form of modernist prejudice. It should be noted, as Professor of Historical Theology Richard A. Muller does, the terms "open world structure" and "closed world structure" can be "misleading prior to explanation, given that [Taylor] means open to God or the sacred vs closed to God or the sacred—note the opposite sense in Alexander Koyré's classic work on the history of science, *From the Closed World to the Infinite Universe*." Richard Muller's comments are from personal e-mail correspondence, May 29, 2016. In this essay, open and closed world structure will have Taylor's meaning.

Open World Structure	Closed World Structure
In an open-world structure, all creation, all universes, all reality is dependent on Being-as-Such. All of nature exists at all at the sufferance of its source of being, God.	In a closed-world structure, all of nature is a closed system that just is and is now, this universe, from which it emerged. There is no source of being.

Figure 1: Broad description of open- and closed-world-structure views.

In an open-world structure, true transcendence, the gods, and ultimately the High-God above all gods are not only likely but fundamentally required. In this world picture everyone sees and interprets reality as a whole and their place in it in the light of the transcendent reality beyond. It is from within this world picture that the Hebrew psalmist can say, "The Heavens declare the glory of God" (Ps 19:1) and the poet Gerard Manley Hopkins says, "The world is charged with the grandeur of God."[6] Through the interpretive lens of an open-world structure, everyday experience and personal meaning are made sense of in the light of the grander transcendent reality. A closed-world structure flattens everything to what I'll call the "contingent" plane of existence. The contingent plane is the one on which science operates, the ever-changing world system of materiality in which one state of being is dependent on another state along the same plane of reality but is undisturbed by questions of the system's dependence on anything beyond itself. This shift is like the change in the prevailing cosmological model that Lewis refers to. In a closed-world structure, the always-contingent universe just is and requires no gods or God. This is the prevailing modern "backcloth," as Lewis calls it, and what Taylor calls the modern "cosmic" imaginary. In a closed-world structure there is no transcendence. The shift in the fundamental world picture has led to what Taylor calls the modern "conditions of unbelief."

In a cultural world whose fundamental intellectual and social conditions default to unbelief, it is very hard to imagine how it can be otherwise. This is what Taylor calls the "social imaginary." Every culture has a "social imaginary," he says. The backcloth or cosmic imaginary provide the background that shapes the way we make sense of the world, our social practices and mores. The social imaginary is our "lived experience" of the cosmic imaginary, our backcloth. It shapes and establishes the default lens through which a culture interprets the world and understands meaning and significance. Taylor says,

6. Hopkins, *Poems and Prose*, 14.

> Just as the social imaginary consists of the understandings which make sense of our social practices, so the "cosmic imaginary" makes sense of the ways in which the surrounding world figures in our daily lives: the ways, for instance, that figures in our religious images and practices, including explicit cosmological doctrines; in the stories we tell about other lands and other ages; in our ways of marking the seasons and the passage of time; in the place of [and, I suggest, the very meaning of] "nature" in our moral and/or aesthetic sensibility; and in our attempts to develop a "scientific" cosmology, if any.[7]

The prevailing social imaginary in every age just seems obvious and unchallengeable—a self-evident truth that all reasonable people operate in. It is the framework that enables everyone to grasp life. A culture in which the cosmic imaginary is an open-world structure, the prevailing social imaginary is disposed toward belief. It is all but impossible not to believe in God. In a closed-world structure, the cultural conditions are toward unbelief. It just seems obvious that all things transcendent and religious are irrational. "From within the [closed-world] picture," Taylor says, "it just *seems obvious* that the order of argument proceeds from science to atheism, through a series of well-grounded steps."[8] This is why in the year 1500 it was virtually impossible not to believe in God, while today it is, for many, almost inescapably difficult.[9]

A closed-world-structure way of seeing and interpreting the world is commonplace in Western culture today. It is the default position of modernity. For most who interpret reality this way, to believe in a transcendent God is a purely subjective thing. It's not the way things really are. In this view, we know the way things really are through rational and empirical confirmation, most explicitly through science. If science cannot demonstrate the reality of divine transcendence, those who continue to hold on to such realities must admit they are mere "beliefs," not something called facts. Such

---

7. Taylor, *A Secular Age*, 323.

8. Ibid., 565 (emphasis mine). Taylor's broad argument to this point is addressed in chapter 15 of *A Secular Age*, "The Immanent Frame," 539–93. Commenting on Taylor's argument that unbelief is more than subtraction, James K. A. Smith says, "The 'secular' is not just the neutral, rational, areligious world that is left over once we throw off superstition, ritual, and belief in the gods. This is because the secular is not just *un*belief, or lack of specifically religious belief. . . . The emergence of the secular is also bound up with the production of a new option—the possibility of exclusive humanism as a viable *social imaginary*—a way of constructing meaning and significance without any reference to the divine or transcendence. . . . We . . . had to be able to *imagine* within an immanent frame. . . . " Smith, *How (Not) To Be Secular*, 26.

9. Taylor, *A Secular Age*, 25.

beliefs are deemed a giant leap of faith, and skeptics cannot make that leap. Some who interpret reality this way wind up committed atheists (such as in the group known today as the New Atheists) and some agnostics (those who believe transcendence and God are very unlikely and are perhaps still open to the possibility but are persuaded we cannot actually know for sure). Thus, today's prevailing Western default conditions of unbelief or doubt[10] yield an outlook something like the following:

- Religious belief is in fundamental conflict with science
- The only knowledge we should have confidence in is empirically based
- The only "authority" we should hold to is reason, not texts (e.g., scriptures) or priests
- Faith-based beliefs are irrational and reason-based ones are rational
- Things we call good and evil and morality are human constructions, nothing more
- From a postmodern perspective, perhaps nothing is real but only a human construction
- Phenomena called transcendence (e.g., love, beauty) are neurology, biology, psychology
- What is real is probably only the natural world and universe, not something in or beyond
- If there is anything beyond, we simply cannot know it or know enough to be sure

Is this outlook intellectually coherent? What lies within the backcloth of this model? Let's look.

KEY INTELLECTUAL CONUNDRUMS ABIDING IN THE BACKCLOTH OF CLOSED-WORLD MODERNITY

To illustrate the importance of the backcloth we'll consider a few example intellectual elements that reflect the passage from an open- to a closed-world structure.

---

10. To reiterate from Charles Taylor, this doesn't mean a culture where belief no longer exists nor even one where belief is still prominent, as in America; but rather it means a culture where belief is hard in the sense that default hurdles against belief are prominent because the prevailing conditions are toward unbelief and doubt.

These intellectual backcloth elements, while only an example set, make all the difference on many big questions, such as God, of course, but also a wide variety of downstream social, ethical, political, legal, economic, and arts and literature ideas. They shape the prevailing intellectual outlook about what's rational or not and about what seems reasonable. Though not often talked about, they affect daily life.

On Being and Sense-Making

This is the big element, the one from which all others flow. The simplified open- and closed-world structure descriptions provided in figure 1 above reflect these two different outlooks. They show the answers each view gives to the question of reality: What is? What has being?[11] More specifically, why is there anything at all rather than nothing at all?

In his book *The Experience of God: Being, Consciousness, Bliss*, David Bentley Hart begins his section on the question of "being" as follows:

> The beginning of all philosophy, according to both Plato and Aristotle, lies in the experience of wonder. One might go further and say that the beginning of all serious thought—all reflection upon the world that is not merely calculative or appetitive—begins in a moment of unsettling or delighted surprise. . . . It is the astonishing recollection of something one has forgotten only because it is always present: a primordial agitation of the mind and will, an abiding amazement that lies just below the surface of conscious thought and that only in very rare instances breaks through into ordinary awareness. It may be that when we are small children, before we have learned how to forget the obvious, we know this wonder in a more constant, innocent, and luminous way, because we are still trustingly open to the sheer inexplicable givenness of the world. In the dawn of life we sense

11. For Christians reading this section, I should make a comment here. I'm well aware of the inter-Christian discussions over how proper it is to appeal to natural reason and philosophy (what is often called "natural theology") as the starting point for a discussion about the nature of the being of creation; as well as the debate between Christian philosophers over Classical Theism and Theistic Personalism. For those who wish to engage with these two topics I recommend the following: on natural theology, see Vanhoozer, *Remythologizing Theology*. Vanhoozer seeks to reconcile Barth's *analogia fides* and Aquinas's *analogia entis* through *analogia dramatis*. See also McGrath, *The Open Secret* and *A Fine-Tuned Universe*. On Classical Theism and Theistic Personalism, see Feser (blog); Davies, *An Introduction to the Philosophy of Religion*; Moreland and Craig, *Philosophical Foundations for a Christian Worldview*; and Plantinga, *Does God Have a Nature*. For my purposes I will accept natural theology as a legitimate Christian enterprise and I will accept Classical Theism.

with a perfect immediacy, which we have no capacity or inclination to translate into any objective concept, how miraculous
it is that—as Angelus Silesius (1634–1677) says—"Die rose ist
ohne warum, sie blühet, weil sie blühet": "The rose is without
'why': it blooms because it blooms." As we age, however, we lose
our sense of the intimate otherness of things; we allow habit to
displace awe, inevitably to banish delight; we grow into adulthood and put away childish things. Thereafter, there are only
fleeting instants scattered throughout our lives when all at once,
our defenses momentarily relaxed, we find ourselves brought to
a pause by a sudden unanticipated sense of the utter uncanni-
ness of the reality we inhabit, the startling fortuity and strange-
ness of everything familiar: how odd it is, how unfathomable,
that anything at all exists; how disconcerting that the world and
one's consciousness of it are simply there, joined in a single ineffable event. . . . One realizes that everything about the world
that seems so unexceptional and drearily predictable is in fact
charged with an immense and imponderable mystery. In that
instant one is aware, even if the precise formulation eludes one,
that everything one knows exists in an irreducibly gratuitous
way: "what it is" has no logical connection with the reality "that
it is"; nothing within experience has any "right" to be, any power
to give itself existence, any apparent "why." The world is unable
to provide any account to its own actuality, and yet it is there all
the same. In that moment one recalls that one's every encounter
with the world has been an encounter with an enigma that no
merely physical explanation can resolve.[12]

The wonder of which Hart speaks is the same as that expressed by the
psalmist David: "The heavens declare the glory of God, and the sky above
proclaims his handiwork." It's probably fair to assume that every human being has experienced such feelings in an encounter with nature, frequently
for many and rarer for some. It is an echo, something we've experienced
and remember, even if faintly. As Hart says, such things are the "astonishing
recollection of something one has forgotten only because it is always present." The ever-presence of our encounter with nature (of which we ourselves

---

12. Hart, *Experience of God*, 87–88. I use Hart's book extensively in this section to
address this mystery primarily because it is a nontechnical work. There are many specialists and sources that can be referenced to address the same points. See, for example,
Craig, "Kalam Cosmological Argument" and "Argument from Contingency"; Kreeft,
"20 Arguments for God's Existence." And more generally on the cosmological and
contingency arguments, see Reichenbach, "Cosmological Argument." For traditional
reference on these and other major Catholic scholastic arguments, see Aquinas, *Summa
Theologica* and *Summa Contra Gentiles*.

are a part) forces us to treat it as mundane in order to get on with life. But even in the ubiquitous everydayness of this encounter lies the "immense and imponderable mystery," the "unfathomable [reality] that anything at all exists" rather than nothing at all. We know the world by experience; it is common to us; yet the universe is "unable to provide any account to its own actuality." "Even if the precise formulation eludes [us]," we recognize that it is a gift. This is the biggest question of nature: Why does anything exist, and in particular, this something we call reality, the universe, rather than nothing at all?

This is the question of *being*. Why does anything at all exist, and what does it mean to exist? The fact that something exists versus nothing is the persistent glaring evidence of transcendence—God.

From within the modern default closed-world structure, the contemporary interpretive frame is so steeped in a naturalist outlook that it restricts *how we answer all questions* to the methods of empirical science. We default to thinking that all *why* questions are "efficient cause" questions, such as what is the beginning cause of the world, to which we might answer the Big Bang or quantum fluctuations in multiverse theory. In this sense we are asking and answering *how* nature has come to be as it is rather than *that* it is at all. Thus, when it comes to the question of being, we think we are asking, "What caused nature as we know it?" But the question "What causes X?" in the sense of what are the prior conditions that gave rise to X, is what the classical and medieval world understood only as the "efficient cause," the third of Aristotle's four causes (formal, material, efficient, and final cause). Asking the question of existence in terms of the question "how did the universe come to exist as it does now?" presumes it is an efficient cause question, a science question. This is this question that Stephen Hawking and Leonard Mlodinow's 2010 book *The Grand Design* addresses. But such answers do not address the question of *being* at all. They only address how what exists in nature might have come to be what it is now.

This is a huge flaw in our modern social imaginary. It even causes us to have in our mind a flawed notion of what the word *God* has meant in the course of history and certainly distorts the Judeo-Christian understanding of God, whose very name is the to-be verb, "I AM." The modernist view assumes God is like the Enlightenment idea that led to Deism—where "God" is the first cause (he started everything) and now the universe runs on its own. This view results in what critics of theism (especially scientific-oriented atheists) call the "God of the gaps." With this understanding of God, Hawking's project of the grand design might succeed, tracing back through the series of all efficient causes to "the beginning" (the originating cause), resulting in no further need for the God hypothesis. "Because there is a law such as gravity," Hawking and Mlodinow say, "the universe can and will create itself from nothing. Spontaneous creation is the reason there is something rather than nothing, why the universe exists, why we exist. . . . It is not necessary to invoke God to light the blue touch paper and set the universe going."[13] This argument and evidence is what is adduced by most science-oriented atheists and skeptics. Looked at from the point of view of science using inductively discovered empirical and logical inferential methods, God is a speculative hypothesis, an ever-reducing God of the gaps as science progresses. If one can scientifically solve the unified theory problem, one has solved what God has covered the gap for.

According to Hawking and Mlodinow, M-theory[14] seems so promising to that end that the God hypothesis is no longer necessary. From the standpoint of "God as a kind of Demiurge," they could be right. This flawed understanding, and therefore the flawed answer to the question of being and existence, has created enormous intellectual confusion. It causes perceived intellectual barriers to be established that really aren't barriers at all.

The problem is that the solutions this approach provides do not address the question at hand—existence as such. That's because it's not the right question. Material and efficient causality, or scientific answers, don't get us any closer to answering the question of why anything exists. Science and scientific methodologies simply cannot answer the question of being—it's not a material or an efficient-cause question. It is a metaphysical question. Science theorizes about and studies only what is, how it works, and how what is might have come to be what it is now. Science assumes existence; existence is the starting point of science. Within this frame of reference, we may be able to discover that the world (our universe) is due to multiple universes or perhaps how M-theory reconciles the quantum world to the cosmological constants and provides us with a unified theory. But these don't help answer why there is anything at all versus nothing. Here is how David Hart puts it:

> As a matter of purely intellectual interest, it would be wonderful some day to know whether the universe was generated out of

13. Joyner, "God Did Not Create Universe."

14. M-theory is a breakthrough in theoretical physics, tied at least initially to an advance in string theory, that suggests the possibility of the answer to long sought unified theory—what Einstein spent the last thirty years of his life working on. For a high-level summary, see Kaku, "M-Theory." For a detailed explanation, see Hawking and Mlodinow, *The Grand Design*. Presenting a critique of Hawking and Mlodinow's claims, see particle physicist Dr. Stephen Barr, "Much Ado About 'Nothing.'" For a lecture by Barr on this topic more generally, see Barr, "The Beginning of the Universe, Physics and God."

quantum fluctuation, belongs either to an infinite "ekpyrotic" succession of universes caused by colliding branes or to a "conformally cyclic" succession of bounded aeons, is the result of inflationary quantum tunneling out of a much smaller universe, arose locally out of a multiverse in either limited constant or eternal chaotic inflation, or what have you. As a matter strictly of ontology [a "theory of being"], however, none of these theories is of any consequence, because no purely physical cosmology has any bearing whatsoever upon the question of existence.[15]

The answers that science and scientific theory can provide may eliminate the need for a deistic demiurge "god" in explaining efficient causes (and to a great extent, they have). But these kinds of answers do not and cannot address the question of why something exists versus nothing at all. There are only two rational responses to the basic question: the closed-world-structure, naturalist view and the open-world-structure, transcendent theist view.

The Closed-World-Structure View

That there is something rather than nothing "just is." This is a way of saying, "I don't know" or of ignoring the actual question. Or alternatively, of deflecting it to questions of how it came to be what it is now. Once again, as we have seen, this is an appeal to science on a different question, the question of beginning cause, or the prior conditions or events that caused the thing in question. But, of course, these are no answer to the question at hand.

Of important note, if one asserts, as the closed-world naturalist must, that from science we can know there is no God because science has proved that everything "just is" and there is no ground for being, it must be recognized that this is a metaphysical claim, but a very weak one—bordering on if not an outright irrational one. Such a claim made ostensibly on the basis of the methods of science is claiming something its methods cannot demonstrate. The reasoning is circular. Such a claim is a faith-based one, one that in terms of logic is far more reliant on blind faith than the alternative.[16]

---

15. Hart, *Experience of God*, 97.

16. For detailed "best explanation" arguments on this matter, see Richard Swinburne's *Is There a God?* and *The Existence of God*.

The Open-World-Structure View

Acknowledging that existence as such—all that we know and can ever discover that has being, which includes all we that call nature, the universe, or the universe of universes as we know it or shall—has its existence, its being, and is sustained in its being, by *borrowing its existence from the source of all being*. This source is the transcendent reality of Being itself, what all the great theistic faiths call "God." Without God, nothing at all would exist.

Here is why this must be so. All of what we think of as concrete reality, whether at the cosmological level or the quantum level, is contingent—always moving from one state of being to another. This reality's existence is dependent on a reality that is not contingent, Being itself.

> *Contingent Dependency:* Hart says, "Everything available to the senses or representable to the mind is entirely subject to *annicha* (to use a Buddhist term): impermanence, mutability, transience. All physical things are composite, which is to say reducible to an ever greater variety of distinct parts, and so are essentially inconstant and prone to dissolution. All things are subject to time, moreover: they possess no complete identity in themselves, but are always in the process of becoming something else, and hence also in the process of becoming nothing at all. There is pure fragility and necessary incompleteness to any finite thing; nothing has its actuality entirely in itself, fully enjoyed in some impregnable present instant, but must always receive itself from beyond itself, and then only by losing itself at the same time."[17]

In summary, Hart says, "one lives and moves and has one's being only at the sufferance of an endless number of enabling conditions, and becomes what one will be only by taking leave of what one has been. Simply said, one is contingent through and through, partaking of being rather than generating it out of some source within oneself; and the same is true of the whole intricate web of independencies that constitutes nature."[18] The question that remains at the end of all the enabling conditions within the contingent plane is, What is the enabling condition of the plane itself? Each of us and the whole of what we call nature and existence are completely dependent on the source and sustainer of all being, Being itself. Hart's comment here is precisely the same point the apostle Paul makes, using some of the same words, when speaking to the philosophers at the public forum Areopagus (also called Mars Hill) in Athens:

17. Hart, *Experience of God*, 91–92.
18. Ibid., 93.

Paul stood in front of the Areopagus and said, "Athenians, I see how extremely religious you are in every way. For as I went through the city and looked carefully at the objects of your worship, I found among them an altar with the inscription, 'To an unknown god.' What therefore you worship as unknown, this I proclaim to you. The God who made the world and everything in it, he who is Lord of heaven and earth, does not live in shrines made by human hands, nor is he served by human hands, as though he needed anything, since he himself gives to all mortals life and breath and all things. From one ancestor he made all nations to inhabit the whole earth, and he allotted the times of their existence and the boundaries of the places where they would live, so that they would search for God and perhaps grope for him and find him—though indeed he is not far from each one of us. For 'In him we live and move and have our being'; as even some of your own poets have said,

'For we too are his offspring.'

Since we are God's offspring, we ought not to think that the deity is like gold, or silver, or stone, an image formed by the art and imagination of mortals."[19]

Nothing in nature that exists has or maintains its existence in itself. We "live and move and have our being" at the sufferance of Being itself, God.

It doesn't matter how far back we trace efficient causality (*how* things came to be); we "still ultimately arrive at only the most elementary contingencies of all, no closer to an explanation of existence than one was before setting out."[20]

In another place Hart explains why we are forced to recognize that we "live and move and have our being" only as the result of the source of all being: "No one lives in a 'naturalistic' reality, and the very notion of nature as a perfectly self-enclosed continuum is a figment of the imagination. It is the supernatural [the hyperphysical; *super naturum*] of which we have direct certainty, and only in consequence of that can the reality of nature be assumed, not as an absolutely incontrovertible fact but simply as far and away the likeliest supposition."[21] This is where such theories as Hawking's *The Grand Design* miss the obvious logical problem with the notion that a spontaneous generation of the universe solves the problem of existence. Such theories reflect the transition of one state of being to another. This

19. Acts 17:22–29, NRSV. Emphasis added.
20. Hart, *Experience of God*, 93.
21. Ibid., 96.

does not account for sheer existence, nor does it account for the rise of existence as such from nonexistence. "An old and particularly sound metaphysical maxim says that between existence and nonexistence there is an infinite qualitative difference. It is a distance that no quantitative calculation of processes or forces or laws can ever overcome."[22] "Cosmology simply cannot become ontology. The only intellectually consistent course for the metaphysical naturalist is to say that physical reality 'just is' and then leave off there, accepting that this 'just is' remains a truth entirely in the excess of all physical properties and causes: the single ineradicable 'super-natural' fact within which all natural facts are forever contained, but about which we ought not let ourselves think too much."[23]

Existence is completely fortuitous, a sheer gift. American Philosophers Richard Taylor and William Lane Craig put it like this:

> Imagine you're on a walk in the forest and come across a sphere. You look at it and examine and wonder where it came from. This is a very normal reaction, because it seems out of place. Surely someone must have put it there. But what is just as obvious, and would surely raise the same glaring question if it were not so familiar to us, is the forest itself, the ground we are walking on, and so on. Or, to use another example, what about the universe and everything in it? None of the things that make it up exist necessarily. They could all fail to exist. The natural question is why? "The question would be no less intelligible or pertinent if we were to imagine the sphere either as expanded to the size of the universe or as contracted to the size of a grain of sand, either as existing from everlasting to everlasting or as existing for only a few seconds. It is the sheer unexpected 'thereness' of the thing, devoid of any transparent rationale for the fact, that prompts our desire to understand it in terms not simply of its nature, but of its very existence."[24]

The question of existence is not "Can we prove God exists by somehow finding the fingerprints of God in nature?" If God is the ground of all existence, it is impossible for there not to be signs of God throughout nature— existence itself is *the* sign. The question is not "Is it logically coherent to

---

22. Ibid., 95–96.

23. Ibid. 98–99. The position of the naturalist that Hart says "just is," philosopher Richard Swinburne calls "brute fact." Both writers argue that this position is less intellectually satisfying and doesn't provide the "best explanation." See Reichenbach, "Cosmological Argument"; also see Swinburne, *Is There a God?*, especially chapter 4, "How The Existence of God Explains the World and Its Order," 48–68.

24. Hart, *Experience of God*, 90–91; and Craig, "Argument from Contingency."

conclude there is a transcendent being we call God who gives and sustains being to all that is?" It is preeminently logical. The question is, what is the rationale for *not* concluding this is so?

The question is not "Did God create and sustain all things?" The source of all being, God, must be its *formal* and *final* cause, and in his being rests the basis and reason for all *material* and *efficient* causes. That we have such a hard time with this explanation today is because we have become prejudiced against it and because we believe that science and its methods can answer all questions given enough time and/or that all metaphysics is conjecture in the wake of the Enlightenment philosophy, especially due to Immanuel Kant's *The Critique of Pure Reason*. While Kant believed that God does exist, because of his chastened view of knowledge of metaphysical reality due to the limitations of human perception, he also believed we couldn't know much about God. Though on this point he himself "was very ambivalent towards his own conclusion. He took the view that the tendency of reason to overstep the bounds of science is both incorrigible and inevitable. The question 'why?' will not go away."[25] The wonder that occurs when we encounter the astonishing beauty of nature, which prompts intuitions of God's presence, is right.

It is because we have become so culturally conditioned that we seek to answer religious or metaphysical questions (such as being as such) with the wrong toolset, empirical science. It's because of this that we think we have answered them when we haven't. Each free person may believe what they wish. But to believe there is no absolute source of being, what we properly call God, we must face the fact that such belief is a metaphysical position, not a finding of science. In this respect, one who holds to a closed-world structure metaphysical position faces challenges that one who holds to the open-world structure position has a more compelling explanation for. The only real alternative to accepting the conclusion of a transcendent deity from which all contingent reality borrows its being is to dismiss the question as illegitimate. For the honest seeker for the truth, this "brute fact" position often creates an existential crisis of meaning. The famous existentialist atheist Jean Paul Sartre found himself here, reflected in his question "why am I?" By dismissing the question we "also answer it, in something like the way Sartre answered it in his early writings."[26] Sartre concluded that without God, life must be absurd.

True Transcendence is the only plausible answer to why anything exists at all—that is to say, "God," not a reduced Deist-like God-of-the-gaps,

25. Scruton, *Face of God*, 14.
26. Ibid.

but a "High-God" above all Gods, of the kind Rodney Stark shows all preaxial primitive religions believed sat above their parochial gods,[27] and the supreme sovereign triune God of Christianity. It is the God that David Bentley Hart says all the major theistic religions acknowledge, including "Judaism, Christianity, Islam as well as Vedantic and Bhaktic Hinduism, Sikhism [and] various late antique paganisms," and it "even applies in many respects to various Mahayana formulations of, say, the Buddhist conception of the Unconditioned, or to certain aspects of the Tao."[28] To say this is, of course, not to say all religions are the same; they are not.[29] But it is to say that all major theistic religions (or those close to theism) acknowledge that reality as we all know and experience it cannot be explained without such a conception of the transcendent, of God. It is our natural intuition when we look at the world.[30] The rationality of it has not been proven wrong or weak by science or philosophy, though today many continue to believe it has.

That the modernist social imaginary defaults against this is only because it chooses not to grapple with the fundamental question of being. This is a huge intellectual blind spot in the modernist myth. We just don't see it hidden within the backcloth. We ignore it and assume that the modernist model has answered the question when it hasn't. The only answer we give is a nonanswer: existence "just is."

The answer to the biggest mystery of all—"why does anything exist rather than nothing?"—is God!

27. Stark, *Discovering God*, 54–63. Note particularly Stark's retracing of anthropological scholarship found in Andrew Lang (in his *Myth, Ritual, and Religion* [1887] and *The Making of Religion* [1898]), who broke with the late-nineteenth-century straight-line evolution theory of religion that suggested all primitive religions had a low, simplistic view of God or gods and that the notion of a High God as "a moral Supreme Being" was a very late development. In the latter work mentioned, "Lang discovered that many of the most primitive groups, scattered in all parts of the world, believed in the existence of High Gods: 'moral, all-seeing, directors of men . . . eternal beings who made the world, and watch over morality'" (56). While this was not fully expressed monotheism but rather "henotheism ('one-Godism')," Stark is saying that without a preconceived prejudice that says all forms of monotheism must be a late-stage development, this clearly indicates that even among the earliest, most primitive peoples there was belief and acknowledgment of a High God above all gods. This I suggest is an echoing memory of a supreme High God above all gods, similar to the Greeks' "Unknown God" of whom Paul spoke on Mars Hill.

28. Hart, *Experience of God*, 4.

29. Nor is it to say such a philosophical understanding of God is adequate to describe the Christian God. It is not. But the Christian God encompasses this understanding of God.

30. This we see in St. Paul, Rom 1:20. In this context, some Christians may be discomfited. To allay fears of unorthodoxy here, I point to C. S. Lewis in "The Rival Conceptions of God," in *Mere Christianity*, 29–31.

In the backcloth of modernity this mystery lies hidden, unaddressed, and unanswered yet always present.

While the Judeo-Christian faiths begin with, or assume, God's existence, in the manner of St. Paul, the Western/Judeo-Christian intellectual tradition informs us through obvious reason that it must be this way. How can any contingent being supply its own existence? It cannot. It obtains and sustains its existence from a necessary being. God alone is "necessary," that is, is not dependent on anything other than himself.

Based in this fundamental yet reasonable conclusion of logic, reason itself abides in God. The world, the universe (or universe of universes) is rational, to the extent it is, because God is Rational. Our rationality, our reason is an endowment from God, a gift from God. Human reason and the reasonableness of all things is not something that just spontaneously came to reside in inorganic-turned-organic matter. No, reason itself is another way in which the created order participates in God.

All things that exist do so in God. The whole natural order is reasonable because reason itself resides in God, and all rational beings obtain their rational capacity from God. This is the explanation for why we can make sense of things at all—truly, even if not exhaustively.

The Idea of Human Knowledge and the Notion of Truth

That humans can know anything that should yield anything like truth is a mystery, just as existence is. That we obtain knowledge of any sort is not debatable. Why we do and that the knowledge we obtain should yield truth is.

The Open-World-Structure View

In the open-world-structure view, particularly the Christian view, the capacity that humans have for knowledge is directly related to God. We know, "through a glass, darkly," because God knows. Human beings are a reflection of God, and all true human knowledge reflects The Truth that abides in God.

How we obtain knowledge is diverse: it is through natural reason, including logic, and rational-sensory experience (and experimentation); it is through imaginative, artistic and poetic life, which C. S. Lewis says is the meaning that gives reason its fodder; and it is through God's special revelation of himself to his creatures, including God's self-disclosure in his acts, his Spirit's disclosure to and through people, and most fully in his self-condescension into his creation in his son, the Logos of God. All of these are thoroughly rational and consistent with God who is in constant relation with his creation, upholding it in its being. Without God there would be no being as such nor any actual knowledge and truth, or at least none that we should have any confidence constitutes actual knowledge and truth.

In an open-world structure—at least in something like traditional Christian metaphysics—all knowledge is ultimately sourced in God, even if not acknowledged. In at least this sense all knowledge is about God. If, as Christianity maintains, God is truth, all knowledge therefore finds its truthfulness in God. In the broadest terms, without a transcendent source, human knowledge that yields anything like truth is either a mystery (like the "brute fact" faith of the naturalist on the question of existence) or, more likely, incoherent (and in deep conflict with the empirical science the naturalist so relies on).

The Closed-World-Structure View

In the closed-world-structure view, human knowledge is sourced in the world and in the knower. What counts as knowledge is only that which is about the world found through reason, logic, and rational-sensory experience. Only knowledge about things of the world can be considered actually true—based on the fundamental notion that there is an actual "way things are." Other things we call "knowledge," "true," or "truth" are either expressions of human subjectivity or what a group of knowers agree upon.

What is "true" or "the truth" in a contingent-plane-only reality is always relative. It must be. For all scientists (whether open-or closed-world), for whom the contingent plane of nature is the domain, truth is always relative—or better, tentative—and subject to further knowledge of what is known *now*. For all scientists, there is an assumed "truth of the matter" with respect to material reality. And, all scientists acknowledge that what they know about the "truth of the matter" is *what we know now*. All scientific truth is relative to "from where we stand, with what we know now." This is the way all science works. It is driven by ignorance, coming to know some things which then raise new questions about what is not yet known.[31] Science is primarily a methodology—a way of discovering and inferring what nature is and how it works. Scientists form theories, or "models," that can hold what is known now and form new ones when new discoveries cannot be held in the old theories or models. For the politician or social theorist who adopts closed-world-structure naturalism, notwithstanding the same moniker "scientists," there is no "way things are," no nature as it were.

31. See Firestein, *Ignorance*.

Morality, law, and truth are relative to whatever the society and culture they are part of decide is "true." "Truth" is pure social construction.

For the scientist (all scientists), therefore, truth is measured against what we know now—which is as it must be. But for the closed-world naturalist scientist who steps out of the role of scientist and becomes a metaphysician or social theorist or ethicist and begins to declare what a human being *is* or what *should* be done because we *know* what human beings *are* and what *is* good, just, and true, that scientist has made absolute assertions from provisional knowledge. Science's plane of study is material existence, which is always changing. It assumes material reality. That is its field of study. The measure of truth is against this reality alone. Notwithstanding whatever we may discover by science, in a closed-world structure metaphysic, nonmaterial things, like concepts such as beauty, goodness, morality, justice, personhood, identity, gender, and so on, must be either purely material or physical phenomena or only social constructions (not real).[32]

Furthermore, though all scientists believe there is a "way things are" and we slowly but surely learn more about what that is, once the closed-world structure naturalist metaphysics position is taken, the naturalist faces a conflict with science—one that the theist does not face. In closed-world-structure naturalism, there is no reason we *should* trust that human cognition should yield anything like truth *or* that what we know *should* be or *is* true. This closed-world view *must* hold to a nondirected, wholly random form of cosmic and biological evolution. The problem is not with science or with evolution as such but with philosophical naturalism. Naturalism must on the one hand hold that knowledge is real and rises to the level of real truth about the way things are, and yet on the other hand has no logical explanation for why this should be so. It is wholly illogical to believe that we should trust human cognition to yield true, reliable beliefs or even true knowledge. Those who hold this outlook should doubt whether it is true. And many of the best minds within the camp of naturalism have openly done so. Darwin did: "'With me the horrid doubt always arises whether the convictions of man's mind, which has been developed from the mind of lower animals, are of any value or at all trustworthy. Would anyone trust the convictions of a monkey's mind, if there are any convictions in such a mind?' Nietzsche, Nagel, Stroud, Churchland, and Darwin, nontheists all, seem to concur: (naturalistic) evolution gives one a reason to doubt that human cognitive faculties produce for the most part true beliefs."[33] As

32. For some closed-world-structure idealists and postmodernists, all reality is a human construction, even material reality.

33. Plantinga, *Where the Conflict Really Lies*, 316.

such, naturalists should either seriously doubt their belief that there is no transcendent explanation for the concurrence between our cognitive faculties and what we experience, or seriously doubt their belief that their cognitive faculties are delivering true, reliable beliefs, or knowledge, including the belief that somehow, in some way, a material-only reality caused reliable cognitive faculties to develop such that we should trust them. Either way, naturalism has a problem.[34]

An open-world structure that holds to theism, in particular the Trinitarian theism of Christianity, does not have this problem. It has the most rational, coherent reason for human knowledge and truth: God. With knowledge grounded in God, we obtain an answer to an even more visceral question about knowledge: Why are we drawn so incessantly to pursue it? The answer is found in St. Bonaventure: "All knowledge [is] integrated into a spiritual journey *toward* love; love of God and love of fellow human beings."[35] Even in our pursuit of knowledge, we are longing for God.

The Limits of Scientific Knowledge

The unalloyed mystery that science demonstrates so well is that nature is orderly. Because of this order we can come to know and have a significant understanding of it. But science is limited in scope. It explores and seeks to understand only the contingent plane of existence, what we call nature.

Science, which is primarily a methodology for knowing, is the best way we have for discovering what the makeup of nature is, how it works, and to some extent how what we now observe came to be as it is now. This is an invaluable source of knowledge, especially practical knowledge. But science's scope and its methods have limitations. By default, science can only answer questions within its scope. It cannot answer questions about existence that are not within the contingent plane. Anything beyond the contingent plane, and certain phenomena in it that are not physical properties beyond how

34. This way of framing the problem of knowledge and truth in closed-world naturalism is addressed in Plantinga, *Where the Conflict Really Lies*. The explicit argument is that whereas it is often thought that there is a deep conflict between religion and science and no conflict between philosophical naturalism and science (basically a closed-world-structure view), the reverse is the case. Plantinga shows that between religion and science there is only superficial conflict and that there is deep conflict between naturalism and science, particularly between naturalism and current evolutionary theory in science. Plantinga concludes that "one can't rationally accept both naturalism and current evolutionary theory; that combination of beliefs is self-defeating. [And] there is a deep conflict between naturalism and one of the most important claims of current science." Plantinga, *Where the Conflict Really Lies*, 349–50.

35. Bonaventure, *On the Reduction of the Arts*, 9. Emphasis added.

they work and their chemistry, science cannot address: for example, what consciousness actually is and what love is. Science explains what is in the contingent plane of existence, how it works, and how it moves from what it was to what it is now. It cannot explain whether there is anything beyond the contingent plane, nor why anything in that plane exists except in terms of the processes that explain how they came to be what they are now. Science is impotent on metaphysical questions.

This is not to say that *reason* cannot address such questions, only that science's material and efficient cause-effect methodology cannot. Logic, which is a human capacity that science uses but that is not equivalent with science nor can science explain it, and speculative reason can address metaphysical questions. (This is so, I suggest, despite the Kantian tradition that suggests no such metaphysical knowledge is possible.)

The closest science comes to metaphysical questions is in its findings. Science's findings reveal how improbable the universe (or universes it may theorize) it studies really is. This is seen best in what is often called the "fine-tuned argument." This argument suggests that the contingent reality that science observes and seeks to understand is found to have such narrow tolerances for the conditions necessary to spawn and sustain life that it must have a deeper reason behind it—an intelligence behind it that made it in just this way such that life could develop and be sustained. The staggering coincidences are otherwise too improbable. The most recent theory to explain these improbabilities put forward by closed-world-structure cosmological scientists is the multiverse theory outlined by Stephen Hawking and Leonard Mlodinow in *The Grand Design*. In this view the improbabilities that are present in this (our) universe are accounted for by there being many universes, enough so that it is only reasonable to assume that with enough time, the otherwise improbable constants and chemistry found in our universe that are necessary to sustain life would occur.

Most scientists are not philosophers. Their work, again to use Lewis's comments on models, is to observe the reality they have at hand and perform experiments and come up with theories that can best explain it. They look for the theory/model that can best "hold it all." So it is reasonable that scientists would theorize a multiverse to explain what is observable and use math to confirm the plausibility of their theories of cosmology. It is more than appropriate that philosophers would take this data into account in their pursuits. But in the end, the scope of the scientist's work doesn't and cannot reach beyond its domain—again, as Hart points out, cosmology cannot become ontology.

But no human knowledge-seeking enterprise of any kind operates outside of a philosophical framework. Within this framework are embedded answers to a host of nonscientific questions—whether well considered and articulated or not. Among the nonscientific questions are the question of existence itself, the question of contingency, the question of knowledge, the question of logic, and the question of human cognition and conceptualization, among a host of others.

Being a good scientist does not include or preclude judgments about transcendent reality, or God. Most of the greatest scientists have believed, even if not always in traditionally orthodox terms, that the universe (or multiverse) did not just come about and is sustained on its own but must rely on a transcendent source, God. The limits of scientific knowledge are not a weakness; they are simply a limitation of scope. Listen to Oxford Professor Michael Ward on C. S. Lewis's understanding of the narrow scope of science:

> The smallness of scientific statements is often obscured by their successfulness. Scientific statements succeed in defining and predicting certain pockets of the natural world, definition and predictions which can then be put to use, in curing small-pox, or building the internal combustion engine, or devising the microchip. The magnificence of such scientific achievements is so huge that it can mislead us into thinking that they have said a great deal, when actually they have said relatively little, but said it very well. A true scientific statement has to be relatively small, because it is only relatively small things that can be said with sufficient univocality to be empirically verifiable or falsifiable. You might think it preposterous to describe the mapping of the human genome as a "small statement," but genetics is only one department of biology and biology is only one department of science and science is only one department of human knowledge. Seen in context of all that there could possibly be said about a human being—socially, psychologically, spiritually, economically, historically, geographically, emotionally, visually, audibly, tangibly, olfactorally, racially, anthropologically, dermatologically, psephologically (you get the picture!), any genetic statement, however marvelously correct, is still a minuscule fraction of the total. When you start trying to make larger statements you move into the language of the humanities and then into the arts and then into religion. Religious statements, by saying things which attempt to explain life in the round, use language which is very hard to quantify, to measure, to test. But that is because they are trying to say a very great deal; they are trying to find the unity, the oneness, the heart of all reality. Here

the stake is not a mere thirty shillings, but every penny you have, your life, your soul.[36]

The Idea of Progress

This topic can, of course, be very big, but I will make it very small for our purposes. Almost everyone in the West just assumes the world and human life is progressing forward, advancing. This notion has a long history. But not all peoples have held this view. Most had a circular view. The idea that the world and human life is going somewhere, moving forward, advancing, as we think of this today, began with the Jews. And it was advanced through Aristotle, St. Augustine, and St. Thomas Aquinas, long before it was picked up in modern biological and social evolutionary theory.

The whole story of Western civilization (and now to a great extent the whole world) rests in no small way on the Judeo-Christian narrative. The ancient Jewish idea that history is going somewhere (and is not merely cyclical) emerges from the story of Abraham and his relation to God. This new cast of mind literally changed the world, as Thomas Cahill describes in his book *The Gift of the Jews: How a Tribe of Desert Nomads Changed the Way Everyone Thinks and Feels*.[37] Born when "Abraham went" from Ur in Mesopotamia (c. 1850 BC) and developing through the long history of Israel and Christianity, a whole new mind-set developed that literally made possible Western civilization and the world as we know it today.[38] As this

36. Ward, "Science and Religion in the Writings of C. S. Lewis," 10.

37. For a review of Cahill's book and a list of the reviewer's notable changes identified by Cahill, see Prager, "Cahill's Gift."

38. On the Jews being the first historians, see Halpern, *The First Historians*; and Michael Grant, *The Ancient Historians*, 10–14. Grant's purpose is to show how history writing as we know it began in earnest with the Greeks and Romans. But he acknowledges that there is a preeminent penultimate beginning with the Jews: "Their examination and assessment of the divine aim as displayed in past epochs endowed history with immense importance, far greater importance than it had ever assumed in previous culture. The God of Israel has made a pact, a covenant, with Israel; the working-out of this covenant year after year is history"; and, "Consequently, as G. R. Elton remarks, 'no other primitive sacred writings are so grimly chronological and historical as the Old Testament.' It selects from the course of events those facts and signs which seem relevant to the interpretation of God's Order, advancing from myth and legend to factual annals which selectively compile and edit earlier literary documents. . . . The accounts of their reigns far outdo, in literary eloquence, anything which has survived from earlier peoples or times. . . . There was nothing comparable to the Jewish literature, which had taken such an aloof view, not indeed about the divine purposes, but at least about the rulers who were failing to carry it out" (10, 11, 14).

story encountered Aristotle's ideas of potentiality, actuality, and teleology and were integrated by Thomas Aquinas in the thirteenth century,[39] the notion of a grand story and that history has a destiny became cemented in the Western mind. It's so obvious to us now that it's hard to see it hasn't always been so. It is in this very big idea that we intuit life as a journey, an adventure.

With this Judeo-Christian notion of the world and human life as on a journey, no longer did the fates control. The world lives within the story of the transcendent, sovereign God. The whole of God's creation came about and proceeds within and according to his plan.

The Open-World-Structure View

Within the open-world-structure view, the transcendent God gave rise to and sustains all that is, and God's creation is moving from its beginning toward its consummation. It is and has a story. It is narratival; it has a plot. The narrative and plot is given to it by its creator. It's that simple. The world and all creatures in it, particularly human creatures, live within this narrative and plot. All small stories find their source and meaning within this Grand Story. The intuitive sense of life as a journey is a resonance of this Grand Story. This is one of the echoes of the voice of God we just feel in our bones. For all the historical deconstruction and redaction these days, this sense of a journey is what launched the Western world's journey of exploration—to new worlds like Magellan's and Columbus's journeys and that gave rise to science as we know it. Genius and brilliance arose in many places and in diverse cultures, but only in the West did science and exploration take on the character of advancement. This is a direct lineage of the overarching sense of life as a journey that began with the Jews, advanced in Aristotle's potentiality-actuality principle and telos (goal, end) of all "things," and is fulfilled in the theology of Christian eschatology.

The Closed-World-Structure View

Those who hold the closed-world-structure view may employ the language of progress and advancement, but this language no longer has any actual meaning. The closed-world-structure naturalist adopts the idea of progress in cosmic and biological theory of evolution, yet all this really means is

---

39. See Aquinas, *Summa Theologica*. Specifically related to human beings having an end (telos), see Aquinas, *Summa*, First Part of the Second Part, Question 1, "Of Man's Last End."

change from one state to another. Without a transcendent reason to suggest otherwise, to speak of evolution as an advancement makes no sense.[40] It is tautological. Within a completely contingent world, always changing from one state to another, to suggest "forward" or "backward" is either pure assertion or is a legacy of another outlook—which is, indubitably, the legacy of the Judeo-Christian Western tradition.

Though many of those committed to a closed-world outlook do so regularly, to employ the idea of progress and advancement to the social world, describing it as social/cultural evolution, is sheer assertion. There is no measure against which to assess advancement or decline. It's just movement, change. This extends to ideas of advancement in social justice, the rule of law, the recognition of human dignity, and so on. To speak of these as progress has no logical warrant. Progress or advancement in this view is merely arbitrary. It must be. There is no basis to conclude otherwise. For example, if there is no transcendent justice, what is human justice but arbitrary? The same is true of the notion that the rule of law is better than fiat. To appeal to universal human dignity as the basis, where does such dignity come from? Why should we assume human beings should be treated better than animals? Indeed, PETA asks this very question. In a closed-world-structure world, PETA is just as right as the UN Declaration for Human Rights. The idea of political and social progressivism in a closed-world structure is no less intellectually empty. Everything becomes a matter of assertion. This is precisely what philosopher Richard Rorty asserts, a "consensus reality," what people agree to be the case, not what is actually the case. For Rorty, and what has become generally accepted in today's culture that doubts any transcendent reality, reality is "linguistically constructed"; truth simply *is* "whatever our peers will let us get away with saying."[41]

From the open-world-structure view, the world actually is advancing toward an end, a telos. But under the influence of a closing structure, in the nineteenth and early twentieth century in the West the theory changed. The modern progressivist theory emerges from the idealist theory of history and philosophy of G. F. Hegel as later mediated through the explicitly atheistic philosophies of Marx and Nietzsche. Eventually, supported by reductionist liberal theology, Marxism, and liberal political theory, progressivism came to be viewed as inevitably good, redefining the notion of sin and brokenness as institutional oppression. According to traditional orthodox theology in the Christian tradition, the world is not inevitably getting better due to

40. Except to say perpetuation, of a universe or a species. But, this is not a statement of advancement.

41. See Plantinga, "How to Be an Anti-Realist"; and Sartwell, "'Postmodern' Intellectual Roots."

human sin and the effects of sin in this broken world. The world has been freed from its enslavement to sin and death by the work of Jesus Christ on the cross, but the fullness of this redemption is yet to be realized in this world. The world is being redeemed by God, and as such it is in a state of advancement toward God's end, but it is not progressing in the sense of inevitably getting better. This is an already-and-not-yet time. This full realization will be accomplished in the final consummation of things, when Christ comes again to reign in his kingdom.

From a modernist closed-world structure, to assert progress is simply that: an arbitrary assertion. To suggest otherwise is unconsciously to carry within the modern backcloth remnants from the Judeo-Christian story and the premodern Western intellectual tradition but without the coherence of the full worldview.

The Meaning of the Human Person

This, too, is a big topic—and a controversial one. It has such an effect on so many social, moral, and political dimensions of life that it is hard to over-estimate the impact views of the human person have on the way we see and live in the world.

The Closed-World-Structure View

In a closed-world-structure view, the meaning of a human person is wholly a human construct. Personhood is merely an ascription, a name given to a particular kind of biological organism that developed under conditions just right for its development. The meaning of the human person, if any, is what we who fall into this species have constructed over time. In this view, there is no nature of things, only things of nature.

In a closed-world view, the ascription of personhood to the human organism is a fabrication. Any "meaning" is assigned solely through the semiotic development of cultures over time. The social, moral, and politi-cal significance assigned to the "human person" is, and must be, *only* the cultural and legal accretions that have accumulated like soot on a hearth. The meaning of the human person in this view is historically relative and highly malleable. There is nothing real or permanent in the notion of the human person.

However, people still treat the human person as if it is real and perma-nent. Such practices are, again, the legacy of a former open-world-structure view. Examples include ideas like human rationality and intellect, human dignity, human identity and purpose, human spirituality, and human freedom. But these are nonsensical in a closed-world view, except sociologically and anthropologically. To build social, moral, political, and legal theories and practices on these legacies is arbitrary without a transcendent story—at minimum a teleological one like Aristotle's, in which all things have a purpose and whose being resides in the Unmoved Mover, but even more fully the Judeo-Christian God of all things.

Within a closed-world view, an argument may be made that the accumulated wisdom of human cultures over time is sufficient justification for treating certain aspects of the organism called "human person" *as if* it were real. But this is only pragmatic. In actual fact, in this view, there is no justification apart from the assertion that wisdom has been accumulated; for apart from some form of a social contract between human organisms living together as a society, to recognize certain cultural accretions as "wise" or "just" or "fair" is merely that—a social contract.[42] If another society decides otherwise, it's hard to argue for universality. On the one hand, this is precisely where the world is today in many respects. On the other, the legacy of the West, largely shaped by a Judeo-Christian understanding of the human person and of natural law, has been exported and embraced around the world—even if in only practical terms.

In stark contrast to this view, still held by many even as the world has closed, is the US Declaration of Independence: "We hold these truths to be self-evident, that all men are created equal, that they are endowed by their Creator with certain unalienable Rights, that among these are Life, Liberty and the pursuit of Happiness." The "truths" are discerned in nature that certain "rights" are endowed by the creator.[43] It is contradictory to continue to hold to such truths and rights as permanent and universal without an appeal to a transcendent source. A closed-world structure does not have such an appeal.

The Open-World-Structure View

In an open-world-structure view, the meaning of the human person, like all things in creation, finds its being and ultimate meaning outside itself, from the transcendent God. In the Judeo-Christian tradition (which has become integrally embedded within the Western tradition at large), the human

42. This is what Jean-Jacques Rousseau claimed, and it is even the basis of the UN Declaration of Human Rights.

43. This is the view of John Locke, whose ideas of natural rights significantly influenced the writers of the US Declaration of Independence.

person obtains its meaning and its nature from God. Human beings were created by God in his own image, after his likeness. Human persons were created male and female, and together as one whole they reflect God; and, as depicted in the New Testament, the marriage of a man and a woman, as one, reflects the relationship between Christ and his church. Being created in God's image gives true meaning to human persons.

Being created in God's image does not preclude a developmental process, such as human evolution. Though, because God made and sustains everything, any developmental process is not random chance. Through whatever natural means of development, and modern science has discovered much about such developmental processes, human persons move from potentiality to actuality by God. God is the formal cause and final cause. God made and instituted whatever material and efficient causal processes in nature there are to bring humans about.

Through whatever means, God is the source and sustenance of all life in the universe wherever it exists. He breathes life into and gives every human being their soul. Human persons therefore entail a spiritual dimension of reality, another effect of being created in God's image. All human life, in whatever stage of development, is a person—and is to be nurtured and protected as such.

As such, all human persons, all personhood, has its being, nature, and meaning in God. Human persons are real things and have real meaning.[44]

As with all real things, in the human person there is an inherent nature. The nature of a thing defines its purpose. In the Judeo-Christian tradition, human persons are bodily ensouled rational moral beings made in God's image that are to be fruitful and multiply, be in active loving relation with God, and are to serve as his vice-regents in his creation. A royal position, with a royal purpose, reflecting and representing God as his ambassadors (his image) in the theater of his creation. We are to tend, take care of, and cause all creation to flourish—we are culture makers. The human person is not just a thing in nature. Rather, in accord with the nature and purpose given by God, humans persons move toward fulfillment, their intended purpose, their end.

To fulfill their ends, human persons, made in God's image and likeness, are endowed by God with unique capacities and capabilities among the created order. These include: spirituality; reason and rationality (analogous to God's reason and rationality); creative capacities to make things and make culture in, from, and for ourselves and the wider creation; freedom and a will; and the capacity for conscious love—indeed, humans are

---

44. See Smith, *Moral, Believing Animals* and *What Is a Person?*

fundamentally lovers, worshipers. We can choose well (meaning in accord with our nature and the moral order established by God) or not (departing from and not fulfilling our intended purpose). In this regard, to paraphrase G. K. Chesterton, "The huge modern heresy is to alter the human soul to fit modern social conditions, instead of altering modern social conditions to fit the human soul."[45] But human freedom and love, according to God's intended purposes, are not a license to do whatever we want to do. Rather, we are made to do and live in accord with the ends and purposes for which God has made us.

In their nature, in virtue of their purpose given by God, human persons have real dignity, real worth. It is not a worth defined simply by humanity itself but by God.[46] From this worth, this honor, endowed not by human construction but by God, flows the notion that human beings should receive justice, be treated justly, in accord with their nature and purpose. This justice is not arbitrary but according to justice as such, which resides in God, in accord with our intended ends. Indeed, within this understanding resides the notion of redemption: re-deemed, or deemed again, according to the thing's actual value and worth.

Human beings were given their purpose by God but did not fulfill it. One Greek word used in the Bible for "sin" means to miss the target (which is consistent with *telos*: aim, purpose, end). Human beings missed the mark by willful disobedience, placing someone else or thing other than God above their creator and sovereign: themselves. This St. Augustine calls "disordered love." According to justice, God's judgment fell upon human beings and the whole of creation over which humans were given responsibility. But to our great astonishment, through Jesus Christ, in pursuit of his undeterred love for his creation and the satisfaction of his justice, God set about to redeem the whole creation. By his grace in pursuit of redemption, in our stead God's judgment came to rest upon Jesus Christ, the incarnate son of God. In him, the one who is in himself the very definition of personhood, the human person was fulfilled. In him, in his person and work on the cross, the proper human end and the justice of God were fulfilled. In him we fulfill our intended purpose. And through the grace extended to us in Jesus Christ, God's justice is also fulfilled. In Christ, we now seek to fulfill our original purpose, reflecting and representing God in his creation and causing the world to flourish—by reflecting Jesus Christ in the world. As

---

45. Chesterton, *What's Wrong with the World?*, as adapted by Gay, *Way of the Modern World*, 237.

46. For a theological exploration of Christian views of human dignity, see Howard, *Imago Dei*.

such we are his body in the world, proclaiming and reflecting the redemption wrought by him.

In this view, we see that justice itself is real, not merely a human construct. It is defined by and flows from God. It is part of God's stamp upon us and the whole creation. It is intuitively known by all, just as moral order is known by all. Human cries for justice are a natural-order reflection of God. That human beings cry out in their soul when injustice occurs reflects that human beings were created for a real purpose, one reflecting an endowment by God with human dignity proper to that purpose.

This idea of the special dignity of the human person is embedded in the fabric of Western civilization, initially found in Judaism, later in different forms in the classical Greco-Roman world (e.g., Stoicism[47]), and came to fuller bloom as the Christian church emerged in late antiquity and the Middle Ages. In this tradition, nature itself witnesses to, or reflects, the special dignity and role given to the human being by God. This we see in part in the intuitive sense of human dignity that humans have. It is an echo of God's created intended purpose. Cries for justice when this natural order of things is violated further reveals the uniqueness of the human person. Only as the Judeo-Christian tradition came to institutionally impact the Western world, however, do we see this fuller view of the human person become built into the broader social fabric. Only as Christianity became integrated in the West did this understanding of the human person become the de facto universal meaning in social and political life broadly. This view developed into foundational understandings of the meaning of the human person and of "civilization" itself in the Western world over time. Seeds from this tree have now taken root worldwide and have grown into the fabric of the global culture, political frameworks, and law. Only under the shadows of this tree did these unique ideas of the human person and justice rise to become an aspirational vision, even if not always lived up to. Only in this tradition do they find their root.

In modernity, the vision remains, but the unique, coherent story and the political and legal theories that were established on it are now increasingly being dismantled. In a closed-world structure, the rationale for treating human persons with special dignity associated with who they are by

---

47. See Charry, *God and the Art of Happiness*, 3–62; on Stoicism, particularly Roman Stoicism (e.g., Cicero), see specifically 9–16. For an important example in the Greco-Roman tradition, see Cicero, *Ethical Writings*. It must be acknowledged, of course, that Greco-Roman ideas of human dignity were markedly narrower than in Judaism and especially Christianity. Intrinsic human dignity, body and soul, virtuous or not, slave or free, unborn, child or adult, whole or impaired, is a uniquely Judeo-Christian notion based on the *Imago Dei*.

nature is left largely to rhetorical force. Without the theory and story that give explanation and understanding, the cries of human dignity and for justice have little rational warrant.

Within a Judeo-Christian open-world-structure understanding of the nature and intended purpose for human beings, it is not within our purview simply to choose our own purpose and identity. These are given to us by God and are reflected in nature. In a naturalistic closed-world structure, there is no nature, no purpose, and no actual identity of the human person. It is all cultural construction. In our late-modern or postmodern world, we believe we choose our own purpose and our identity. Yet we still cry out for uniqueness, fairness, and justice. Ironically, we assert an unreal, socially constructed, and malleable, de-natured personhood, yet continue to appeal to real human dignity and real fairness and justice.

The very fact that we continue to hold to human uniqueness and continue to cry out for human justice simply reveals that these concepts are real, built into the world. No purely natural process without a transcendent source can build such things into nature. Acting as if there is no transcendent source and no created nature brings only chaos—a confused conundrum.

The above five examples are just that—examples. There are many more that could be explored, deep mysteries with practical implications. The unstated "model" constituents of our backcloth shape the makeup and lived experience of our social imaginary. They affect fundamental visons of our intellectual, social, and moral life. They affect the way we interpret reality and shape our vision of the meaning and purpose of life and our vision of human flourishing. They shape our private life and our views of public life and of what we consider to be the public good. The prevailing cultural backcloth today is an admixture of both world structure views, but the modern public default today is to a closed-world structure. In practice, modernity precludes a cosmic transcendent order and relegates beliefs in one to personal, subjective speculations, beliefs not to be engaged with on public concerns of everyday life. This modern default "model" has largely adopted only one way of knowing—empirical science—and since science cannot prove transcendence or God, we declare them not to exist. Yet on visceral concerns, like real and universal human rights and justice, etc., we cling to transcendence and God unawares. But we don't see any logical problems with this. We intuitively believe we are the most rational of generations and cultures, yet we cannot see the contradictive irrationality in the backcloth that has developed. Modernity's backcloth is a conundrum. This makes it difficult to make sense of the persisting transcendent echoes. We try to deny them, but like the Albatross, they just won't go away.

THE STORY-NESS & MYTHICAL CHARACTER OF OUR BACKCLOTH & SOCIAL IMAGINARY

Our backcloth is adopted and shaped in us in subtle ways through stories. And our stories give context and meaning to our lived experience. They function like myths. Cultures and individuals are shaped and formed over time by ideas, practices, rituals, beliefs, etc. Rarely do people go through an intellectual exercise to form or even reflect on their own backcloth, nor do many people readily look into what their culture's is. Backcloths are formed through "lived understanding" and become what "we naively take things to be."[48] This formation is narratival. Our cultural habits of mind are shaped by the stories we live in.[49] As English professor Daniel Taylor put it, the cultural habits of mind are constitutive of and reflect our "personal canon of sacred stories." This canon constitutes our controlling narratives. "When young, as . . . [our] canon is being created, we will fairly readily exchange some core stories for others. As we get older, we tend to defend our sacred stories the way Davy Crockett defended the Alamo, preferring to die with our stories rather than surrender them for alien ones."[50] In the modern scientific world, it is easy to forget that we and our worldviews are the product of our stories, some unexamined and inchoate, "born of the dynamics of human experience" and some "the products of pure thought . . . and worked out theoretically."[51] Both as individuals and as cultures, we live as the product of our stories. Our stories shape us. The stories that shape us form our backcloth, our interpretive lens. This lens becomes our unspoken

48. Taylor, *A Secular Age*, 3, 30.

49. On this from a sociological perspective, see Smith, "Living Narratives," in *Moral, Believing Animals*. Smith says, "For all of our science, rationality, and technology, we moderns are no less the makers, tellers, and believers of narrative construals of existence, history, and purpose than were our forebears at any other time in human history. But more than that, we not only continue to be animals who make stories but also animals who are *made by* our stories. . . . We, every bit as much as the most primitive or traditional of our ancestors, are animals who most fundamentally understand what reality is, who we are, and how we ought to live by locating ourselves within the larger narratives and metanarratives that we hear and tell, and that constitute what is real and significant" (64).

50. Taylor, *Tell Me a Story*, 79–80.

51. Naugle, *Worldview*, 137, where Naugle describes Heidegger's view of how worldviews are formed and work.

controlling narrative, the mythos through which we interpret reality. This is how myths work.

Joseph Campbell held that myths are stories that help us relate to the world and link us to a particular society. They are stories that allow us to make sense of the world and find our place in it.[52] Ironically, part of today's body of stories that constitute the prevailing closed-world social imaginary is that we no longer live with mythology. That's the way premodern cultures lived, we say, but we moderns no longer do. This embedded notion is a component of our backcloth. "We live in the age of reason" is the mantra of modernity. Consider Will and Ariel Durant's quip at the beginning of *The Age of Reason*, the seventh volume of their sweeping history of civilization: "Religions are born and may die, but superstition is immortal. *Only the fortunate can take life without mythology*."[53]

The goal of the Enlightenment was to employ human reason to release human beings from the shackles of authority and tradition. Enlightenment thinkers "believed that human reason could be used to combat ignorance, superstition, and tyranny and to build a better world."[54] Enlightenment philosopher giant "[Immanuel] Kant defines 'enlightenment' as humankind's release from its self-incurred immaturity; 'immaturity is the inability to use one's own understanding without the guidance of another.' Enlightenment," he says, "is the process of undertaking to think for oneself, to employ and rely on one's own intellectual capacities in determining what to believe and how to act." This confidence "in human reason is generally paired with suspicion or hostility toward other forms or carriers of authority (such as tradition, superstition, prejudice, myth and miracles), insofar as these are seen to compete with the authority of reason. Enlightenment philosophy tends to stand in tension with established religion."[55] The Enlightenment sought to achieve these goals by establishing an objective, universal way of knowing. Unaided pure reason plus the experimental scientific method were believed to achieve this goal. It is commonly believed that this objective universal rationality was attained, though it was not.[56] The Enlightenment is believed to be the great breakthrough of reason over faith—that we learned to live in the age of reason instead of the age of faith and superstition. Thus, the prevailing belief today is that we are among the fortunate who have learned to "take life without mythology."

---

52. Campbell and Moyers, *Power of Myth*, 22–23.

53. Durant and Durant, *Story of Civilization*, 575, 647, emphasis added.

54. Brians, "Enlightenment."

55. See Bristow, "Enlightenment."

56. See MacIntyre, *Whose Justice? Which Rationality?*, 6.

But listen to famous American intellectual Gore Vidal in an interview with Studs Terkel in 1961:

> You're born into a society and you are shaped by it, whether you know it or not or whether you like it or not. Each of us is born into a prison, of received opinion of superstition and of prejudices. . . . Alfred Whitehead said something fascinating about this. He said, you know you can always determine the nature of any society by the things it does not write about itself. It takes them so much for granted they feel no need to state it. So by the omissions you can begin to determine what a culture is like. . . . The prison is going to break you eventually, but you can at least get a look out; and it is the look out that is art—seeing something that is elsewhere, an alternative to the life that you're leading. *So, to try to see the thing whole.*[57]

Now consider Plato's famous allegory of the cave. In Plato's view the day-to-day world of change and flux in which we live reflects our participation in a more real and unchanging world, what he called to the world of "forms" or ideas. He describes the difference between the two worlds in his famous allegory, where he likens the changing world to people chained together in a cave with a big fire burning behind, the light from which casts shadows of their movements on the wall before them. The people in the cave interpret the shadowed movements as the sum total of reality. Only when a person escapes the chains and makes his way out of the cave, after a period of acclimation to correct his blindness, can he see the truly real world. Like in the movie *The Truman Show*, escaping the cave allows him to understand that the only reality he'd ever known is a mere shadow in comparison to an even more real world. The reality of the everyday world obtains its reality by "participating" in the truer world. The sensible things of this changing world are reflections of and point toward the more real world. But the "sensible" things in the world of those in the cave blinded them to the greater reality. Plato, using his teacher Socrates as the interlocutor, makes the point that even after the person who escaped saw the greater reality and returned to tell his compatriots about it, they wouldn't believe him. Socrates had predicted the outcome: "*Will he not fancy that the shadows which he formerly saw are truer than the objects which are now shown to him?*"[58] Not because

---

57. Vidal, "Gore Vidal on America." Emphasis added. Vidal was an atheist. He was right about the prison of the dominant cultural myth to which every generation is incarcerated unawares; even he was.

58. Plato, *Republic*, 280. Emphasis added.

it wasn't so, but because they preferred their current way of thinking. The prisoners preferred their prison, their blindness.

Were the Durants right? Have we come of age where we can take life without mythology? Or is Vidal closer to right, that we are *all* born into a society and shaped by it such that we are *all* in a prison of received opinion of superstition and of prejudices? Do even we moderns live in a myth unawares? Is it possible that Plato's ancient allegory of the cave applies even to us today? Is it perhaps true that the very movement we now call the Enlightenment, by reducing the meaning of reason, simply created a new and different world of shadows? Is there actually a truer, fuller, richer, more-real world all around us all the time and we just don't see it? Is it possible that our "enlightenment" resulted in new prejudices, such that when we encounter and are told of a truer, fuller, richer, more-real world, we still fancy the shadows that we formerly saw as truer than the objects made known by the true light?

The truth is, there are no fortunate few. There is no enlightened age of reason that can "take life without mythology." As Friedrich Nietzsche, the preeminent modernist atheist, made clear, we fortunate moderns cannot live without myths any more than premoderns; we just create new ones. In the modern age the myths just changed. English professor Thomas Howard put it this way: "The myth sovereign in the old age was that everything means everything. The myth sovereign in the new is that nothing *means* anything."[59]

We all live in the story-ness and mythical character of our backcloth. So let's look deeper into "myth." What does it mean, and how might it relate to the passage to modernity we have gone through?

---

59. Howard, *Chance or the Dance?*, 12.

3

"Myth" & the Prospects of a Whole

THE DURANTS' USE OF the term *myth* corresponds with the Oxford English Dictionary's (OED) second definition: "A widespread but untrue or erroneous story or belief; a widely held misconception; a misrepresentation of the truth. Also: something existing only in myth; a fictitious or imaginary person or thing." This is the most popular understanding of myth today. But Nietzsche's use captures a different sense. Nietzsche made it clear he embraced the closed, this-world-only plane of existence: "God is Dead and we killed him," he writes in *The Gay Science*.[1] In his *On the Genealogy of Morals* he traces how the Western world had long ago fallen prey to the fantasy that there is a real transcendent reality and, in particular, how the Western world drank the Christian "slave-revolt" Kool-Aid that humility and service are the highest virtues. In his *Thus Spoke Zarathustra* he makes it clear that we must accept that this world is all there is, that God is dead, and that we have to mourn this. This mourning he calls the first step of nihilism. But once we do, we must take the second step in nihilism. This kind of nihilism is the creation of a new story: the will to power, the story of the Overman (or Superman). In the Overman, we reconstruct a whole new horizon, a new transcendence, a this-world-only transcendence, made by us, similar, he says, to how the previous horizon came about.[2] This captures the OED's first definition of myth: "A traditional story, typically involving supernatural beings or forces, which embodies and provides an explanation, aetiology

1. Nietzsche, *Gay Science*, 280, as cited in Pearson and Large, *The Nietzsche Reader*, xxv.

2. For Nietzsche the Overman (Übermensch) is like the most important "higher men" in the past, some of whom he identifies as Homer, Socrates, Moses, and Jesus. These men created new horizons, but in his view illusory ones. The Overman does this too but without the delusion of the divine. See Robert E. Wood, *Placing Aesthetics*, 214.

[the study of causation], or justification for something such as the early history of a society, a religious belief or ritual, or a natural phenomenon." Nietzsche's use, of course, eliminates the supernatural beings or forces but he
retains the idea of myth still present in all cultures—the backcloth character
of controlling stories.

These two dimensions of myth constitute the modernist and postmodernist outlooks in which we live today. The first reflects the flattened
(no transcendent) reality of a closed-world structure. The second, in its
Nietzschean closed-world-structure form, reflects that the only reality is
one we construct: cultural and moral relativity whose only reference is to
other contingent things, ideas, and identities. What meaning there is, we
alone construct. And, as Nietzsche says, this includes constructing a new
kind of this-world-only transcendence, a new horizon we fabricate out of
whole cloth. In such a world, the hardened-materialist version focuses all
the energy on skepticism, asserting that empirical fact demonstrates that
any notion that there is merit in age-old myths is spurious. They are delusions, the fantasy of faith in superstitious ghosts. This is bad for the world
and must be overcome: only the fortunate can take life without mythology.
The Nietzschean revised version of myth focuses on recasting the myth with
new horizon lines, including remaking and redefining culture and ourselves
within the constraints of a this-world-only imagination. The result is endless
self-refashioning and identity-making—e.g., Rachel A. Dolezal's "I identify
as black" and Bruce "Caitlyn" Jenner's claim that "the identity that fits her
inner sense of self" is a female body.[3]

But there is a richer, deeper sense to myth that in the midst of our current cultural moment we hardly ever consider, something poetic or mytho-
poeic.[4] In his *Poetics*, Aristotle uses the Greek term *mythos* to describe what
we now call *plot*. The literal meaning of ancient Greek *mythos* is a report,
tale, or story. In the broadest sense, Aristotle's *Poetics* is about epic poetry,
in particular tragedy and comedy (though all that survives today is his writ-

3. Brock, "Caitlin Jenner." For a more thorough review of identity politics, see
Heyes, "Identity Politics." Citation of gender identity change here as an example of self-
refashioning is not intended to dismiss genuine gender confusion. It is to point out that
in a this-world-only closed world structure myth, identity means nothing real.

4. See Tolkien's use of the term. Mythopoeia (also mythopoesis, after Hellenistic
Greek μυθοποιία, μυθοποίησις, "myth-making") is a narrative genre in modern literature and film where a fictional mythology is created by the writer of prose or other
fiction. This meaning of the word *mythopoeia* follows its use by J. R. R. Tolkien in the
1930s. The authors in this genre integrate traditional mythological themes and arche-
types into fiction. This term is first introduced by Tolkien in his poem "Mythopoeia,"
prompted in part by the evening conversation Tolkien, Dyson, and Lewis had about
myth. Tolkien expands and analyzes its use in his essay "On Fairy-Stories."

ings on tragedy). For Aristotle, such writings included Homer's *Iliad* and *Odyssey* and Sophocles' *Oedipus the King* among others. As time went along, long poems and narratives with similar sweep and scope were called epics: e.g., ancient Mesopotamian mythology like the *Epic of Gilgamesh* and Babylonian mythology like *Atrahasis and Enuma Elish* and later in the Roman Medieval and Modern periods like Virgil's *Aeneid*, Ovid's *Metamorphoses*, *Beowulf* (anonymous), Milton's *Paradise Lost* and *Regained*, Blackmore's *King Arthur*, Southey's *Joan of Arc*, Yeats's *The Wanderings of Oisin*, and Tolkien's *Lord of the Rings*, among others.

Aristotle's *Poetics* outlines and describes certain features that an epic poem, a play, or a dramatic narrative should have.[5] "Mythos" was the first of six parts: plot, characters, diction, thought, spectacle, and melody. He went on to describe four features of plot: 1. It must be a whole, including "beginning, middle and end"; 2. it must be "'complete,' having 'unity of action'"; 3. it must be "'of a certain magnitude,' both quantitatively (length, complexity) and qualitatively ('seriousness' and universal significance)"; and 4. it must be "either simple or complex, although complex is better. Simple plots have only a 'change of fortune' (*catastrophe*). Complex plots have both 'reversal of intention' (*peripeteia*) and 'recognition' (*anagnorisis*) connected with the catastrophe. Both *peripeteia* and *anagnorisis* turn upon surprise."[6] Plot in these senses calls attention to how stories, poems, and plays can help us see an overarching "plot" to our lives that makes sense of them. It shows how the plots of epic stories help us make sense of who we are as individuals and societies. This is how myth works. That myth works this way suggests a grand plot, a true epic, a true myth that makes sense of and gives true meaning to life.

This sense is the general meaning of plot: the main or guiding story of a narrative, or the "pattern, rhythm, sequence" of the story that guides and makes sense of, gives meaning to the actions of the characters. In his book *Tell me a Story: The Life-Shaping Power of Our Stories*, author Dan Taylor points out that "many locate the origin of narrative and plot in the very beginnings of human experience," that stories and plot are the "first rituals—and therefore the first step toward art and religion." Plot is the "ability to recognize the patterns, and to pattern one's own actions after them" and increases "the odds of surviving. It still does. We live better and longer if we can find a pattern, a plot, to our lives. [Alasdair MacIntyre] claims that when someone complains that their life is meaningless, they often are really saying that 'the narrative (story) of their life has become unintelligible to

---

5. Aristotle, *Poetics*.

6. McManus, "Outline of Aristotle's Theory."

them, that it lacks any point, any movement towards a climax or a telos."[7] All of our lives are guided by plot, stated or unstated.

The age of reason did not eliminate guiding myths by which the peoples of the world live. The myths just changed. Human beings are mythmakers. It's no less true now after the passage through the Enlightenment into the age of reason. A question should arise in our minds when we realize this: is it possible that our mythmaking nature is the echo of a Grand Myth, one written not *by* us but *in* us, *in* creation by the creator?

This is what dawned on C. S. Lewis when he was still skeptical before he became a Christian. He had a life-changing conversation one night in 1931 with his friends J. R. R. Tolkien and Hugo Dyson. "Lewis had never underestimated the power of myth. Far from it, for one of his earliest loves had been the Norse myth of the dying and rising god Balder. . . . [His friend Owen] Barfield had shown him the crucial role mythology had played in the history of language and literature. But he still did not believe in the myths that delighted him. Beautiful and moving though such stories might be, they were (he said) ultimately untrue. As he expressed to Tolkien, myths are 'lies and therefore worthless, even though breathed through silver.'"[8] While Lewis was enamored of myths, he didn't like Christianity because he simply believed that it could not be true.

Lewis had invited his friends to have dinner at his home in Oxford. After dinner they went for a walk and were discussing Christianity and myth. After Lewis had told Tolkien and Dyson his feeling that while fascinating, myths were worthless lies, Tolkien said, "*No . . . they are not lies.*" Reflecting back on this conversation later, Lewis recalls that just as Tolkien spoke there was

> "a rush of wind which came so suddenly on the still, warm evening and sent so many leaves pattering down that we thought it was raining. We held our breath."
>
> When Tolkien resumed he took his argument from the very thing that they were watching.
>
> You look at trees, he said, and call them "trees," and probably you do not think twice about the word. You call a star a "star," and think nothing more of it. But you must remember that these words, "tree," "star," were (in their original forms) names given to these objects by people with very different views from yours. To you, a tree is simply a vegetable organism, and a star simply a ball of inanimate matter moving along a mathematical course. But the first men to talk of "trees" and "stars" saw things very differently. To them, the world was alive with

7. Taylor, *Tell Me a Story*, 58.
8. Carpenter, *The Inklings*, 42–43.

mythological beings. They saw the stars as living silver, bursting into flame in answer to the eternal music. They saw the sky as a jewelled tent, and the earth as the womb whence all living things have come. To them, the whole of creation was "myth-woven and elf-patterned."

This was not a new notion to Lewis, for Tolkien was, in his own manner, expressing what Barfield had said in *Poetic Diction*. Nor, said Lewis, did it effectively answer his point that myths are lies.

But, replied Tolkien, man is not ultimately a liar. He may pervert his thoughts into lies, but he comes from God, and it is from God that he draws his ultimate ideals. Lewis agreed: he had, indeed, accepted something like this notion for many years. Therefore, Tolkien continued, not merely the abstract thoughts of man *but also the imaginative inventions* must originate with God, and must in consequence reflect something of eternal truth. In making myths and practising "mythopoeia" and peopling the world with elves and dragons and goblins, a storyteller, or "sub-creator" as Tolkien liked to call such a person, is actually fulfilling God's purpose, and reflecting a splintered fragment of the true light. Pagan myths are therefore never just "lies": there is always something of the truth in them.[9]

They continued to talk. Lewis expressed his hesitations about the core of the Christian story. While he had extensively reviewed and studied the sources and documents of Christianity and had become convinced it did actually happen, he expressed to Tolkien his misgivings about the core elements of the story. "How," he said, could "the life and death of Someone else (whoever it was) two thousand years ago . . . help us now—except in so far as his example could help us." Lewis was put off by the notion, right there at the center of the Christian story, of "propitiation," "sacrifice," and so on. How could the death and resurrection of Christ save the world? Tolkien responded to Lewis consistent with what he'd been saying before but with a bigger idea and specific to the Christian story: "Had he not shown how pagan myths were, in fact, God expressing himself through the minds of poets, and using the images of their 'mythopoeia' to express fragments of eternal

9. Ibid., 43. For further explanation of Tolkien's view of myth as a reflection of truth, see Pearce, *Tolkien Man and Myth*. Pearce writes of Tolkien's view "In his mythical creations, or sub-creations as he would call them, he shows how the unseen hand of God is felt far more forcefully in myth than it is ever felt in fiction. Paradoxically, fiction works with facts, albeit invented facts, whereas myth works with truth, albeit truth dressed in fancy disguises. Furthermore, since facts are physical and truth is metaphysical, myth, being metaphysical, is spiritual." Pearce, "J. R. R. Tolkien: Truth and Myth."

truth? Well, then, Christianity (he said) is exactly the same thing—with the enormous difference that the poet who invented it was God Himself, and the images He used were real men and actual history." Tolkien continued: "Here is a *real* Dying God, with a precise location in history and definite historical consequences. The old myth has become fact." Tolkien suggested to Lewis that he see the Christian story in a different light but clearly within the bounds of Lewis's understanding of how myths are used in classical literature. He said, "Could [you] not transfer that attitude, that appreciation of story, to the life and death of Christ? Could [you] not treat it as a story, be fully aware that [you] could draw nourishment from it which [you] could never find in a list of abstract truths?"[10] This was a major turning point in Lewis's eventually embracing the Christian faith.

Following from this conversation, in his own short essay called "Myth Became Fact," Lewis recounts a dialogue with another friend, Corineus. In this conversation Corineus appealed to the definition of myth as superstition and Lewis responded with the definition of myth as explanatory story and with Tolkien's grand idea of myth. According to Corineus "Christianity is something so barbarous that no modern man can really believe it: the moderns who claim to do so are in fact believing in a modern system of thought which retains the vocabulary of Christianity and exploits the emotions inherited from it while quietly dropping the essential doctrines. [He] compared modern Christianity with the modern English monarchy: the forms of kingship have been retained, but the reality has been abandoned. . . . 'Why not cut the chord?', asks Corineus. 'Everything would be much easier if you would free yourself from this vestigial mythology.'" Lewis provided the following response:

> To be sure: far easier. Life would be far easier for the mother of an invalid child if she put it into an Institution and adopted someone else's healthy baby instead. Life would be far easier to many a man if he abandoned the woman he has actually fallen in love with and married someone else because she is more suitable. The only defect of the healthy baby and the suitable woman is that they leave out the patient's only reason for bothering about a child or wife at all. "Would not conversation be much more rational than dancing?" said Jane Austen's Miss Bingley. "Much more rational," replied Mr. Bingley, "but much less like a ball."
>
> In the same way, it would be much more rational to abolish the English monarchy. But how if, by doing so, you leave out the one element in our State which matters most. How if the

10. All references to this conversation between Lewis and Tolkien are taken from Carpenter, *The Inklings*, 43–44.

monarchy is the channel through which all the *vital* elements of citizenship—loyalty, the consecration of secular life, the hierarchical principle, splendor, ceremony, continuity—still trickle down to irrigate the dustbowl of modern economic Statecraft?

The real answer of even the most "modernist" Christianity to Corineus is the same. Even assuming (which I most constantly deny) that the doctrines of historic Christianity are merely mythical, it is the myth which is the vital and nourishing element in the whole concern. . . . It is what Corineus calls the myth that abides; it is what he calls the modern living thought that moves away.

This is no less true with the modern and postmodern myths. If the truth of the matter is that the story of Christianity is the grand myth authored and told by God, then it would be much more than the result of mere human language, imagination, and writing utensils, as creative as human beings are. It would reflect the infinite creativity, power, and resources of discourse of the Triune God. What if God used the artistic fodder of infinite imagination and the writing utensils of a real cosmos, real things and real human beings? What then? Then the myths we construct ourselves, even the modern and postmodern ones, are shadows of the real thing. "Those elements even in modernist Christianity which Corineus regards as vestigial, are the substance: what he takes for the 'real modern belief' is the shadow."[11] In other words, though human beings construct stories and myths, and though they might provide something of a guide to our lives and enable us to make some meaning in and of them, these are shadows of a bigger truth. These small stories, smaller myths, are reflective of a grand myth, a true myth, written not by us but by the great artisan, the creator himself. In this story all other stories fit.

The Judeo-Christian story is the Grand Model, the Grand Story, the Myth Become Fact. It is the Grand Plot, the guiding story of all our personal narratives, the pattern, rhythm, and sequence of the story that guides and makes sense of and gives real meaning to the actions of us all who are the characters in God's story. As we shape our lives into the patterns, rhythm, and sequence of *his* story, the odds of surviving are better. In God's story all our small stories have real meaning. Their source is in God's story.

11. All quotations in this section referring to his conversation with Corineus are from Lewis, "Myth Became Fact," 63–65.

4

Reweaving the Tapestry
Finding the Whole in the Parts

IN MY INELEGANT POEM "Hallowed Terminal," I began with the image of an airport terminal at Christmastime—the hustle and bustle of people going this way and that trying to get to their gate on time to get home in time for Christmas. The feeling is a form of organized chaos. Amid all the competing sounds of roller-bags clicking across the tiles of the floor, the voices of people chatting, kids crying, and people like me just wanting to get home, there remains the constancy of muted sounds coming over the public address system. There, in and through the cacophony of it all, emanating from above the fray, is a voice that echoes softly. We must listen closely, intently to hear it. Only that voice gives order to the chaos. Only in that voice do the echoes have meaning.

There is a bigger story reflected in the echoes of a constant mysterious presence—transcendent yet concrete, too, echoes of the voice of God. But just as the mysterious presence often eludes us, so also is the closed world brought about by aspirations of the intellect to overcome the perceived naiveté of superstition and authorities. Like Coleridge's captain in *The Rime of the Ancient Mariner*, we moderns embarked upon a grand passage of adventure to discover new worlds. Along the way, at least at first, when faced with a dense fog in treacherous waters, we listened intently, and we were rescued by the great Albatross—the echo of the voice of God in the human soul— and we made it through. But as we traveled on in calmer waters, the bird annoyed us, so we shot it and hung it around our neck as an achievement, a trophy. But it echoes on in a still, small voice. We remain disturbed by its persistence, as expressed in the angst of Knight in the *Seventh Seal*[1] and Jean Paul Sartre's atheistic existentialism. We can't live well and often not long with the deep anxiety over the meaningless absurdity of it all.

Believing ourselves to have become wise by our narrowed rationalism, and though we have used it to astonishing success in our modern science, we have flattened reality onto a contingent plane of random, disparate interactions. Like the people in the land of Shinar in the biblical story of the Tower of Babel,[2] despite successes that have produced many great things, the result is confusion, a fragmented world of pieces and parts. We still encounter the echoes, but because the world is now closed, they make no sense. They just bounce around. Our analysis says they are nothing, but our soul says there's more.

It is commonly believed that doubts about God and a grand story arise because they conflict with reason and rationality. It is far more a loss of imagination. In a closed-world social imaginary where science is king, it's about analysis and not about seeing things whole, as Gore Vidal points out. Imagination is the synthetic faculty that can weave the pieces and parts into a whole—not an imagin*ary* whole, but a *real* whole.

In classical literature and drama, stories had a beginning, middle, and end, with five parts: exposition, rising action, climax, falling action, and denouement. The denouement is the point in a story where all the action, rabbit trails, and subplots come together to allow for resolution to the overall plot. It's not the end but the beginning of the end. It provides a sense of coherence to the story and the characters' actions and portends a sense of resolution. In the fragmented, closed-world modern and postmodern outlook, there is no mechanism to see and sense a denouement to the world's story. The prevailing sense within the backcloth of modernity is that there's not one. There can't be in a reality of pure contingency. But we still act as if there is one, and we keep searching for it. We long for coherence.

---

1. Kreeft, *Heaven*, 52–53.
2. Genesis 11:1–9.

> *Imagination* is the "synthetic faculty; that is, it brings things together (synthesizes) rather than breaks things apart (analyzes). . . . it is an image-making faculty; that is, its tendency is from the abstract to the concrete, and not vice versa."
>
> THOMAS HOWARD, *CHANCE OR THE DANCE* (1969)
>
> The word *religion* is derived from the Latin *religāre*, or "re-ligate," literally, "to bind together," "to re-ligament," "to see the whole." *Analysis* is derived from the Greek *análusis* from *aná*, meaning "on, up," plus *lúō*, "to unbind," "to loosen."
>
> DEVELOPED FROM THE OXFORD ENGLISH DICTIONARY

Imagination is the ligature of the pieces and parts to see the thing whole, connecting the head with the heart to find the meaning. It enables disparate words, ideas, concepts, and actions to make a narrative, which enables life to be experienced as a grand drama. It allows us to see concrete things as windows. If this book were a drama, this chapter is the top of the dramatic arc, the climax that leads to the denouement.

We need not less imagination to see things whole and make sense of the pieces and parts. We need more. This chapter shows how imagination enables the denouement of a grand story of reality to be recognized.

I invoke C. S. Lewis again here for his relatively unique combination of deep analytical skills and extraordinary imaginative capacity.

To begin let's consider an image Lewis casts to allow us to see the effects of our modern way of approaching everything. In his short essay "Meditation in a Toolshed," he says we moderns are like Lewis himself standing in a darkened shed.[3] This essay shows the consequences of the tendency to "look at" rather than "look along" a light beam. Here's the setting: Lewis is standing in a darkened toolshed, and there is a narrow light beam streaming in from a crack at the top of the door. "Everything else was almost pitch black," he says. "I was seeing the beam, not seeing things by it." To look *at the light* or look *along the light*? When the focus is trained at the light beam as a beam, all that is seen is the light beam and the particles of dust appearing in the otherwise dark toolshed. "Then I moved, so that the beam fell on my eyes. Instantly the whole picture vanished. I saw no toolshed, and (above all) no beam. I instead saw, framed in the irregular cranny at the top of the door, green leaves moving on the branches of a tree outside and beyond that, 90

---

3. All quotations that follow are from Lewis, "Meditations in a Toolshed," 212–15.

odd million miles away, the sun." Looking along the light, the beam of light as a beam vanishes, and a whole other world outside comes into view.

Lewis's point is obvious: the angle of our vision, what we're focused on, is crucial. Analytically focusing just on the light-beam, we can obtain a certain measure and a certain kind of knowledge. We can inspect every particle of dust in the beam and understand it in great detail very well. We can, if we choose, put a prism into the beam and analyze the distinctive colors that make up the light. This intense analytical focus is metaphorically like looking through a microscope. This is the way we arrive at our disbelief in God in our prevailing closed-world structure and why we dismiss the persistent echoes of the voice of God. By intense analytical focus it becomes easy to conclude that what we can see when staring at the light beam is all there is. We discover many interesting and useful details with this angle of vision—this is what science does, and must do. But when we look along the light and lose awareness of the light as a beam, we see *by* the light. It sheds light on everything else.

Recall Oxford research professor Michael Ward's comment about the smallness of scientific statements (on pages 39–40). By its nature science must be analytical. To do its job it must ask narrowly focused questions, and its answers will invariably be small. "When you start trying to make larger statements," Ward says, "you move into the language of the humanities and then into the arts and then into religion. Religious statements, by saying things which attempt to explain life in the round, use language which is very hard to quantify, to measure, to test. But that is because they are trying to say a very great deal; they are trying to find the unity, the oneness, the heart of all reality."[4] Herein lies our problem.

The passage to modernity brought with it a new way of approaching almost everything. We are analysts. The question is, is analysis enough? Can it possibly discern a grand story to reality if there is one? It cannot, for several reasons. Among the most important are two: first, the intensity of analytical focus causes us to be blinded to the imprisonment of our own cultural moment, as Gore Vidal's comments capture. Second, as Lewis's metaphor of the light shining in the toolshed calls attention to, an analysis-only outlook forces us to miss the whole, the reality beyond which is the source of the light.

There is too much reality that is missed or swept under the rug in an analysis-only approach. Our predilections to this kind of analysis today, along with having educated ourselves into a predisposition to a closed-world structure, cause us to think we are maintaining the most rational view of

---

4. Ward, "Science and Religion in the Writings of C. S. Lewis," 10.

things. As we have seen, this is not the case. Despite our current restrictive, reductive social imaginary, we continue to live and act as if things still really mean something. We also saw that many of the biggest questions and mysteries that have always loomed out there still do. Through the few examples we discussed, we see that what are often perceived as intellectual barriers to belief in God and a transcendent grand story are false barriers. The ways we live continue to serve as a sign of real transcendence and a true grand story, even when our modern cultural conditions of unbelief suggest otherwise.

We must re-ligament the world of pieces and parts that our preoccupation with analysis has pulled apart. This is what imagination enables. It's what it always does even if we don't recognize it. Though science and scientists extensively use metaphors (recall that forming hypotheses and theoretical models requires the act of imagination) and then use them to abstract and generalize the way certain features of reality work, we easily forget this. As noted earlier, for laymen over time "the scientific metaphors . . . become fossilized: we quickly forget that they are metaphors and assume they are literal."[5]

To illustrate, consider this exchange between Gradgrind and Sissy Jupe in Charles Dickens's novel *Hard Times*. "Teach these boys and girls nothing but the Facts," says Gradgrind. "Facts alone are wanted in life. Plant nothing else. You can only form the minds of reasoning animals upon Facts: nothing else will ever be of service to them." In Gradgrind's class he once asks his students to describe what a horse is. He sees a new young student, "girl number twenty," Sissy (Cecilia) Jupe, whose father "belongs to horse-riding." He asks about Sissy's father: "Your father breaks horses, don't he?" Sissy starts talking about what breaking means, that it occurs in "the ring," and Gradgrind interrupts. "You mustn't tell us about the ring, here. Very well, then. Describe your father as a horsebreaker. He doctors sick horses, I dare say?" "Oh, yes sir," Sissy says. "Very well, then. Your father is a veterinarian surgeon, a farrier, a horsebreaker. Give me your definition of a horse." She proceeds to describe what her father does and the horses she knows. Gradgrind, irate, says, "We don't want to know anything about all that, here." And, he says, Sissy "possessed of no facts, in reference to one of the commonest of animals!" According to Gradgrind, Sissy doesn't know what a horse is. He then calls on the boy Bitzer. "Describe a horse," he says. Bitzer answers, "Quadruped. Graminivorous. Forty teeth, namely twenty-four grinders, four eye-teeth, and twelve incisive. Sheds coat in the spring; in marshy countries, sheds hoofs, too. Hoofs hard, but requiring to be shod

---

5. Holyer, "Lewis on the Epistemic Significance of Imagination," 220.

with iron. Age known by marks in mouth.' Thus (and much more)." "'Now girl number twenty,' said Mr. Gradgrind, 'You know what a horse is.'"[6]

Through Gradgrind, Dickens shows how easy it is in our modernist default perspective to conclude that if we just have "the facts," we know all there is to know. But Sissy Jupe shows us there is more, much more than abstracted analytical facts alone can deliver. We intuitively know the horse contains an invisible life, a form or essence. This is what Sissy perceives. It was this that Sissy understood to be what a horse *is*, what it means to *know* what a horse is. "The essence of [things,] bread, for example, is grasped intuitively by the mind regardless of the sensory 'accidentals' of color, shape, and so on, and in this way the universal idea of bread, or bread-ness, is achieved. . . . That the invisible life, the form, is *in* the thing, not elsewhere. [Unless we train it otherwise] . . . the mind, the soul . . . correspond with this invisible reality."[7] Such intuitions are the resonance we encounter with things in this world prior to pulling them apart, abstracting them. When we pull them apart, dissonance emerges. This is the angst we feel: we intellectually believe and use the language of Gradgrind but in our bones we feel what Sissy does. We just know a horse is more than its factual, abstract description.

Imagination is the synthetic faculty that pulls the two worlds together. As we peer at the light, we can continue to discover and find astounding uses for the pieces and parts. But with that alone we experience little meaning. To experience an integrated reality and know true meaning and see the vast vistas beyond the darkened toolshed, and to find the source of the light of integration, we must turn our heads and look along the light. We must see things whole.

6. Dickens, *Hard Times*, 10–11. I am indebted to Ken Myers and Jay Wood for this illustration and passage in Dickens found in Myers, "Lost Sense of Learning," 14–15; and Wood, *Epistemology*, 184–85.

7. Taylor, *Poetic Knowledge*, 18. I am aware that the precise acceptance of "universals" as expressed in Plato, Aristotle (in his own unique way), and Augustine is widely debated, even by Christians. However, even if their specific articulations are debatable, Nicholas Wolterstorff makes a strong case for universals as "kinds" (e.g., a performance of Beethoven's Ninth symphony is a kind of symphony, where symphonies are just as real as a particular performance), though he does not hold that Plato's notions of forms are like paradigms to be imitated nor that medieval theology's notion that universals are exemplars "for anyone's creative activity." Wolterstorff's limitation on the practical use of universals does not limit their reality or the sense that particulars (including particular human beings) participate in them. See Wolterstorff, *On Universals*. On the question of universals, also see Armstrong's three volumes: *Universals: An Opinionated Introduction*; *Nominalism & Realism: Universals & Scientific Realism*, Vol. 1; and *A Theory of Universals: Universals & Scientific Realism*, Vol. 2.

SEEING THINGS WHOLE

Philosopher Martin Heidegger famously suggested we are "thrown into existence," by which he meant we simply find ourselves here with no rhyme or reason. Albert Camus wrote a book about this notion, *The Myth of Sisyphus*, in which he discusses the absurdity of existence. The book takes its title image from the figure in Greek mythology who was condemned to repeat forever the same meaningless task of pushing a boulder up a mountain, only to see it roll down again. For Camus this is a picture of modern existence without God and any eternal, enduring values or truth. In a famous section of *Walden*, Henry David Thoreau writes, "The mass of men lead lives of quiet desperation. What is called resignation is confirmed desperation. From the desperate city you go into the desperate country, and have to console yourself with the bravery of minks and muskrats. A stereotyped but unconscious despair is concealed even under what are called the games and amusements of mankind. There is no play in them, for this comes after work. But it is a characteristic of wisdom not to do desperate things."[8]

Everyone at times feels as if we have been simply thrown into existence, that life is absurd, and therefore we live lives of quiet desperation. But why is it a "characteristic of wisdom not to do desperate things"? Why do we keep pushing the rock up the hill, believing in our bones there is something to it, beyond it, something more? Why do we keep trying to find the meaning in things, in our daily lives? Why do we find the stories of our lives and those of others interesting, perhaps even compelling? The most plausible answer is because there is a real mythos—a real plot—to our lives.[9] As with poems there is a historical, ruddy concreteness to our lives, yet there is more

8. Thoreau, *Walden*, 8–9.

9. Sociologist Peter Berger coins the term "plausibility structure" in his *The Sacred Canopy*, 45–48. In this book and later in Berger, Berger, and Kellner, *The Homeless Mind*, the term is applied to describe how the plurality of social worlds of modern life confuse us: how, for example, we create separate spheres and plausibility structures for religion and public life, to enable us to make sense of the whole. In a world where we both continue to encounter signals of transcendence (see Berger's *A Rumor of Angels*) and yet the cultural institutional structures do not accommodate them, the formerly integrative plausibility structures don't work anymore. There are no anchors for the reconciliation of the two worlds we live in. What I am suggesting here is that the most plausible answer to the intellectual and social confusion we experience in modern life, where our default closed-world social imaginary says there is no transcendence and yet we continue to encounter signals of transcendence, is that we actually live in a Grand Story, the grand story of God, but we have lost a way to see it because in our modernist analytical mode we've broken our experienced reality into pieces and parts. To be reconciled to the plausibility of a Grand Story, we must see things whole.

there to *see through them* than momentary existence. There is a transcendent drama written and directed by God.

As Walt Whitman suggests when querying about life's meaning,

> The question, O me! so sad, recurring—What good amid these,
> O me, O life?
> *Answer.*
> That you are here—that life exists and identity,
> *That the powerful play goes on, and you may contribute a verse.*[10]

There is a grand drama occurring, and we are part of it. As far back as we can look, we have always seen glimpses of it in our natural inclination to reach for it in reason, in art, literature, music, in our ordinary daily lives, and in our religious proclivities. In this inclination we encounter pieces and parts of the actual truth. We retain an intuition of the Grand Story even though it is often fleeting, seemingly there for the moment but quickly gone, as if passing by. We resonate with it, as if it is a call from a "home" we have yet to fully know while also seemingly to have known it forever. But through the passage to modernity, resulting in a closed-world image of reality, we have made things even harder—we stare too intensely at the beam rather than looking along it. Though the powerful play goes on and we may contribute a verse, we no longer believe there is a grand drama but only an infinite set of meaningless scenes that we write each day.

To see the more, to see our dramas within a grand drama, we must see things whole.

From the time he was a boy, C. S. Lewis had always been enamored of the great myths—particularly those of Adonis, Bacchus, Balder, and others. He "always found the heart of these pagan stories . . . to be 'profound and suggestive of meanings beyond my grasp even tho' I could not say in cold prose "what it meant."'"[11] For Lewis, reason, to which he was always committed, "could only operate if it was first supplied with materials to reason about, and it was imagination's task to supply those materials."[12] "For me," he says, "reason is the natural organ of truth; but imagination is the organ of meaning." Further, he says, "meaning is the antecedent condition of both truth and falsehood, whose antithesis is not error but nonsense."[13] So it is important to stress that for Lewis and for our purposes, discussion of imagination is not something separate from reason but is integrally linked to it, and the goal is

10. Whitman, "O Me! O Life!" Emphasis added.
11. Ward, "Good Serves the Better," 64.
12. Ibid., 60–61.
13. Lewis, "Bluspels and Flalansferes," 265.

always truth. Lewis struggled with what the myths that captured his imagination meant. There was something elusive in them that he wanted to know.

This elusiveness was, for Lewis, even more confounding when it came to "joy." He would eventually come to see the resolution for both the meaning of myths and for joy in the same source. From the time he was a teen in boarding school, Lewis was fascinated by joy. He was constantly in search of it, persistently hoping to capture precisely what it was, what it meant. In his autobiography about his journey to faith, *Surprised by Joy*, he describes the elusiveness of it:

> All that such watching and waiting ever could find would be either an image . . . or a quiver in the diaphragm. I should never have to bother again about these images or sensations. I knew now that they were merely the mental track left by the passage of Joy—not wave but the wave's imprint on the sand.[14]

He would come to define this "joy" as something similar to what the German Romantics called *Sehnsucht*, which in a rather bland translation means simply a deep yearning. But Lewis draws out the richer meaning, calling it an "inconsolable longing" that has "a stab and a pang," "distinct not only from pleasure in general but even from aesthetic pleasure."[15] For Lewis joy was not an emotion or a sentimental feeling. "It is not some feeling we get when we look at a painting or when we hear an uplifting song. It is rather that intense sense we have when, in looking at a painting or hearing a song, we know and long for something more; something greater than what we are seeing or hearing," says Joe Pucker. For Lewis, Pucker says, "Aesthetic feeling is the feeling we get when we are content or satisfied with the beauty of people or things. When we use the word 'joy' we usually are thinking of something that is pleasant or satisfying and we almost always know what is bringing us to this feeling." Joy in this "usual sense," for Lewis, "refers to something (usually identifiable) that *removes* any discontentment. However, Lewis's word 'Joy' is more like the appreciation for all that is beautiful and inspiring on earth even *while* in a state of uneasy discontentment with it. . . . For Lewis, *Sehnsucht* is 'an unsatisfied desire which is itself more desirable than any other satisfaction. [Something] that anyone who has experienced it will want it again.'"[16] I call this kind of longing "the residue of grace" after a brief encounter with God.

14. Lewis, *Surprised By Joy*, 219.

15. Ibid., 72.

16. Pucker, *Apologetics of Joy*, 22. For a deeper exploration into Lewis's understanding of "Joy," see McGrath, "Arrows of Joy: Lewis's Argument from Desire," in *Intellectual World of C. S. Lewis*, 105–28.

It is this longing that Lewis expresses through Psyche in his novel *Till We Have Faces*:

> It was when I was happiest that I longed most. It was on happy days when we were up there on the hills, the three of us, with the wind and the sunshine. . . . It was so beautiful, it set me longing, always longing. Somewhere else there must be more of it. Everything seemed to be saying, Psyche come! But I couldn't (not yet) come and I didn't know where I was to come to. It almost hurt me. I felt like a bird in a cage when the other birds of its kind are flying home.[17]

It was this sense, this persistent deep longing—the wave's imprint on the sand, triggered by nature, in nature, even in himself, but which was ever so there-and-gone elusive—that captured Lewis as a young boy in school. This is what he saw in but that was never fully captured by the great myths that so fascinated him. It is what drove him to find the meaning in things, which could not be achieved through aloof, abstract analysis. There was truth there, the Truth. He could sense it. But it wasn't easy to get at. It could not be captured or contained.[18]

The first step along Lewis's way of discovery was reading George Mac-Donald's *Phantastes*, which he would later say was when his imagination was baptized. From that point on, for Lewis, imagination and reason had to work together. Both had to be satisfied, and only then could the "'command center,' the will, . . . turn about and receive the supernatural truth."[19]

Lewis continued to study at Oxford and to master the classics, philosophy, Greek poetry, and literature and to study the great religions and their sources, including Christianity. Through the years after World War I, he had ongoing conversations with his friend Owen Barfield about reason, imagination, and myth. Fifteen years after Lewis first read MacDonald's book, when he was thirty-one, he would have that fateful after-dinner conversation with his friends Tolkien and Dyson about myth, which was the penultimate step to his ultimate conversion. What troubled Lewis was not the facts of things; it was the imagination. He would later write to his friend Arthur Greeves, "'What has been holding me back . . . has not been so much a difficulty believing as a difficulty in knowing what the doctrine *meant*.' Tolkien and Dyson showed him that Christian doctrines are not the main thing

17. Lewis, *Till We Have Faces*, 74.

18. This realization by Lewis is the same idea David Bentley Hart alludes to when he says "beauty crosses boundaries." It is that "unmasterable excess contained in the object of beauty." Hart, *Beauty of the Infinite*, 20–21.

19. Ward, "Good Serves the Better," 64.

about Christianity. Doctrines are *translations* into concepts and ideas of that which God has already expressed in 'a language more adequate: namely the actual incarnation, crucifixion and resurrection' of Christ." Michael Ward, commenting on this, says, "The primary language of Christianity is a lived language, the real, historical, visible, tangible language of an actual person being born, dying and living again in a new, ineffably transformed way."[20]

Once Lewis stopped trying to analyze the myths and even Christianity—or, expressed as we've been saying, stopped "pulling things apart" or "translating" them into concepts—but accepted the story on its own terms first, he began to see what they *meant*. To focus on doctrine *before* seeing the meaning of the story, on its own terms, is to fall into the modernist trap.

Lewis's problem coming to faith is the same modern problem we've been describing. We moderns are so stuck on analysis that we can't see beyond it. To us, truth is found only in analysis. It was for Lewis, too, and this was a barrier. But he came to see that for the truth to be recognized, he needed to step back and see the meaning. Once he did, he describes it this way: "I believe in Christianity as I believe that the Sun has risen, not only because I see it, but because *by it I see everything else.*"[21]

All too often many religious believers today, Christians included, fall into the same trap as Lewis, emphasizing doctrine first over the whole story—or perhaps better, they mischaracterize doctrine in abstract terms. As Michael Ward says, commenting on this problem for Lewis, "Doctrines, though useful, are the product of analytical dissection; they recast the original, equivocal, historical material into abstract, less fully realized categories of meaning."[22] This is merely the effect of the modernist cultural outlook working itself out within the Christian community. It's no less hazardous there than in the culture at large. This is surely why, at least in part, theologian Kevin Vanhoozer recently published two scholarly works that address this problem: *The Drama of Doctrine* and *Remythologizing Theology*.

Vanhoozer, adapting famed twentieth-century philosopher Paul Ricoeur, says, "*Mythos* is a mode of discourse that configures human action so as to create a form of wholeness (i.e., unified action) out of a multiplicity of incidents. 'Poetics' refers to how authors create meaningful wholes (viz., stories) that allow one to make sense of what would otherwise be a chaotic jumble of unrelated events. A dramatic plot or *mythos* thus 'configures' a totality of time out of a succession of events. Ricoeur suggests that the *mythos*

20. Ibid.
21. Lewis, "Is Theology Poetry?" 140. Emphasis added.
22. Ward, "Good Serves the Better," 65.

of drama is to time what an icon of painting is to space."[23] This, Vanhoozer would say, is the proper role of doctrine, to make the story whole, not pull it apart.[24]

Imagination is necessary, as Lewis says, in order for the faculty of reason to have material of meaning to work with. But imagination alone does not yield truth. Reason is necessary too, otherwise imagination yields only an "imaginary world." But in the end "imaginative reason" is also insufficient. It cannot rise to the supernatural on its own. "Imagination and reason together," for Lewis and I suggest for us all, work not to serve themselves but to serve the will. They are enabled by God's Spirit to change the will. "The good serves the better and both serve the best. The best is the will, the heart of a person, and this must be reoriented by a meeting with the divine."[25]

No amount of argument or intellectual credibility will by itself cause anyone to have life-transforming faith in God. But a genuine encounter with God always will. Listen to Roger Scruton commenting on the great polymath Blaise Pascal: "Nobody who has the experience of [the real presence of the mysterious thing we call the transcendent one] is likely to think it to be simply an illusion: it comes to us with a self-verifying character that silences skepticism. . . . The night of 23 November, 1654, for two hours, [Pascal] experienced the total certainty that he was in the presence of God—'the God of Abraham, of Isaac and of Jacob, not the God of the philosophers and the wise men,' in other words a personal God, intimately revealed, not conjured by abstract argument."[26] In the end, there is no intellectual or other hurdle so great that a genuine encounter with God cannot overcome it.

23. Vanhoozer, *Remythologizing Theology*, 6.

24. To be clear, neither Tolkien, Dyson, Vanhoozer, nor am I saying doctrine is unimportant and that truth is unimportant. They are. It's simply to say that to focus on doctrine first and in an abstract, theoretical way, and then to generalize as if that were all there is, is to miss the drama of doctrine. This is to do in theology what Michael Ward says the scientist does, to make perhaps true statements but relatively small ones. Though perhaps "marvelously correct, [they are] a minuscule fraction of the total." When you start trying to make fuller statements, you move into the drama or *mythos* of doctrine.

25. Ward, "Good Serves the Better," 76.

26. Scruton, *Soul of the World*, 11–12.

THROUGH THE LOOKING GLASS

I'll tell you all my ideas about Looking-glass House. First, there's the room you can see through the glass—that's just the same as our drawing room, only the things go the other way.

—Alice in Lewis Carroll's *Through the Looking-Glass*

"This must be a simply enormous wardrobe!" thought Lucy, going still further in and pushing the soft folds of the coats aside to make room for her. Then she noticed that there was something crunching under her feet. "I wonder is that more moth-balls?" she thought, stooping down to feel it with her hand. But instead of feeling the hard, smooth wood of the floor of the wardrobe, she felt something soft and powdery and extremely cold.

—C. S. Lewis, *The Lion, the Witch and the Wardrobe*

One enduring thing we human beings are is storytellers and story-livers. Charles Dodgson, known to us as Lewis Carroll, is one of the best storytellers, as is C. S. Lewis. Carroll is most famous for the wonder-filled world of *Alice's Adventures in Wonderland*. Alice's adventures continue in *Through the Looking-Glass*. Carroll's yarns are among the best. They're exciting, and their resonance, especially with children, bespeak the seemingly innate, untaught ability in us all to imagine worlds beyond our own. Indeed, what *is* our world and the meaning we find in it? Is there only whatever meaning *we make* from the stuff of our lives—along the lines of the fashionable sentiment expressed in the 2015 movie *5 to 7*: "Life is a collection of moments; the idea is to have as many good ones as you can"? Are the stories we live, the adventures of our lives, only make-believe or merely fatefully adventitious? Or are the stories we live in truly *about* something? Do our lives really *mean* something? Is it possible and plausible that we participate in a bigger story? Is there anything *beyond* the wardrobe for Lucy? Is there really anything for us to see, like Alice, *through* the looking-glass?

ℭ

These are the questions we've been exploring. We have seen how imagination, as Professor Thomas Howard said, is the "synthetic faculty; that is, it brings things together (synthesizes) rather than breaks things apart (analyzes)."[27] This includes in our reasoning (including science), art, the daily rituals of our lives, the music we make, even the flickers of truth we find in the great myths and religions, and in and through the plots of our lives. Recall what atheist Gore Vidal said in his interview with Studs Terkel: we must "try to see the thing whole." Ironic though it is coming from Vidal's lips, this notion captures the difference in the root meanings of the words *religion* and *analysis*. *Religion* literally means "to bind together; to re-ligament; to see the whole." The human plausibility of a true grand story rests in wholes instead of just parts. We must see along the light to the transcendent reality that makes sense of everything else, to see the source of the light that sheds light on everything else.

We have explored a variety of aspects of the voyage to the modern world and can now better understand our culture of doubt and why we remain thirsty even with water all around. We live in a fragmented world of pieces and parts. In the old-world cast of mind, the way reason was conceived allowed us to encounter concrete things and through them to see more. In this older cast of mind, reason acknowledged intuition and imagination to be the integrators (the synthetic faculty) of how we know and how what we know bespeaks what really is there to be known. In the old world, few believed that the integrative faculties of reason told of the precise details of transcendence, but no one thought it wasn't there. Further, contrary to popular belief, in the old world people distinguished and discounted unwarranted superstition.[28] In the new world we have reduced reason to analysis, and a specific kind of analysis established on the foundation of doubt. A legitimate goal of the Enlightenment was to overcome unwarranted superstition, but in its wake doubt took over. Over time we came

---

27. Howard, *Chance or the Dance?*, 24

28. Charles Taylor spends extensive space on this in his *A Secular Age*. As a small example, take the festival Carnival (still celebrated in New Orleans as Mardi Gras, as well as in South America, particularly Brazil's Carnival). A "French cleric [describes what Carnival really was in the minds of the church and culture] in the technology of the day: 'We do these things in jest and not in earnest, as an ancient custom is, so that once a year the foolishness innate in us can come out and evaporate. Don't wine skins and barrels burst open if the air-hole is not opened from time to time? We too are old barrels'" (46). I would point out that just as Lewis shows how models and metaphors created and used by scientists for specified purposes become fossilized and come to be thought of as "the way things really are," so too can religious practices and festivals established for a particular purpose, like Carnival, take on a kind of reality never intended for the religious culture at large. This is the kind of superstition the Enlightenment rightly sought to eliminate, and the kind we should eliminate in our day.

to treat as knowledge only what can be proven through empirical methods, theories, and logical probabilities within the closed world of nature, that is, the modern scientific method. This new, highly disciplined, yet truncated model of reason was not wrong—indeed it was part of and an outgrowth of the older, more robust and integrated model of reason. It was just too narrow to accommodate the whole. The problem arose when the modern backcloth foreclosed the wider view of reason so that it could not speak to the whole. One thing that contributed to this is that we came to believe erroneously that there are models of knowing that are completely disinterested and outside of an interpretive milieu. The notion that "the facts speak for themselves" presumes a kind of god's-eye view of "objectivity" that is faulty. The delusion of an objective standpoint blinds us to our own controlling narratives and latent a priori philosophical commitments, ones more religious in character than scientific, and ones that do not fit the very narrow meaning of reason and rationality that is asserted to be "reason itself."

The modernist, truncated view of reason forced a hermeneutic of suspicion to anything that falls outside of its restricted domain of the possible. Its foundational premises require that it be blind and deaf to the possibility of anything more than the sum of the parts. If anything more, the closed-world postmodernist would say, it must be found in the parts not a whole: in our own discrete stories and the meaning we construct from them, but only subjectively and culturally valuable or practically and politically useful, not from anything transcendently real. In the old world, the cultural rituals formed us in ways that enabled sight and ears to hear, not with unreflective credulity, but also not without prejudices.[29] The cultural rituals of the new world shape us, educate us, and form us, like the captives in Plato's cave, to analyze the shadows cast against the cave wall and conceive of them as the only reality there is. Though the echoes of Coleridge's guiding Albatross still reverberate, they only annoy us now. We consider them to be the vacuous noise of troubled delusions. So we try to kill them. Yet in our effort to kill them, they become an Albatross around our neck and choke the life out of us.

The modernist social imaginary that inclines us no longer to see correspondences of transcendence in the world is not *more* reasonable and rational than that of the old social imaginary. Further, we still live as though

---

29. The older social imaginary was not without its own credulities, its own prejudices, its own superstitions, of course. These are what Will and Ariel Durant took note of in their comment that "religions are born and may die, but superstition is immortal. Only the fortunate can take life without mythology." The elimination of these very credulities and prejudices is the laudable motive of the Enlightenment's pursuit of a neutral, objective, universal reason. But that goal was never met and cannot be. Each generation must work to overcome its own unreasonable credulities, unjustified prejudices, and unwarranted superstitions.

there are real correspondences that speak of a transcendent world.[30] Science and analytics to the contrary, we simply do not live without transcendent reference. This is yet another sign that, in truth, we live within a grand story. Not one we simply construct for ourselves but something real.

So what can we see happening here? Just as Tolkien explained to Lewis, myths mean more than their details. In and through them we see that this world we live in is God's very own myth, his Grand Story, his Grand Drama. In God's myth, these details, these images are us and the whole created order. Just as all poems use concrete language and images and yet speak of more through them, the concrete things, images, and words of our stories and of the whole of reality as God's story serve as *looking-glasses* for us to recognize him as our source of being, identity, and meaning.

As Alice looks through the glass, she sees more, and more fully as from the other side. Through the passage of Lucy's wardrobe there's a Narnia beyond the furs. For the Samaritan woman who came to draw water at the well, when she met Jesus, she found a kind of water that quenches a thirst she didn't know she had in a way such that she will never thirst again. Jesus himself was and is that Water.

---

30. "Correspondence" here might be a confusing thing. Though it would take us too far afield of my primary purpose, I would point to C. S. Lewis in another of his rich and imaginative essays—"Transposition"—in which he says, "Where we tend to go wrong is in assuming that if there is to be correspondence between two systems it must be a one-for-one correspondence—that A in the one system must be represented by *a* in the other, and so on. . . . And there never could be correspondence of that sort where the one system was richer than the other. If the richer system is to be represented in the poorer at all, this can only be by giving each element in the poorer system more than one meaning. The transposition of the richer into the poorer must, so to speak, be algebraical, not arithmetical." This comment by Lewis calls attention to how the concrete world of the everyday (the poorer system) corresponds to the world of divine transcendence, what we often call the "spiritual world" (the richer system), not in a direct one-to-one way but rather in different orders of magnitude. Or, in my terms, the concrete, while altogether real, corresponds to a transcendent reality in such a way that the concrete is carried into, subsumed within perhaps, the transcendent. To use an illustration Lewis uses, it's like a picture drawn on paper or painted on canvas that accurately conveys the real world but with lines and shadows and colors—the three-dimensional, real world is conveyed in two-dimensional space. For someone who had never seen the real world but learned of it only through well-crafted pictures, to say the real world is sort of like this but with no lines, such an explanation would sound unimaginable—not real at all. But while the truth is that pictures *can* convey a different reality in their own dimension of flatness, the higher reality depicted differs by orders of magnitude. The paper or canvas is part of the "higher reality" (it is subsumed within it), but the three-dimensional reality is that and much more. Correspondence can be this way between the concrete world and the transcendent reality of which the concrete is both a picture and a window. See Lewis, "Transposition," 98–99.

To see more, as C. S. Lewis says in *The Abolition of Man,* we must see *something through* the concrete: "The whole point of seeing through something is to see something through it."[31]

Let us therefore turn now to the Grand Story: The Nightingale of the Heart and the Poetry of God.

---

31. Lewis, *Abolition of Man,* 91.

PART 2

The Nightingale of the Heart
& the Poetry of God

God is love.

1 JOHN 4:8

The Long Journey Home

The captain is asleep in his quarters as the boat rocked gently with the rolling swells in the long night in the vast ocean. Deep in his dreams he still has a strange awareness of the real world surrounding him. But as he sleeps, his dream is the only form in which he can know and interpret the world he inhabits. He hears the dull clank of the alarm bell on the deck above, not fully in use but with a hollow sound triggered only by the boat's rhythm. But he interprets it as the tolling of the bell in a high tower of the church on the hill in the small town of his boyhood. A gentle breeze enters through the window of his room on the marine vessel. To him it is the wind blowing through the valley in which he stands and gazes up at the grand tower. The soft wind makes the edge of a tarp above his quarters flap; in his dream he hears the window of the bell tower jostling, being opened to make way for the sounds to escape. The first pale light of the morning reaches him from the window in his quarters, but to him it is the last pale light of evening as the prior prepares for Evensong. He hears the voice of someone trying to rouse him from his sleep because it is time for him to awake, but to him it's the call of the bell from atop the hill, "Come home!"

Having caught a fresh wind and sailed for weeks and weeks, on the far distant horizon the sailors see what looks like land. Can it be? They've traversed the treacherous and foggy waters around the Horn though the Tierra del Fuego, being led safely by the Great Bird. On their voyage they've circumnavigated the globe in extraordinary discovery. The captain looks through his scope and confirms: "Land ho!" The closer and closer they get, the more familiar it looks. "Can it be that in all our exploring, we have arrived where we started and yet know the place anew, as if for the very first time?"

IT WAS A SILENT night. There in the vastness the sounds were far off yet very close to him. They coalesced as if forming a language. Not of an ordinary kind, though, with mere human words. It was a language and vocabulary of the heart somehow—one he understood immediately but had never been taught, telling a story he'd never known yet somehow known forever, a story that seemed both foreign to him but so familiar, encompassing and wrapping him as if in a blanket. It produced a satisfaction so fulfilling that he'd surely never known it before, yet deep inside he'd ever and always known. He was waking. Morning was breaking. His dreams from the far-off country were on the horizon of the real world. Love was beckoning him home.[32]

> Awake, you who sleep,
> Arise from the dead,
> And Christ will give you light.[33]

---

32. This little story is inspired by a similar one told by David Bentley Hart in his *Experience of God*, and a couple of phrases are direct quotations from Hart's story. This story also alludes to Coleridge's *Rime of the Ancient Mariner*, and the final line is adapted from T. S. Eliot's *Four Quartets*.

33. Eph 5:14, NKJV.

At the beginning of part 1, we saw Coleridge's Albatross calling out in the fog, guiding the ship through the treacherous waters of the long journey, a journey of exploration that, for Coleridge's and our purposes, led to a new, modern world. As *The Rime of the Ancient Mariner* captures, early on the journey to navigate the world of the unknown, we trusted the voice of the Albatross, the voice of Christ as reflected in the human soul. But after we passed through what we thought was the danger zone, we believed ourselves to have become emancipated from any need for the bird and shot it. Only later, after arriving in the expansive ocean of the new world and having stalled with no wind in our sails and after the persistent still, small voice had become a burdensome Albatross around the neck, we found ourselves adrift and thirsty. There was water everywhere but not a drop to drink that would satisfy our parched souls. In Coleridge's poem and in today's world we know there's more but can't seem to find it. In another poem that Coleridge wrote around the same time, he uses the image of the evening thrush, the Nightingale, to capture how in and through all our exploring, we have come to perceive ourselves as grown up and to have put away childish things only to become deaf to the things that can only best be grasped with the childlike wonder of a first-time encounter with the songbird. This, Coleridge would say, is due to making secondary things primary and primary things secondary. We remain thirsty. Our souls cry out.

Our soul's cry seems to be a kind of deep longing, perhaps from somewhere like Psyche spoke of to her sister, or perhaps from someone as if being spoken to in a unique language and vocabulary of the heart. Peter Kreeft calls this summoning call the "Nightingale in the Heart," like Knight struggled against in *The Seventh Seal*. Kreeft says, "We try to quiet this . . . tiny voice. We feed the nightingale dog food and cat food and monkey food. . . . But it keeps crying for nightingale food, and we cannot find nightingale food. Yet, though we do not feed it, it does not die. We can muffle it, but, like Bergman's knight, we can't kill it."[34] The transcendent real is the Nightingale of the Heart. It is the Albatross pointing the way in the fog, the soul pointing to a kind of food that fully satisfies, a true fulfillment that C. S. Lewis says is the fully real. This satisfaction, this fulfillment, is the love of God.

Even once we rediscover, as we have, that belief in divine transcendence is rational, and even when we come to believe that the best and fullest explanation of reality is interpreted through a theistic lens, these philosophical ruminations are only explanation. Even when we rediscover the linkage between reason and imagination and begin to reweave the tapestry and see things whole, we are still at risk of believing the world story is only

---

34. Kreeft, *Heaven*, 53.

about understanding. We moderns have explored the world, and it has led to great knowledge. But even when life is understood as a journey where we accumulate rich and varied experiences and vast and deep knowledge, we will not have discovered the full story. The Grand Story is not merely an elegant lens to explain the world nor merely a great journey, though it is those things too.

The story is much closer to a love poem, told in a language that satisfies both the mind and the heart. It is unrelentingly concrete yet echoes in a transcendent sphere vast and unending. It is the place we see eternity touch time. But it is not about mere explanation or even understanding; it is about encountering Love himself. The Nightingale is singing. "Love alone is credible," Hans Urs von Balthasar says.[35]

This love is never far away. With renewed imagination, we can see that it is reflected *in* us and refracted *through* the whole of creation everywhere all the time. Then it comes to abide with us: the person of Love. "This sign imprinted on nature, however," von Balthasar says, "comes to light only when the sign of absolute love appears: the light of the Cross makes worldly being intelligible, it allows the inchoate forms and ways of love, which otherwise threaten to stray into trackless thickets, to receive a foundation in their true transcendent ground."[36] The Grand Story is the story of the love of God in his condescension into the world as the true dying and rising God, the true myth in which we find home.

In part 2, we turn to the Judeo-Christian story. This story is a real historical story, as if a poem where the concrete imagery, the real places and people, are reflective of and windows into a whole other world (like Lucy entering Narnia). We can see contours of the transcendent story both *in* and *through* the concrete, like a symphony reverberating in musical space. But it only becomes fully known as the center point of all stories, in which each of our specific stories are encompassed, as God himself steps into history in the person of his son, Jesus Christ.

This story I tell in three parts and an appendix. For most, especially in the West, the Judeo-Christian story is familiar and straightforward—so much so, especially in our postmodern moment, that we conceive of it as just one among many other discrete culturally formed stories from which to choose, and in doing so we miss its full universal scope. So we begin in chapter 5 with "The Grand Story—in the Artist's Hand" first by looking at how nature itself witnesses to a grand story through art as an expression of a language and vocabulary of the heart, then by looking at a particular artist

35. von Balthasar, *Love Alone Is Credible*.

36. Ibid., 142.

and work of art, T. S. Eliot's *Four Quartets*. Then in chapter 6, "Rediscovering the Grand Story—as a Whole," we look anew at the old familiar story but in a simple, even childlike, poetic way to avoid becoming too easily caught in the weeds of modernist analysis yet expounding on this in its full historical narrative form in an appendix that summarizes the biblical story. Finally, in chapter 7, I provide an overall summary conclusion.

5

The Grand Story—in the Artist's Hand

Eo mens est imago Dei, quo capax Dei est et particeps esse potest.

The mind is the image of God, in that it has the capacity for Him and can be
partaker of Him.

St. Augustine, *De Trinitate*

BEFORE WE REDISCOVER THE sweeping Grand Story of the overflowing and
self-manifesting love of the divine Logos of God as told in the Christian
story, we shall explore how the story is reflected *in* us and *through* the world
and human experience at large, particularly in the artist's hand. This reflection is another natural sign or echo of a grand story in creation. Though we
cannot grasp the whole story from nature alone, we can see witnesses in
nature to a grand story; and through human poetry in a mythopoetic form,
we can see this story told through the concrete natural world.

Human beings have the innate capacity to know God, as St. Augustine
says. Twelfth-century mystical theologian Hugh of St. Victor's called this
capacity the *oculus contemplationis* (eye of contemplation), and sixteenth-
century Reformed theologian John Calvin called it *sensus divinitatis* (sense
of divinity). This capacity doesn't mean we always see or are aware of God
in the world, nor does it ensure that even when we do, we accurately grasp
God. Indeed, our awareness and perception of God are always distorted,
unless or until corrected by God's self-manifestation and -disclosure. Despite our innate capacity, the capacity alone certainly doesn't mean we know
God. But it does indicate that we can. This capacity is not limited to those

83

who have already come to know God. Evidence of it is ubiquitous, as noted, for example, in Tolkien's comment to Lewis the night they were discussing myth that even in the ancient mythmakers we can see fragments of eternal truth. This capacity, at least in some respects, seems particularly astute among some mystics, reflective thinkers, and artists.

Why is this so? Certainly it is because we have been created with this capacity. But what does this capacity tell us about ourselves and about God in relation to his creation? The most dominant image of the Christian story is the "Word," in Greek *logos*. St. John put it this way, harkening back to the Genesis story of Creation: "In the beginning was the Word [*Logos*], and the Word was with God, and the Word was God. He was in the beginning with God. All things came into being through him, and without him not one thing came into being. What has come into being in him was life, and the life was the light of all people. The light shines in the darkness, and the darkness did not overcome it." And just a bit later, "The Word became flesh and lived among us, and we have seen his glory, the glory as of a father's only son, full of grace and truth." (John 1:1–5, 14, NRSV). *Logos* has a variety of meanings or uses. Among the most often cited meanings are "reason" or a "principle of order and knowledge" or "the logic behind an argument," even the "generative principle of" and "divine animating principle pervading" the universe.[1] St. John certainly had all these in his mind when he wrote his Gospel, in part because he lived in a Hellenistic Greek-minded world and wanted the scope of his declaration about Jesus Christ to be all encompassing. However, even among all these varied meanings, the most straightforward and base meaning of *logos* is "discourse," as in speaking, having a conversation, communicating, even intimacy, as one has in a relationship. This means the most dominant image in the Christian story is one of relationship. God's Logos/Word relation to his creation is not distant, abstract, or capricious but fundamentally relational. It is not so just in that he has and does actually speak, in word and deed, though he has and does. It is *fundamentally* the way God relates to his creation. There is a discourse relation between God and creation built into nature, an expression of overflowing and incessant love.

This basic Logos/Word relation between God and his creation is what I call the "language and vocabulary of the human heart."[2] It is not just with

1. See "Logos" in Liddell and Scott, *Lexicon*; "Heraclitus" in *Cambridge Dictionary of Philosophy*; Hülsz, "Heraclitus on Logos," 281–301.

2. In support of this idea, see Candler, "Tolkien or Nietzsche." In particular note Candler's comment that for Tolkien in comparison to Nietzsche, "Christ is capable of 'transubstantiating' all moments of human *poiesis*. The Word who is before all worlds, who creates all worlds, who was made flesh and dwelt among us—does not all creation

words that we have the capacity know God. His word-language relation with creation is a basic, fundamental way we experience his presence. This is why the metaphor of mythopoesis, or story, is more than just a metaphor. It is real. This is a natural expression and therefore a natural sign of our participation in God's Grand Story. It is an indicator of *capax Dei*, the capacity to know God.

To see this capacity as a sign and an expression of the story, we shall look first at how human art is an expression of the cosmic language and vocabulary of the heart. Then we will look at a few dimensions of T. S. Eliot's poem *Four Quartets* as he sees the Grand Story *through* his own life in mythopoetic form.

ART IN ACTION—AN EXPRESSION OF GOD'S LANGUAGE AND VOCABULARY OF THE HUMAN HEART

Human art is an expression of God's language and vocabulary of the human heart. It reflects a human resonance with the language of the Author of creation, the Grand Artist. Conceiving art as part of a cosmic language is analogous to the Westron, Elderin, or Tengwar languages created by J. R. R. Tolkien in his *Lord of the Rings*. The characters in Tolkien's story know these, can and do use them, and they actually communicate when spoken to one another. But even their local cultural use reflects their own creator because they are a language and vocabulary built into them by their author. They are a sign of the author. Human art as part of the language and vocabulary of the heart is a gift given by God the creator and as such points to him as the Author of the story of the world. Conceived as part of this "language and vocabulary," human art can be recognized as a natural way we are aware of the Author's reality and presence in ordinary life. We can grasp something about the Author as "Word." We become aware of the Author's ubiquitous presence in us and through creation and sense a grand story being told. But we discern it only in outline form. As characters within the story, we still see "through a glass, darkly." To grasp the whole story, the storyteller must

---

speak, in an infinite variety of tones, keys, timbres, and tongues, of that Word? Does not the Word made flesh render all flesh in some sense *articulate*?" (123). Editor Ralph Wood, in his introductory comments on Candler's essay in *Tolkien among the Moderns*, says, "Tolkien is not at all troubled by the linguistic character of both divine revelation and human truth. Rather than leading to nihilism [Nietzsche's contention], our irreducible linguisticality proves, in Tolkien's work, to be our abiding hope, since human beings are sacramentally created to participate in the life of the triune God, who creatively speaks all things into being" (3).

speak within the story. So though it is a real sign, human art as part of the language and vocabulary of the human heart is but a haunting presence.

Haunting here captures a couple of senses. In the first sense it draws attention to an "awareness of presence" that enraptures us, as when we encounter beauty in this world, both natural and captured by artists. In this sense, while there is an awareness of presence, we seem aware of it only indirectly. The second is the Middle English sense, haunting as a force calling us "home." It is a longing in our heart for the Author, our true home. Art as a haunting is a sign of the presence of the Author of the Grand Story. It is part of a language we know yet have never been taught. It is part of the *capax Dei*, our capacity to know God.

The arts help us see how these hauntings function as a special language and vocabulary, unique both to being human and also to how this particular way of being human shows how *humanitas*[3] itself points to another reality in and through the way we live out our humanity. The other reality is both the "real" that writer and literary critic John Gardner refers to when he says, "Art opens up for us . . . 'the real,' a treasure vastly beyond the value of the key [to understanding the work of art]."[4] And it is the "fully real," the ultimate satisfaction, that C. S. Lewis refers to in "The Weight of Glory."[5] The real and fully real are both part of (the real) and yet beyond (the fully real) the reality we call our world.

There are many ways to consider art as a sign of the Grand Artist and Storyteller and of our capacity to know of his presence and something about him. But the one we will focus on is what philosopher Nicholas Wolterstorff, in his book *Art in Action,* calls art as world projection.

To avoid any confusion, let me be clear at the outset what this idea does *not* mean. Art as world projection, including word art such as stories, myths, and poetry, does *not* mean God is a human projection, as Ludwig Feuerbach or Sigmund Freud or Karl Marx said. Quite the reverse, in fact. Further, as you read on, you might be tempted to think I am promoting some kind of amorphous nineteenth-century Romanticism or twentieth-century radical postmodernism. I assure you I am not. Read carefully.

Wolterstorff says, "World projection is perhaps the most pervasive and important of the actions that artists perform by means of their artifacts. Not every artifact of art is used to project a world. 'Pure' music and 'abstract'

---

3. *Humanitas*, as I am using it here, is the endeavors of the human person as reflected in "major themes in the arts, social sciences, and humanities." This is exemplified in the Humanitas Project at Oxford University. You can learn more at http://www.torch.ox.ac.uk/humanitas.

4. Gardner, *On Moral Fiction*, 14.

5. Lewis, "Weight of Glory"; and Lewis, *Great Divorce*, 69.

art constitute exceptions. Yet, a vast array of works of art are used to do so, works of high art and other art alike; and in their being so used, we human beings over and over find their fundamental significance and worth."[6] The core meaning of the artist's action of world projection that Wolterstorff has in mind is that the artist is "presenting to us a world for our consideration." He clarifies what he means by asking whether poets and fiction writers are telling lies, a criticism that David Hume leveled against fiction. Wolterstorff makes it clear the answer is no, the artist is not lying, yet the artist is not doing philosophy or science—that is, the artist is not "making claims about the actual world. And so of course he is not asserting things which are false. He is not claiming things to be the case which are not the case. Instead . . . he is projecting a world for us." The world the artist projects is normally not completely compatible with the actual world, but neither is it completely incompatible. "Some of the things comprised in the world of Macbeth occurred, [but] the totality of them did not. . . . What makes fiction as we know it possible is not our human ability to make claims about the actual world but rather our ability to imagine a world distinct from the actual world." This goes to man's power of envisagement. "Between the ancient classical vision of the artist as imitator of actuality and the Enlightenment vision of the artist as repudiator of actuality, a middle course must be found." To clarify this point, Wolterstorff cites J. R. R. Tolkien's essay "On Fairy Stories," in which Tolkien points out that a work of art is a "sub-creation," that the work of art is distinct from this actual world, and yet "if it is at all good, [it] will be believable; we will find ourselves according to it what [he] calls 'Secondary Belief'":

> [Tolkien says,] That state of mind has been called "willing suspension of disbelief." But this does not seem to me a good description of what happens. What really happens is that the story-maker proves a successful "sub-creator." He makes a Secondary World which your mind can enter. Inside it, what he relates is "true": it accords with the laws of that world. You therefore believe it, while you are, as it were, inside.

But there are "many stories that never accord 'Primary Belief'—fairy stories chief among them. We do not find them likely to have occurred. We do not find them, in that sense, plausible. Nor is it at all necessary to our enjoyment that we do so. Sometimes the opposite":

6. Wolterstorff, *Art in Action*, 122. All references in this paragraph down through the second indented Tolkien quotation are from 123–24. All references in this section to art as world projection are from "The Action of World Projection," 122–55.

[Tolkien says,] Fantasy, the making or glimpsing Other-worlds, was the heart of the desire of Faerie. I desired dragons with a profound desire. Of course, I in my timid body did not wish to have them in the neighborhood, intruding into my relatively safe world, in which it was, for instance, possible to read stories in peace of mind, free from fear. But the world that contained even the imagination of Fafnir was richer and more beautiful, at whatever cost of peril. The dweller in the quiet and fertile plains may hear of the tormented hills and the unharvested sea and long for them in his heart. For the heart is hard though the body soft.

Though Wolterstorff introduces his point about world projection in the arts through fictional literature and fairy stories, he makes it clear that world projection is common throughout the various arts, including poetry, drama, sculpture, painting, music, dance, and so on. He also makes another clarifying point about fictional world projection. The creation of an alternative world through art does not mean something true about reality is not or cannot be communicated through the alternative world. Some aspects of reality, he says, may be better shown through such fictional worlds. Wolterstorff provides seven benefits of the action of world projection in the arts, summarized here below.[7]

1. The confirmatory function of art: some art confirms what its community believes is true. For example, "the stories, the dramas, the paintings, the sculptures, serve more as an expression of the religious convictions of the artist's community, and to confirm that those convictions, than to lead to new ones." But it is more than just a confirmation of religious convictions. Art in this sense is also a form of remembered history. Why does this keep happening in art? Wolterstorff says that, among other things, it is that there is a longing deep inside human beings for the concrete. Art makes community beliefs and history concrete.

2. The illumination function of art: in short, this is the prophetic function of art. In art this function *shows* us something different about actuality rather than *tells* us. In this way art is illuminating. This is part of Gardner's point about art opening up the "real."

3. The world-altering function of art by presenting another world: this is partly what Tolkien was referring to when he described how he preferred the Faerie world; it was "richer and more beautiful." Sometimes art serves the purpose of distraction from actuality, "to escape the drudgery and pain, the boredom, perplexity, and disorder of real

7. All citations in this summary are from Wolterstorff, *Art in Action*, 144–50.

life." And, though the desire to escape the real world may be normal in the sense of momentary relief, the world-altering function of art by presenting a different world that offers this momentary relief may also bespeak an actual escape from this world to another actual world that doesn't have the same problems of real life.

4. The mystery of the emotional impact of art: "Aristotle gave central position to the fact that the projected worlds of tragedies evoke emotions in us—specifically the emotions of pity and fear. "Plato . . . [insists] that representational art has some special impact on our emotions. . . . How does one explain the fact that the world of painting, of a film, of a novel, of a play, moves one profoundly?" There is little debate about this, yet little is really known about why it is so. I suggest (admittedly mostly as an intuition on my part) it is because the arts are fundamentally a part of a language and vocabulary of the heart.

5. Art as a modeling function: art in various ways makes us dream about being different and as such to act and to some extent become like what we encounter in a work of art.

6. The communication function of art: for many people this may be the first thing that art can do by projecting a different world. While Wolterstorff acknowledges this benefit of world projection in art, he believes this actually happens less frequently than most people think.

7. The consolation function of art: Wolterstorff again appeals to Tolkien's "On Fairy-Stories"[8] to make his point here. I strongly recommend you read Tolkien's essay, but for our purposes I'll summarize a few key points that Wolterstorff is stressing. Tolkien says that fairy stories always have a form of consolation in them, but not mere "Happy Endings." He calls it *Eucatastrophe*, a good that unexpectedly emerges from a catastrophe, what Tolkien calls "the sudden joyous 'turn' . . . ; this joy, which is one of the things which fairly stories can produce supremely well, is not essentially 'escapist', nor 'fugitive'. . . . [I]t is sudden and miraculous grace: never to be counted on to recur." Tolkien says this is not a denial of the terribleness of the bad and sorrowful aspects of the catastrophe (what he calls *dycatastrophe*), "the possibility of these is necessary to the joy of deliverance." But in the end, beyond all expectation, there is good news (what he calls *evangelium*, which is the Greek word for "gospel"). Here Tolkien says:

8. Also see Tolkien, *Tolkien on Fairy-Stories*.

The peculiar quality of the "joy" in successful Fantasy can thus be explained as sudden glimpse of underlying reality or truth. It is not only a "consolation" for the sorrow of this world, but a satisfaction, and an answer to that question "Is it true?" The answer to this question that I gave at first was (quite rightly): "If you have built your little world well, yes: it is true in that world." . . . But in the "*eucatastrophe*" we see in a brief vision that the answer may be greater—it may be a far-off gleam or echo of *evangelium* in the real world. . . .

The Gospels contain a fairy-story, or a story of a larger kind which embraces all the essence of fairy-stories. They contain many marvels—peculiarly artistic, beautiful, and moving: "mythical" in their perfect, self-contained significance; and among the marvels is the greatest and most complete conceivable eucatastrophe. But this story has entered History and the primary world; the desire and aspiration of sub-creation has been raised to the fulfillment of Creation. The Birth of Christ is the eucatastrophe of Man's history. The Resurrection is the eucatastrophe of the story of the Incarnation. This story begins and ends in joy. It has pre-eminently the "inner consistency of reality." There is no tale ever told that men would rather find was true, and none which so many sceptical men have accepted as true on its own merits. For the Art of it has the supremely convincing tone of Primary Art, that is, of Creation. To reject it leads either to sadness or to wrath.[9]

For our limited purposes, let me mention only a few dimensions of the relation of these benefits of world projection in human art to art as a sign of the Grand Artisan and the Grand Story. The human capacity for art, specifically art as world projection, reflects the *imago Dei* (image of God) in man, just as the capacity for all human creation is.[10] Human artifacts echo the creative nature of God reflected in his creations. God creates *ex nihilo*; humans out of the stuff God created, including we ourselves, along with our ability to project imagined worlds. God's world-projection creation—this real world—is a confirmation of his love. It confirms what is good, beautiful, and true. His creation, this real world, its very existence and sustenance given and held by him, confirms his desire to make his love concrete. His creation contains real stories, dramas, paintings (think of sunsets), sculptures (think

9. Tolkien, *Tolkien on Fairy-Stories*, 77–78.

10. For a specific reference to this human capacity in art, see Sayers, *Mind of the Maker*, and Cowan and Guinness, *Invitation to the Classics*; and for broad understanding of the human capacity for creation as an expression of the *imago Dei*, see Crouch, *Culture Making*, and Crouch, "To Play and to Pray."

of majestic mountains), and so on. Indeed, it *is* these things. Cosmic and human world history are gathered up in God's memory *as* the story of his love in relation with his creation. God illumines his world and people by the light of his Word. He does this through direct locutionary speech acts, through illocutionary acts (performative acts—communicating by doing something), and perlocutionary acts (prompting his people to go and act or say) as reflected, for example, in Moses' going to Pharaoh, in the Old and New Testament prophets, and by the ongoing illumination of his people by his Spirit. God's world-altering dimension of his world projection is seen in the whole redemption story and specifically as fulfilled in eschatological vision in the final consummation. The emotional impact dimension of God's world projection is noticed in the many ways his creatures are affected by the encounter of him in his world. God's world is sacramental in that we encounter him through it. This is particularly seen the mystery of the Eucharist in human worship. This is a reciprocal reflection in the divine drama of redemption of the whole world and all of world and human history as gathered up, past, present, and future, in a single point—the Cross—and remembered and replayed in the Eucharistic meal (indeed metaphorically in every human meal). We'll see this again later in Eliot's *Four Quartets*. The most striking dimensions of art as modeling in God's world projection are the apparent teleology built into the world—it is drawn toward a future fulfillment—and the love through which we are drawn to him in the person and work of his son. And clearly two dramatic dimensions of the communication aspect of world projection from the perspective of God are seen in the psalmist's "the heavens declare the glory of God," and most especially in the incarnation of God in Jesus Christ. Finally, and most dramatic of all, the consolation dimension is best seen in the redemptive story in full bloom in the *evangelium* (Good News) and *eucatastrophe* (good catastrophe).

Human art as world projection is an echo of the language and vocabulary of God as seen in the world, a natural sign of his presence. In and through God's artifact—the whole of his creation but uniquely in his human creatures and the art they create—this cosmic and concrete language is spoken.

Before we conclude our review of the overall significance of Wolterstorff's explanation of art as world projection for my purposes, let me make a few comments about language and how it is used in respect to world formation and the interpretation of meaning in language. In today's more radical postmodern outlook, words don't have any objective reference or meaning. Everything is mere social construction. It is generally agreed, however, even among radical postmodernists, that there is discernible meaning in texts (and in speech), at least as signs and senses, although this meaning is always qualified by the context of the world of the individual and specific communities. But within these constraints, as Gerhard Sauter asserts, "language itself and as a whole," even apart from specific meaning, resides in a "sensory picture, a mysterious web of relations forming the world which encloses us and out of which we cannot fall." Words as used come "to indicate all that which we find to be significant for us."[11] The words we use and their specific sense and meaning *to us* have the capability of forming new worlds. This is an analysis from modern linguistics. Embedded in this notion is something important that can easily slip by us. Words carrying meaning in human use show us how their world-forming capacity can hold us in a world "out of which we cannot fall." This can be easily understood when related to fiction literature and even fairy stories, as Tolkien points out. But let's look at this complex notion relating to art as world projection and the Grand Story.

World projection in human art and language is fundamentally the way the language of art works. This human artistic capacity accounts for why we resonate so much with art as a kind of language—an echo of God, the Grand Artist. Our own actions of world projection in art are analogous to the way in which the Grand Artist has spoken. To repeat for emphasis what was said above, the language and vocabulary of the human heart is a natural resonance we all experience in, for example, play, humor, music, human body/dance, images/pictures, romantic love, and even story itself. We can analyze how language and the language of human art works and relativize the meaning of texts and of the interpretation of art.[12] But this doesn't tell us what language, including the language of art, actually *is* or *why* it is. In a world of true transcendence, a world in which human beings are creatures of a creator, these natural human capacities reflect sub-creation and a kind of *re-cognition* of God our creator. Artistic world projection echoes the Grand Artisan. It's a sign of God's mythopoesis in the world.

The very practice of art as world projection is a built-in sign of whose we are—the progeny of the Grand Artist. Because we so persistently project specific worlds, worlds of consolation, redemption, and *eucatastrophe*, this kind of world projection "may be a far-off gleam or echo of *evangelium* (good news) in the real world," as Tolkien says. That we use fairy tales, myths, and poems to tell abiding truths artistically should not surprise us. The creator himself used such artistic devices in the Grand Story. We are his workmanship, his images in this world. Jesus Christ is the archetypical

---

11. Sauter, *Question of Meaning*, 7.

12. To be clear, this comment is not in support of the absolute relativity of all language. Indeed, I hold that because the ultimate reference of language is to the objective truth of God, all language is not truly relative. For some help reconciling this question, see Smith, *Who's Afraid of Relativism*.

image of God; in him all the fullness of Deity came to dwell in bodily form, and in him we humans come into our fullness.[13]

Now to return to the relevance of the linguistic point. If it is true, as I assert, that human art is part of the language and vocabulary of the heart, the linguistic and language interpretation comments above explain why there are so many varied interpretations and tastes in the arts and yet why there is a universal resonance in them. The language of the arts is part of the language and vocabulary of the Grand Storyteller with his creation. It is built into us. We naturally "know" this language, and we resonate with it even when we don't understand it to be saying anything to us specifically. This explains why individual artists can create (project) specific worlds from this language, why some resonate with that particular world more and some less, and yet why everyone can still understand the basic language of the art. Art is a reflection of the fact that there is a language and vocabulary "out of which we cannot fall." It is the language and vocabulary of the Grand Artisan, God's story out of which we cannot fall.

As such the language of the arts can also be understood as a natural sign of the Grand Storyteller.

The overall point of this discussion of Wolterstorff's *Art in Action* is that art is a universal, persisting, haunting presence and an expression of the love of God, the creator and sustainer of all. It is part of the language and vocabulary of the heart, a natural sign throughout the world and world history that we are participants in a grand story. The fact that art and so many other concrete and fundamental human characteristics function like a kind of language—think further about the universal language of music—means we can see even in them that there is a person to person relationship between God and his human creation. It is no surprise, then, that the instrument of God the creator and sustainer of all to make and sustain his creation is the Logos, the Word. We have a hard time grasping this today because we default to a closed world and are too analytical and narrowly focused.

Let us now look at a specific artist and work of art, a poem that both exemplifies art in action and is an expression of the whole story even while being tightly anchored in the world of human experience.

AN ARTIST AT WORK—A PICTURE OF THE WHOLE

"Language gets encrusted," says English Professor Thomas Howard, "and the poets have to come at the barnacles with hatchets."[14] Partly because

13. See Col 1:15 and 2:9–10.

14. Howard, *Dove Descending*, 14.

the Judeo-Christian story is so embedded in the story of the West and in keeping with the idea of trying to see things whole, we will now look at the Grand Story through a poem. This depicts the "seeing through" quality of all poetry so lost in our modern vision.

To further illustrate this vision problem, let us imagine how the closed-world modern/postmodern way of seeing things compares to poetry. From within the prison of this world picture, modernity and postmodernity as poetry would be either a thoroughly concrete world and nothing more or one so thoroughly translucent and imaginary that there's nothing left to see. The hard-nosed modernist is all and only about the concrete—the empirical world of science, cosmology and quantum mechanics, chemistry and biology, sociology and anthropology, and neurophilosophy. The radical postmodernist is all and only about a reality as images socially constructed—one in which nothing is really real or truly meaningful, one that with full-orbed creativity and infinite malleability we construct from whole cloth.

Poetry in an open-world-structure view (a view maintained at least in some manner in most Western poetry until the early twentieth century), while always concrete and emotionally evocative, grounds us in the here and now while allowing the everyday world to open upon the transcendent dimension of reality. In poetry (as in all art) immanence and transcendence coexist.

The Grand Story is not *merely* a poem, but it *is* one of a sort: a true, dramatic mythopoesis written by God. By his own Word, the Logos, the transcendent creator himself created a kind of myth. But rather than using human writing utensils and materials, he uses a real created order, the whole of nature including real human beings, to write the story. The whole of creation—its time, order, and its being, indeed the whole of human history—these are the elements and characters of this story. We are God's creative world projection. In due time, he inserted himself in it in the condescension of his son. The Word became flesh and dwelt among us in real history. He is the center of the story. He is the real dying and rising God. This is the true myth of which all other myths are an echo, the myth become fact. "As myth transcends thought, Incarnation transcends myth," Lewis says. "The heart of Christianity is a myth which is also a fact. The old myth of the Dying God, *without ceasing to be myth*, comes down from the heaven of legend and imagination to the earth of history. It *happens*—at a particular date, in a particular place, followed by definable historical consequences."[15] The grand myth is a grand drama.

---

15. Lewis, "Myth Became Fact," 66.

In this Grand Drama, to adopt Walt Whitman's phrase, "life exists, and identity . . . [and] the powerful play goes on, and you will contribute a verse." The author of the drama stepped into the play and became incarnate, as if Shakespeare might step into Hamlet and thus disclose who he is and why and how everything in the play—the players and the whole of their reality—invariably bespeak him. The Grand Story is compelling on its own as a dramatic human story, like all good stories and poems are, but it is also the true cosmic story.[16] It is the *"lived language*—the real, historical, visible, tangible language of an actual person [God himself] being born, dying, and living again in a new, ineffably transformed way."[17]

This mythopoetic drama is the story of love overflowing, the story of love condescending, the story of love dying, and the story of love rising again. It is *this* story toward which all reason yearns, in which all loves abide and are a reflection, and against which all distorted loves are measured. It is the story in which all human knowledge, language, culture, art, and experience reside and to which they refer. In this story all plots find resolution and fulfillment. In this story we all "live and move and have our being."

To see how a human poem can be a window onto the timeless, transcendent Grand Story, let us look at T. S. Eliot's *Four Quartets*, first published between 1941 and 1942. As it must be, Eliot's poem is in a way his own story, and yet he finds his true home in the Christian story. This poem critiques our modernist prejudices and uses his own story as a window into the Grand Story. This poem is a kind of verbal icon. Its scope is an expression of cosmic and concrete mythopoesis. The poetic rhythm from the concrete to the transcendent divine reflects a Christian sacramental ontology.[18]

Eliot's poem is long and complex. It is used here only as an illustration of a kind of mythopoetic drama of the Grand Story. I will rely on Thomas Howard's excellent exposition of the poem, *Dove Descending,* and Daniel Taylor's review of Howard's book.

Eliot received the Nobel Prize for Literature in 1948. He was born in St. Louis, Missouri, in 1888, went to college at Harvard, and did graduate

16. Ibid., 63.

17. Ward, "How Lewis Lit the Way." Emphasis added. For a more detailed exposition of the relation of imagination and reason in C. S. Lewis, see Ward, "Science and Religion in the Writings of C. S. Lewis." See also Holyer, "Lewis on the Epistemic Significance of Imagination." For a compelling presentation of the Christian story as a lived language in poetic, symbolic, sacramental form of *leitourgia* (liturgy) from an Eastern Orthodox point of view, see Alexander Schmemann's extraordinary little book *For the Life of the World.*

18. See, for example, Boersma, *Nouvelle Théologie* and *Heavenly Participation.* For comments on this topic from an explicitly Evangelical Reformed perspective, see James Wood, "Reformed Sacramental Ontology."

work in philosophy "at the Sorbonne, Harvard, and Merton College, Oxford. Eliot has been one of the most daring innovators of twentieth-century poetry. Never compromising either with the public or indeed with language itself, he has followed his belief that poetry should aim at a representation of the complexities of modern civilization in language and that such representation necessarily leads to difficult poetry."[19] There is little question he succeeded at representing complexities that make his poetry difficult. Eliot is undoubtedly one of the greatest poets of the twentieth century.

Four Quartets, as its name indicates, consists of four poems in one: "Burnt Norton," "East Coker," "The Dry Salvages," and "Little Gidding." Three of these are places in England and one off the coast of Massachusetts, each a location that bore a special significance to Eliot. Eliot is perhaps best known for his poem The Waste Land, for which he attained great fame. Later he wrote the Four Quartets following a reflective period of spiritual searching. "Eliot found his escalating fame meaningless, even painful, in the face of his sense of personal failure."[20] Despite his success, he didn't feel it himself. Like the Prodigal Son he "never ceased from exploration" and all but lost his faith. But Four Quartets reveals that he "arrived where he started and knew it for the first time." He returned home. His newfound faith created great consternation among his friends, for example, Virginia Woolf: "'He has become an Anglo-Catholic, believes in God and immortality, and goes to church. . . . A corpse would seem to me more credible than he is. I mean, there is something obscene in a living person sitting by the fire and believing in God.'"[21] For Eliot it was his recognition of his corpse state enlivened by "this Love and the voice of this Calling"[22] that brought him home. Eliot is like us all. Like his poems, he was a concrete man, with concrete struggles, in concrete places, in search of our True Home, the Shalom of God.

Daniel Taylor says, "Even those who allow Christians a right to life are sometimes unhappy with the style of the poem." Some think it's too "talky." Taylor recalls his "graduate school professor, many years ago, complaining [Eliot] had lost his 'objective correlative,' Eliot's own term for conveying emotion (hence meaning) through concrete images, situations, or objects rather than through assertion." But, Taylor says, "he may talk a lot, but he is talking through place. Better, he is thinking and feeling through place. That is, Eliot is using concrete, temporal, experiences of these four very real and rooted places to meditate on things beyond the physical. At Burnt Norton

19. See "T. S. Eliot—Biographical."
20. Taylor, "Rest for the Weary."
21. Ibid.
22. Eliot, Four Quartets, 59.

the formal gardens through which he walks become an 'objective correlative' for the possibility that pattern lies behind (and within) the seeming chaos of the temporal flux."[23] This pattern that lies behind and within is the voice of God in symphony.

Not seen often in current publications of the poem, below the title Burnt Norton are two Greek phrases. Thomas Howard says the "translation would run like this: 'Although Reason is common to all, most people live as though they had wisdom of their own'" and "The way up and the way down are the same." Howard says, "We have enough sense ('Reason') to know that Death will most certainly seal off everything that we have known so far of ourselves and the world, but that we do our best to sweep the baleful fact under the rug. Reason trumpets the fact to us; but we caper, or blunder, or dawdle, along as though we knew something *else* (some private wisdom of our own that notifies us of some exemption to doom). We will find in 'Burnt Norton' lines that will peel the veneer from this idiocy."[24] The candor we see here in facing our delusional state is a preamble to finding home.

The opening line seems less like poetry and more like Albert Einstein: "Time present and time past / Are both perhaps present in time future." Howard says, "Anyone who has ever scratched his head over the riddle of time will no doubt have fancied that perhaps the whole sequence rolls up, like yarn, into some Ultimate Ball. We don't like the notion of things simply fraying off into the ether. Might it not be (we venture) that the present and the past are not *nothing*. Or, Eliot continues, time future is perhaps contained in time past." Here we begin to see in Eliot what I alluded to in my application of Wolterstorff above: the divine drama of the redemption of the whole world and human history as gathered up, past, present, and future, in a single point—the Cross—and remembered and replayed in the Eucharistic meal. As Howard continues, "Time as we know it is the strand of yarn being pulled out into a long length, so that what *will be* (the future) is somehow already *there* at the beginning, designed, foreseen, or 'in the cards', so to speak." Eliot is struggling to make sense of and say something about time. It almost has a physics or cosmology character to it or a philosophy of time character. And though Eliot is a long way off from declaring the answer, Howard says this is an early allusion to it as a "case in point." The Mass is the answer he eventually gives, the "point."

> The notion at work in the Mass is that that which "was" eternally true (the Lamb of God "slain from the foundation of the world"), and which "will be" unveiled in the consummation of all things,

23. Taylor, "Rest for the Weary."
24. Howard, *Dove Descending,* 23–24.

namely, the eschatological appearance of the Mystical Lamb pictured in Saint John's Apocalypse, is *here*—*now*—*on this altar*. It
may be ten o'clock on Sunday morning at Saint Paul's Gloucester
Road (Eliot's parish) in 1942; but all of eternity—"past," "present," and "future"—is here, both in time and in this place. Where
are we—or, in what *when* are we—at Mass? We are with God
in a past eternity when Redemption of the world was hatched;
and we are in the Eden when animals' blood had to be spilled to
clothe the guilty Adam and Eve; and we are in the Holy of Holies
with Aaron with the blood of lambs; and we are at the Last Supper; and on Golgotha; and in the eschaton (heaven) before the
Eternal Altar.[25]

Here, at the very beginning, in the preamble and in the first line, we get
a glimpse of the whole story of redemption, our own delusional hubris (sin),
and the answer to it: the Cross, the Mass.

Time is a constant reference throughout the whole of *Four Quartets*.
In the fifth line Eliot writes, "If all time is eternally present / All time is
unredeemable." "There is nothing we can do about it all if the only 'reality' is
this moment, and everything else (past and future) is an illusion. Eliot raises
the stakes here by introducing the word 'redeem.' He is obviously nudg-
ing us toward something more sober than mere nostalgia for the past or
pipe-dreaming for the future. To redeem something is to *get it back*. A piece
of property, say, or a prisoner. But time? How can we speak of redeeming
time? In the next few lines Eliot draws toward a word that will turn out to be
pivotal in the whole poem. 'Point.' . . . Everything that has been undergirds
this moment, and everything that will be proceeds from it. And nothing is
lost. Furthermore, all that has been, or even *what might have been*, 'points'
to this moment."[26]

Dan Taylor says, "The single most dominant theme in the poem is that
only in and through time is the waste of mere time made right. He alludes to
this in the opening epigraph, citing the assertion of Heraclitus that the way
down and the way up are the same. The way up is a reference to the transcendent vision that promises unity with God. The way down is immersion
in and acceptance of our life in time. One gets to the Promised Land only by
way of the wilderness. One gets to transcendence only through immanence."
This is Eliot's "sacramentalism—the belief that eternity intersects time at
physical points, be they the cross or Communion or creation itself." Taylor
comments further that when Eliot says in Burnt Norton "'Only through

---

25. Ibid., 24–25.
26. Ibid., 26–27.

time time is conquered.' . . . time is not so much defeated as it is redeemed—giving meaning and the potential for significance. Time, in effect, realizes its purpose. . . . Why only glimpses of the still point—scattered for Eliot, as for us in different places at different times, and only for a moment? Why cannot we simply live continuously in that timeless moment—in the beatific vision? Why, as the English Romantics lamented, does the 'visionary gleam' always flee? Why after the beautiful or powerful or good is there the morning after? Eliot's answer . . . : 'human kind / Cannot bear much reality.'"[27]

These momentary glimpses are like those C. S. Lewis describes as his unceasing pursuit to find Joy, only for it to elude him again: "The passage of Joy—not wave but the wave's imprint on the sand."[28] This, again, is what I call "the residue of grace." The ever-present but always elusive realities of beauty, goodness, truth—joy, love—are not objects to be grasped or understood, as if capturing lightning in a bottle, but to be *embraced by*.

And finally, for our purposes, in the last quartet "Little Gidding," we see that these glimpses, the evidences of the "wave's imprint on the sand," the residue of grace that we experience even in the after effect of what we call joy, is the love of God that is calling us home: "*With the drawing of this Love* and *the voice of this Calling.*" And, we can see that, as for Eliot so too for us all, after all our exploring,

Will be to arrive where we started
And know the place for the first time.[29]

Where to? To the river that overflows. "All those fleeting moments that pierced us with *sehnsucht* [longing, yearning, craving, desire]: Shall we follow this river all the way to its unexplored source? Hark! Is that a waterfall there *au fond du bois*?"[30] Have we found our way to the river?

Everything in the poem is an allusion—points to something more. There are echoes, there are roses. There is the Thrush—the Nightingale. And everything in the poem has reference to the "point." The center of all things past, present, and future culminates in the *point*, the Cross. The incomprehensible love that is drawing us, the voice calling us, is the transcendent God who gives and sustains all things in in their very being. He is the one who condescended into his creation, and demonstrated his love in the person of his son, Jesus Christ. Christ is the Nightingale of the Heart, the source

27. Taylor, "Rest for the Weary."
28. Lewis, *Surprised By Joy*, 219.
29. Eliot, *Four Quartets*, 59.
30. Howard, *Dove Descending*, 146–47.

of the river that overflows, the water that satisfies the deepest thirst and the heart's deepest longings.

Eliot's poem is his own story, but with extraordinary detail and complexity it tells the whole story.

Some will say, "Well, this is a poem—a difficult poem, a good poem, but just a poem!" Indeed, it is a poem, but not just so. It is a human piece of art, projecting a world emerging from Eliot himself, envisioned and articulated by him. Eliot himself and his own story, as told through the concrete places of his life—at Burnt Norton, East Coker, the Dry Salvages, and Little Gidding—serve as a picture of each of our own stories, even while echoing the Grand Story of the world. It is a word picture of our very existence.

Theologian Kevin Vanhoozer said, "Hans Urs von Balthasar identifies the key question: 'whether God can enter a drama that takes place in the world and play a part in it, without becoming mythological.'"[31] He can and has in the incarnation of his son, Jesus Christ. "At the heart of Christian theology, as an intellectual activity, there lies the continual interpenetration of dramatic and ontological."[32]

The Grand Drama is God's mythopoetic ontological drama of all of existence. The Christian story of love is God's Grand Drama in which we all play a part. Like poems, we earthly concrete things are windows onto transcendent things. We intuit that we are responders to a bigger reality. We see this persistently in the transcendent echoes, including as cocreators (as Tolkien and Sayers say) of the world we live in. The concrete and imaginative things we make are windows onto an even more real, transcendent, and grander world. The concrete things and malleable words of this world reflect real presences (as George Steiner says), presences of Being that upholds all being. We encounter it in the simple things, like the "thou" in others' faces, even those we see but don't know like some folks I met in a small church in Zihuatanejo. Despite the barrier of language, we *knew* each other. In living our own particular concrete stories, like my ordinary story or like your own story, we *participate* in the grand one. And like Lucy Pevensie when she stepped through the wardrobe into a larger and grander world, we see a depiction of the Grand Story. As Roger Scruton suggests, we participate in a symphony of musical space, where in and through the cacophony of noise that we live there is more than the mere pitched sound the acoustician

31. Vanhoozer, *Remythologizing Theology*, 2.

32. MacKinnon, *Themes in Theology*, 234, as cited in Vanhoozer, *Remythologizing Theology*, 1.

hears.[33] It is the melody of the Nightingale of the Heart, the heavenly *music* interpenetrating everything we do.

Our practice of science and philosophy resonates with and is an expression of cosmic reason. Our very search for knowledge is a pull toward Rationality himself, the Logos. And our capacity for the social construction of reality and culture making bespeaks and has its ultimate reference in a grander community, the community of the interpenetrating love of the triune God. Everything we see, hear, and do, every word in a poem that evokes a sense of place and visceral feelings, displaying action and capturing the imagination, is about something more—the Grand Story, the Word of the story itself. "In Christ, poetry and philosophy have met together. Meaning and truth have kissed."[34]

The language and vocabulary of the heart as seen in human art and Eliot's mythopoetic verbal icon echo God's Grand Story of the world. As St. Augustine says, this reflects our capacity for God and that we can be partakers of him, and our hearts are restless until they find rest in him.

33. Scruton, *Soul of the World*, 37–38.
34. Ward, "How Lewis Lit the Way."

6

Rediscovering the Grand Story— as a Whole

THE RECOGNITION THAT THERE is a grand story reflected in a cosmic language and vocabulary of the human heart, a language that is the language of God, is still by itself only another natural sign that witnesses to the Grand Story. As a natural sign it cannot tell us what the whole story is. In Eliot's poem we see the Grand Story being told through his own story, but the Grand Story he tells through his story came not in a discovery he made through nature but by special divine revelation. To know the Grand Story in its fullness is not first about us stepping "through the wardrobe" into the world of God but about God stepping through it into ours. God first crossed the threshold, disclosing himself in divine revelation, a revelation that we can recognize and understand because of our capacity to know God.[1] But once we are encountered by God's special divine revelation and respond to it, we cross back over the threshold into a whole new world. Revelation is a "world-constituting" event.[2] Though we all hear echoes of it in our own stories, God's self-manifestation comes to us in a specific story—the story of a distinct people whose small story is a microcosm of the story of the whole world. This unique historical story encompasses all our stories, like a grand oak growing from a single seed.

Even with all we've discussed, for some today—ironically, even some Christians who have imbibed deeply from the narratives of modernity and

1. The phrase "crossing the threshold of divine revelation" is adopted here from the book of the same title by William J. Abraham.

2. Abraham, *Crossing the Threshold of Divine Revelation*, 104. For an explication of this idea, see Abraham's chapter 5, "Crossing the Threshold of Divine Revelation," 79–94.

postmodernity—it will still be hard to see the Judeo-Christian story as any-thing other than a discrete, culturally bound story. This again is because in our moment we remain so entrapped in a world of only pieces and parts with no sense that there is a whole.

Even for those who come to terms with the truth that a contingent world cannot be and be sustained in being without borrowing its existence from noncontingent Being, it is all too easy simply to say that the reality of the world depends on an amorphous presence in the world that is Being itself, and, therefore, that all things of the world and all discrete stories in it are merely contingently participating in a kind of immanent world spirit, as with Hegel's Geist or Spinoza's pantheism and similar notions found in many animistic and Eastern religions and philosophies. While these ideas are relatively new to the West, they are not new at all. They are quite old, in fact, and are deeply embedded in many mythopoetic stories that underwrite some of the great non-Western cultures of the world; and, though different in fundamental ways, they are also seen in Western Platonism, Neopla-tonism, and the Stoic philosophy.

The importing of Eastern ideas into the modern West and the mixing of them together with core Western ideas can be confusing. Indeed, this confusion is what largely accounts for the modern aphorism "I'm spiritual but not religious." In some respects, what we've discussed would appear to support some of these ideas—e.g., the notion of true transcendent "pres-ence" everywhere all the time and seeing a grander reality *through* concrete reality. This is precisely what in many respects developed in the German and English Romantic movements and the American Transcendentalist movement.

What we see at work here, however, is again what Tolkien pointed out to Lewis on their walk that evening when they were discussing myth. These notions capture part of the truth about reality, those fragments of eternal truth found in all myths that Tolkien called Lewis's attention to. The big difference between the admixture of today's religious and philosophic mi-lieu and the ancient world is that the old world anticipated a fulfillment of their fragmentary understanding—a center making a whole. The center the ancient world anticipated reflects the *sehnsucht* (longing, yearning, desire) in their religion and philosophy. Today, however, we no longer believe there is a fulfillment, no center making a whole.

What could not be anticipated in the amorphous-presence views but was glimpsed in Balder's dying and rising God, however, is that the fulfill-ment was a person. The person *is* the presence. Not except in Judaism do we see that God, the "I Am," the source and sustainer of all being and the one whose abiding transcendent presence is always present yet distinct from his creation, is personal. Not except in Christianity do we come to understand with fullness that the very meaning of "person" is found not in us but in the Word of the Grand Story, as the Word himself condescends to be with us as the true dying and rising God. Only then do we understand God as love in father, son, and spirit.

It is not except *in* and *through* the discrete, historical Judeo-Christian story that we see that the story of the world is the truly Grand Story told by God. And not except in Jesus Christ do we find the center and fulfillment of the story and that the fulfillment is not mere understanding but is the satisfaction of mind and heart found only as love. The story of the world in the deepest sense is of the condescending love of the transcendent King of kings in whom we "live and move and have our being."

From very early on, beginning with the early Church Fathers, the Judeo-Christian story itself became an interpretative lens by which all reality and all history is understood. This was enabled in part by a unifying religious and philosophical synthesis that emerged in the early church as the Church Fathers adapted and transformed the prevailing philosophical outlooks of the day. The Christian story did not spontaneously erupt in a vacuum. It was born within a culture, multiple cultures, a plurality of religions and philosophies, and from its own heritage, Judaism. Hans Urs von Balthasar puts it this way:

> The Church Fathers presented this message against the backdrop of the world religions. . . . Christianity thus stands out against this background as the fulfillment of the fragmented meaning of the world (*logos spermatikos*), which in the Word Made Flesh (*Logos sarx*) achieves its unity and fullness and redeemed freedom. . . . Against this backdrop, Christianity represented not only a fulfillment, but also a conversion, insofar as all of the fragmentary *logoi* absolutized themselves and thus put up a sinful resistance to the true Logos. . . .
>
> This approach was possible because these Christian thinkers took over the identity between philosophy and theology that had prevailed in the ancient cultures as a self-evident fact. Equally evident to them was the unity of the natural and the supernatural orders. God had been manifest from the beginning of the world and from Adam onward, and the pagan world failed to recognize that which is clearly there to be seen (Rom 1:18f); it had "no excuse" for rejecting obedience to the eternal power and divinity that has been made known" and was thus punished with humiliating idolatry. In short, the ancient world's unifying principles—the Stoic cosmic Logos, the Neoplatonic hierarchy

of being that tends from matter to the superessential One, the abstract majesty of Rome's world-unifying power—are redeemable schematic prefigurations of the personal God-Logos, who has drawn close to the world through the history of Israel, a history that fulfills the cosmos and various religions [Ökumene]. The world was created in the Logos, the true "place of ideas," and can therefore be understood only in the light of this Logos. Christianity marched triumphantly to Rome and from Rome to the ends of the earth—what more was needed to prove that this fulfillment was not only an ideal but also real? . . .

The world, as the ancients saw it, was sacred and, in a formal sense, lacked nothing but a center. With the establishment of the center, God's *agapē* [love] appeared to fulfill the cosmic powers of love to overflowing. . . . The transition that fulfilled the philosophical universe in the Christian-theological one granted to reason, enlightened and strengthened by grace, the highest possible vision of unity.[3]

The story of Christianity in the early days made sense of the world, as the world was understood. It was a story of *fulfillment*, a kind of fulfillment that could be recognized because the world into which Christianity was born acknowledged a common vision that there was a unity—but one that, as yet, had no center. The Logos of God was (and indeed still is) that center, and it made sense intellectually. But in his comments von Balthasar is actually describing how over time the story of love as the center, as revealed in Jesus Christ, has been reduced merely to another philosophy and how when this happens, it becomes unconvincing and unsatisfying. This remains today in our analytical times. We reduce the love of God to intellectualism. But the biggest difference between then and now is not only that we reduce love to the intellect but also that we no longer believe there is a center. Things have fallen apart. There are only pieces and parts. We sit no less today than the past in a culture of a plurality of religions and of philosophies, even more so. And there remains no less need for a center now than then. Again, as William Butler Yeats's famous poem suggests, things are falling apart and the center cannot hold.

But just as the ancient world hoped for, there is a center. And that center is the same now as back then. It's not science, or philosophy, or rationality as such, though it subsumes them all and it is their center. By themselves they cannot hold. Without the Christian story, we cannot truly understand the world, ourselves, or the extended reach of reality apart from truly *knowing* the God of infinite love.

3. von Balthasar, *Love Alone Is Credible*, 15–18.

To begin to grasp the wider interpretation of the story of the world, including that this Grand Story is the "fulfillment" of the multiplicity of religions that are longing for the good, the true, and the beautiful, we must grasp the "center." The Christian story as Person: the love story of God. In this we discover the "center" that holds, a life of renewed conviction and direction to our passionate intensity.

To see things whole, consider here a simple rendition of the grand love story of God in Jesus Christ in a simple mythopoetic form. (For a detailed summary of the biblical story, see Appendix 2.)

The Story of the King

Once upon a time, a long time ago, even before time began, there was a King—one so royal, so hallowed that from his unbounded majesty and power we call all kings King.

Reigning forever, before forever began, the King decided to speak—to tell a story of a kind that had never been told, in a language and grammar that had never been known. When the King spoke, things came into being where there had been nothing at all. The very first utterance caused an explosion. All of a sudden everything that is everything began to unfold. In what seemed chaotic, there was an order ordered by the King's own word. Into the darkness the light of lights shone. Carried on stardust, the story of time became known: the light from the heavens partitioned the night from day, the new from the old. The King by his word stretched his canvas where his story would be told.

From the stuff of his word the King now shaped his kingdom. On a small speck of the stardust, called Earth, he made a garden. There he put all kinds of plants and rocks and animals, and he installed a rich rhythm of drink and drought for delight and dependence and light and darkness for replenishment and rest. To mark his kingdom and reflect it with his very being and to share intimate fellowship with his creation, from the stardust he fashioned an image, an icon of himself. The icon of the King was shaped to live in mutual love and communion with the King; male and female he made them to live together in a community after his likeness, and in a special union together, with him, they would procreate new life and fill the garden. Fashioned in his own image, the King breathed his life into them and he commissioned them as his regents to care for his creation. From the stuff he had made from nothing, as his cocreators they would shape, make, invent, and manage the kingdom and rule over it on his behalf. In his image they would reflect his kingship, and his presence would be known. This they did, and it was very good!

But not long afterward the icons sought kingship on their own, to tell a different story separate from the King. Bereft of his life and communion, their identity was lost, and they became confused. Aimless and deluded, they declared themselves supreme. Yet in keeping with their mission, they multiplied and filled the holy realm. They shaped and made so many things, a legacy of the King, but were left with just opinions as to what it all should mean. It was a broken story now, distorted and misshapen. The majesty of the kingdom became warring tribes and fiefdoms, mere shadows of the dream. It was very bad!

So the broken story goes for many, many generations. By all rights and justice, the Mighty Hallowed King could have simply spoken judgment and put to right all things. But the King was infinite in mercy and longsuffering, and he refrained. The light was dimmed but not out!

Then one day the King did utter a new word, a quieter word, not of fiat or of judgment, but of promise—a promise to search for and find his lost icons. As a Shepherd King, he would bring them home again. A new chapter began, a story retold, one of redemption and restoration would unfold. The story began with a *planet* chosen from the heavens where the kingdom would be made; to restore his reign and redeem the story, he chose a *people* and began with a single, simple aide. Through him and his seed, he would make a people, a kingdom people, and make his kingdom come.

But it would not be easy, and it would not be fast. The seed of treason still flowered. Wanderlust remained.

Yet the King persisted. He brought about a people, a family called his bride, his children. In the marriage, they would make a pledge, a vow of faithfulness: he the Husband-King and they the people, his bride; and he the Father-King would provide for them and protect them, and they, his children, would honor and obey him. The progeny of the King's small family would bear the fruit of redemption for the whole lost kingdom.

Despite the King's faithfulness, the bride, the children strayed—as wife they committed adultery; as children they disobeyed. Though provided for, loved, and nurtured, their eyes and hearts still wandered; their fealty was filled with fickleness and empty formality. Yet the King remained faithful in mercy, grace, and love.

Many years passed. The King's people, still afflicted with temptation, still wrestling with their rebellion, were themselves the story of redemption repeatedly retold. But in it was a glimpse of a final recompense, of an Upright One who would be redeemer and redeemed, the one in whom the icons of the King would be judged aright again—an Icon King from heaven, the Savior King for all.

So in liturgy and ritual the story was retold. With encouragement from oracles, the voice of the King would sing of eagle's wings foretold. And in faithfulness a remnant still pined and dreamed the dream of soaring with the King. But as the years went by, for many, there grew doubts about it all.

Then one day in a still quieter voice, one hardly to be heard, the King spoke again.

In the cool shade of an olive garden in a small village in an out of the way place, a special messenger came, an emissary from the King, to a young peasant girl. He told her of a new story, one so unexpected, so earth-shattering, that she could not begin to believe it. That she, though not yet married, and by all accounts could not, would bear a child. And this child would be like none other. He would be *the* icon of the King. The very word of the King himself would be born of the selfsame dust as all icons of the King. He would live among them on the very speck his first utterance caused to be.

In the fullness of time, on a silent night in another small village, the stars aligned and shined brightly upon a tiny trough in a barn. There, in the muffled cry of childbirth, the King of kings was born. There in a stall, with only hay on which to lay his head.

What could this mean about a king? No pomp, no circumstance, suckling strength from his mother's breast in utter humility. Have the wandering years so tarnished it that we should miss the meaning? That to bear his image is to bow down and kiss his ring.

And so it was. In the beginning was the Word, the Word of the King, and the Word was the King. He is the Light and Life of the world, the one by whom and in whom all things hold together. Yet this sovereign Word of power descended himself as an image of the King that we might truly be redeemed. And from the depths of his immeasurable love, the King himself became a slave in his own creation. A castaway by his people, by them and for them he was executed. The very Word of heaven became the crucified King. In his love and justice he took away the sin of the world and put to rights all things.

> Yet it was not the end. The author of the story did also rise again. Indeed, what seemed an end would but portend: on earth all heaven to descend. The one who cast the heavens and made it all begin, in descent and death and resurrection a new garden to begin.
>
> The story of the King of all glory, majesty and power, is of condescending love—a story where all wanderers finally find their home and where all identity and meaning are fully finally known.

POETIC RUMINATIONS ON THIS GRAND STORY

> Poetry depicts the world of human experience; it reveals to the reader a secret inner meaning, a deeper and transcendent reality which underlies and permeates that experience.[4]

Read as a poem, the Judeo-Christian Grand Story of Creation, Fall, Redemption, and Consummation is ruddy in its concrete historical details in the world of human experience. And it is rich in revelation of inner meaning, the deepest of all transcendent reality. It permeates every square inch of the lived experience of the chosen people of God. The God who fulfilled his promise to Abraham has wrought redemption for the whole of his creation in the person and work of his only son, our Lord Jesus Christ. In this concrete story everything *means* something, the something more of love: the incomprehensible becomes comprehensible as the transcendent one condescends and enters the story.

Søren Kierkegaard puts it like this. Imagine there was a king, an absolute monarch, who loved one of the peasants in his kingdom. He could merely command she be brought to him, but instead he wants to know whether she really loves him—commanded love is not true love, and he must know if she loves him. He concludes that to really know, he must become a peasant too and risk that she might reject him. "Only in this way can he communicate his love so that she can love him in return."[5]

This story and its image derives from a poem found in the second chapter of the apostle Paul's letter to the Philippians. It is sometimes called

4. "Poetry," 1.

5. Evans, *Why Christian Faith Still Makes Sense*, 131, commenting on Søren Kierkegaard, *Philosophical Fragments*, chapter 2. Kierkegaard develops this illustration through his pseudonymous character Johannes Climacus. A longtime friend, Tim Sheppard, captures a similar image in his song "The Serf and the King."

the *kenosis*, or "emptying," passage. It tells the miraculous true story of the immeasurable love of God displayed in the incarnation, life, death, resurrection, and ascension of Jesus Christ:

> who, though he was in the form of God,
> did not regard equality with God
> as something to be exploited,
> but emptied himself,
> taking the form of a slave,
> being born in human likeness.
> And being found in human form,
> he humbled himself
> and became obedient to the point of death—
> even death on a cross.
>
> Therefore God also highly exalted him
> and gave him the name
> that is above every name,
> so that at the name of Jesus
> every knee should bend,
> in heaven and on earth and under the earth,
> and every tongue should confess
> that Jesus Christ is Lord,
> to the glory of God the Father.[6]

The very sustainer of all creation, the Word, became flesh and dwelt among us—he who was with God, who is God, came in condescending love to redeem and renew his creation. This story tells us who we were meant to be, who we became, and who we are in Jesus Christ. As we were "in Adam," subject to the law of sin and death, so we can now be "in Christ," the Second Adam, the True Human, heirs of life eternal.[7] As God made a covenant and brought about a people, "Israel" (those who would live under the reign of God), to be a blessing to all people, all creation, so now "in Christ," all who would live under God's reign in him would now be the New Israel, the fulfilled Israel. The new covenant people would no longer be restricted to historical Israel but would through them, in Christ, encompass all peoples. The walls of separation broken down. Those who were once aliens and strangers

---

6. Phil 2:6–11, NRSV.

7. See Rom 5 for St. Paul's explication of this reality.

were adopted into the family, the worldwide people of God. In Christ and through Christ we reflect the True Adam who lives under God's reign as it was intended to be—as vice-regents of the King. This is the church's mission. It succeeds only when its first and true love is God; then all other loves become rightly aligned. It fails when another love takes first place.

As Abraham stood watch over his sheep on the hillside and as David protected his flock from the wolves, as the shepherds tended their flock that silent night when Jesus was born, so too does the Shepherd King keep watch over us all with the staff of his love. Now as his image bearers (his iconic witnesses), his incarnate hands and feet, for and on his behalf, we extend his love throughout his vast domain. As the wanderer in us all awakens and we turn from our squandered ways and ask and are received again by our Father, now on his behalf—as the Bishop of Digne did with Jean Valjean in *Les Misérables*—we run out and meet other returning wanderers. And with the same prodigality with which God showed us his welcome, we give them the best robes and shout to everyone: "This one who was lost has come home." We all celebrate. As von Balthasar says, "The majesty of absolute Love that approaches man in revelation goes out to meet him, and elevates him to an inconceivable intimacy."[8]

This story is the story of God's immeasurable, incomprehensible love, overflowing in creation, unremitting in redemption, even in the face of our persistent, unfaithful hubris and our distorted loves.

Just as in each of our ordinary stories, in everything that happens in the historical Judeo-Christian story, in each of the smaller stories that make up the bigger story, there is the grand transcendent story of the world. We see this in Jesus' simple, everyday encounter with the Samaritan woman at the well.

Once there was a man who had stopped at a well, called Jacob's well from a time long past. A woman came to draw water, in her usual custom. Being a woman and a Samaritan, she was taken aback when the man spoke to her and asked for a drink.

> She is surprised, but is she also wary? Do we detect an edge to her voice in her reply, "How is it that you, a Jew, ask a drink of me?" (John 4:9) Does she mistrust this man sitting at the well? It would seem she had good reason to. She is a woman hard-used by life. Later in the narrative we will find she has been married five times and now was living with a sixth man without the benefit of marriage. It is not difficult to conjure a scenario of serial rejections, multiple failures, year by year accumulating wounds

8. von Balthasar, *Love Alone Is Credible*, 57.

and scars in mind and body. For her, to be a woman is to be a victim. To be near a man is to be in danger. . . . After opening the conversational exchange at the well, Jesus starts talking in riddles. "If you knew the gift of God, and who it is that is saying, 'Give me a drink,' you would have asked him, and he would have given you living water." (4:10) Soon it becomes clear to us that Jesus is using the word "water" as a metaphor with the Samaritan woman. The word "water" that initially referred to well water pulled up by a bucket is now being used to refer to something quite different, something interior, "a spring of water gushing up [in her] to eternal life."[9]

This is known to all Christians as the story of the woman at the well. It is so everyday and yet so out of this world at the same time. Not merely because Jesus is able to "read her" in her deepest self. In the concrete everydayness of life, where water is so essential, quenches thirsts, and meets the needs for meal preparation, there is something more: a bigger reality is simultaneously operating, where there is a kind of water that quenches a kind of thirst that is far more than this woman was even aware of. A kind of thirst that is a deep longing—*sehnsucht*. The kind of desire whose satisfaction Tolkien alludes to in his "On Fairy-Stories," in which there is something far more important than a *mere* happy ending. It is a picture, as C. S. Lewis says, of how all our natural desires, while having their own temporal satisfactions, bespeak a kind of satisfaction that is beyond this world. Our deepest thirst, a kind that is pictured and pointed to in our everyday thirsts, is fully satisfied in God alone.

Even in the concreteness of our everyday lives and even in the thoroughgoing earthiness of the life of Jesus, there is a bigger story going on—all the time. This is the true Grand Story, the story and promise of Christianity that is so hard to hear today but won't go away. Echoes of the voice of God, from *home*.

9. Peterson, *Christ Plays in Ten Thousand Places*, 16.

7

Passageway Home
Echoes of the Voice of God in Symphony

THE ECHOES OF THE voice of God that we hear faintly are the song of the Nightingale of the Heart. We so often dismiss them because we have consciously or unconsciously adopted either the truncated vision of a modernist, closed-world reality or a radical postmodern, self-constructed reality in which all we do is talk past each other and nothing really means anything. This I call living in a "being there" age of sardonic tales and comic relief.[1] For many the conclusion is, this kind of world is the best there is, so we dismiss that still, small voice singing softly but persistently. We try feeding the bird with all kinds of different food, but nothing will make it stop crying out. We shoot it and hang it around our neck as a trophy, but it becomes an Albatross, and the pang worsens. We cry out as Knight does in Ingmar Bergman's *The Seventh Seal*, "Why can't I kill God within me?" Or, like philosopher Thomas Nagel, we deny the music of the Nightingale because we can't accept that it might be true: "It is not just that I do not believe in God,

---

1. This reference to today's radical postmodern, free-floating, incoherent, and disintegrated cultural narrative and way of being is captured poignantly in Jerzy Kosiński's 1971 novel *Being There*. I have adopted the phrase "being there age of sardonic tales and comic relief" because it provides a sophisticated intellectual hinge-point between modernity and postmodernity by its connection to twentieth-century philosopher Martin Heidegger and because the movie version of Kosiński's novel captures with sardonic hilarity the shallowness and incoherence of our cultural moment. To grasp the import of the reference back to Martin Heidegger, one needs to recognize that most of all of advanced postmodern philosophical thinking today (especially of the continental strain) finds its roots in Heidegger. His most famous book is *Being and Time*, and the most famous word in his philosophy is the German *Dasein*, which literally translated means "being there."

and, naturally, hope that I'm right in my belief. It's that I hope there is no God! I do not want there to be a God; I do not want the universe to be like that. . . . My guess is that this cosmic authority problem is not a rare condition and that it is responsible for much of the scientism and reductionism of our time."[2]

Like the sailor waking from a dream in the story I opened part 2 with, having traveled the world, been stranded in a wide ocean, water all around with nothing to drink, we have caught a new wind and can see anew the horizon, land is in sight. The closer and closer we get, the more familiar it looks. The closer we get, the louder the echoes get, and we wonder. Is it possible that what we perceived as mere sounds, distant echoes, are a melodic theme in musical space,[3] playing in the language and vocabulary of the heart? Is it possible that the echoes are the voice of God in symphony?

As we have seen, there is every reason to believe that the echoes of God we hear amid the cacophony are indeed the ineffable music of God's love. There are signs of a grand story all around, ones that we all experience in one form and another. These signs are concrete and existential. We experience them in our everyday lives, and we are awestruck by them and cry out in our souls when they are reduced to pieces and parts as if they are not real. We also see that in the midst of our modern and postmodern worlds of reduction and flotsam, there is a vocabulary of the human heart that seems "just there," one we never were taught but always knew—a language and story out of which we cannot fall. There are chords we so persistently resonate with, such as those persistent unexplained mysteries and others such as wonder and beauty, beneficial order, the sense that there is something wrong and the cries for justice play out; those most human resonances such as humor, music, and the human body (like the transcendent beauty captured by Degas's ballet dancers and, as Roger Scruton describes in his *The Face of God*, the mystery of the face of God as seen in the human face which when encountered we are intuitively confident there is something more to see *through* them). These are the fodder of our personal stories, the song of the Nightingale. There's a very story-ness to things. We are narratival in our souls. We've seen the Grand Story in the story we live in the West, an outgrowth of the Judeo-Christian story. It is an expression of the flow of time (as Eliot might say) that punctuates the phrases in musical space that lie so deep in the human soul. We cannot imagine they never existed before. The very ideas of "civilization" and "justice" we carry with us in our backcloth are the essence of a particular story, an outgrowth of the Grand Story—our

2. Rea, "Divine Hiddenness," 266–75.
3. For this image, see Scruton, *Soul of the World*, 37–38.

cries for liberty and justice are rooted in the Judeo-Christian understanding of the world. The very desires that pull us along in life are a sign of the
grand musical score—the very nature of desire is for fulfillment and that,
like all things poetic, while our natural desires have their own fulfillment,
their own satisfaction, they also bespeak an ultimate fulfillment: like the difference between the water sought by the woman at the well and the stream
of living water of which Jesus spoke.

In our modern social imaginary, we have a hard time imagining that
the natural signs and the language and vocabulary of the human heart are
echoes of the voice of God. We live in a culture of skepticism, of disbelief.
We all have a natural tendency to suppress the truth, and yet we have made
this tendency worse in our day. We have thrown the mirror down, and it has
broken into millions of little pieces. All we see now is the flickering of the
light as we walk along, and even if we occasionally see a patterned mosaic, it
makes no sense to us. We do this on the one hand because we are so focused
on analyzing "the facts" that we cannot see any sense of the whole. On the
other hand we do this because we don't believe there is really anything there
to see, that everything is just a language game, the free-floating ether of
words untethered to any real meaning. We live in a waste land, strewn with
pieces and parts with no whole, no center.

We can look back, if we will, and see that this is not the only way and
that where we are now is not the natural advancement of human progress.
Our "advancement" is not merely that we have grown up to a mature state.
If we look, we can see that along the way, we shed our ability to see that what
we live in *is* a whole, not just pieces. We can see that nature and grace are
not two separate worlds that don't touch each other, but are one. When we
separate them and reduce them in various forms of rationalism, our soul
reacts, as in Romanticism and Existentialism. But the modern mind-set became established, and with it we lost our ability to interpret vast dimensions
of reality. As Dr. James Patrick puts it,

> When, after the fits and starts of the sixteenth and seventeenth
> centuries, it turned time to try to put the intellectual world
> back together, the lynch pin of the whole system, that highest
> intellectual virtue, insight, that grandchild of the agent intel-
> lect, had gone missing. That wonderful little hand in the head
> called the agent intellect was nowhere to be found; there was
> no way to talk about knowing another something really, only
> pieces of thoughts such as the belief that all knowledge came
> from the senses, not in the way Aristotle meant, through the
> ability of the intellect to abstract knowable forms, but empiri-
> cally, through the ability to touch and describe; or, that failing,

the only alternative was to claim a knowable world was that knowable simply because God put the ideas of things in one's head—as in Descartes. Broadly, the result of this breakdown was the creation of two difficult-to-relate worlds, one in the mind and one out there in things.[4]

With a hubristic veil pulled over our eyes and stoppers in our ears, we dismiss the natural signs of God's presence with us all around. And in our day we have made it even harder to see by establishing cognitive confusion with our flattened, truncated closed-world outlook, resulting in a culture of doubt.

In our advanced, enlightened culture of disbelief we came to believe the answer, if there is one, must be obtained through discursive logic and empirical science, that there are insurmountable intellectual barriers to belief in true divine transcendence. But as we have seen, this is a narrow view of what reason is and how it functions, and it leads to unjustified intellectual prejudices. Notwithstanding the great advancements modern science and scientific thinking have wrought in modern life, the big questions that prompted the pre-Socratic philosophers as well as Plato, Aristotle, and all of premodern Western philosophy remain: What are reality and reason, and how do we make sense of things? What precisely is knowledge, and why should we trust human cognition to yield anything at all like truth? Why do we believe in the notion of progress and life as a journey, an adventure? What is the meaning of the human person? And so many more. We see that to such basic questions as these, the modern skeptical mind with its truncated methodologies simply has no good answer. We see that the best answers, the most rational answers, come from classical and Judeo-Christian tradition and reasoning. In contrast to common modernist belief, there is no neutral, objective practice of rationality. We all operate within a backcloth of sacred stories, and most of the visceral things we cling to are legacies of the Judeo-Christian story we've now rejected. And because of this, in our modernist outlook what is thought to be "rational" in its dismissal of such beliefs as divine transcendence is nothing more than a philosophical leap that cannot be supported by the very methods that cause the skepticism to begin with. Everyone operates within a metaphysical outlook, whether acknowledged or not. And the Judeo-Christian outlook, which is a classical one transformed by the insights of divine revelation, is far more compelling than the closed-world, naturalistic one that prevails in modernity.

Unshackled by the unwarranted constraints of a faulty closed-world, naturalist outlook, it is eminently reasonable to acknowledge that God has

4. Patrick, "Limits of Skepticism."

revealed himself and spoken to his creatures—both in and through nature and in special ways. It is also eminently reasonable to accept that, in a manner not dissimilar to the fact that human beings have the native capacity to reason at all and obtain real knowledge, we also have a native capacity to "see" God in and through nature and to recognize his voice when he speaks to us. When we are honest, like philosopher Thomas Nagel, we can see that we often don't see God in nature or hear the transcendent echoes *as* his voice both because we intentionally suppress what we know to be true (or at least most likely true) and because we have trained ourselves not to recognize him and hear his voice *when* we see him and hear him. Thus, we feel that God is hidden from us, even when he is present with us all the time and everywhere, and not least in our heart's deepest longings.

But the Nightingale continues to sing. The grand symphony plays on and reverberates through everything we call everything. Just as our very being cannot *be* apart from God, in whose being ours resides, so too the very concrete world we live in cannot avoid declaring the glory of God. It cannot because his creation is, in a very substantial way, his abiding place. While the Kingdom of God is not *of* this world, this *is* his world, and it is at all because and only because of his unbounded, overflowing love.

The deafness we now know to the echoes of the voice and our blindness to God's real presence with us is not new, of course. It began a long time ago. As with Israel of old, despite our impudence and hubris, God's love continues to overflow. He did not leave us deaf and blind; he came to us and became one of us so that we might hear and see again and flourish as he intended. The very Word of Being himself that spoke in overflowing love condescended in his love to ransom us from our prison. As the poet speaks in the vernacular of concrete experience and yet bespeaks grander transcendent realities, God spoke in this world and refreshed us with water from the well and daily bread from the baskets, and the very source of this nourishment and satiation yet flows from a deeper river and a far more extravagant banquet table. He is the spring of water gushing up to eternal life, and he himself is the Bread of Life.

Just as Juliet pined in her heart for Romeo on the balcony overlooking the garden below, so too do we pine in our hearts with longing for our deepest Love. Not of a distorted kind, the object of which St. Augustine says cannot satisfy, but of a kind that when we find it, our hearts are no longer restless but are at *home.* Just as Juliet's question about what's in a name raises the question of being completely changed, swallowed up by something so much more real than the confines of her family progeny, so too are we when our hearts are swallowed up in the name that is above every name, Jesus Christ the Lord.

After all of our exploring we have arrived where we started and know the place for the first time.

> Awake, you who sleep,
> Arise from the dead,
> And Christ will give you light.[5]

HOME AGAIN: SHALOM

These pages are reflections from my own life and study. They emerge from a passage I went through many years ago when I was struck in a life-changing way by an echo I came to realize was of God. This essay results from my lifelong reading of books and study of others who themselves were struck by the same echo as I, especially C. S. Lewis, T. S. Eliot, and N. T. Wright, but also many, many more. Each of us all, I am convinced, can hear the echoes of the voice of God amid the competing sounds in our day and come to know them as the voice of God. When we do, we will come to see that our own personal stories are subsumed and made sense of from within his Grand Story. This is the story of the ancient High-God, the Greeks' Unknown God, the one true God. This God we come to know in and through the concrete Judeo-Christian story, like a Grand Poem. It is in this story that we make sense of the persisting echoes and the constant reach seen reflected and re-fracted in the world's great myths and religions and in our varied pursuits to know, including in science and the arts, and in the ruddy work of daily human life. It is the God of this story that best accounts for that reach, even if we do not know him by name (e.g., as with the Greeks' Unknown God). This God is the resonance we experience as the language and vocabulary of our hearts. He is the Nightingale of the Heart. The "love alone is credible" that wells in the heart is the mysterious Triune God, whom we know in the condescension of Jesus Christ, the instrument, source, and sustainer of all creation, the one in whom we live and move and have our being.

---

5. Eph 5:14, NKJV.

Appendix 1

The Past as Prologue

THIS APPENDIX SHOULD BE read as an expanded footnote to chapter 1. Because this work is written to a broad audience, I take it to be fair to assume that many readers may not have much of a historical background of the premodern world. And while this appendix is no meaningful survey of this history, it will suffice to provide a bit of additional context to the passages discussed in chapter 1. For those who wish even more, at the end of this appendix I have provided a few suggested works.

BROAD HISTORICAL PERSPECTIVE: FROM THE CLASSICAL TO THE MODERN PERIOD

The ancient or classical period of antiquity in Western history began around 800 BC and extends to around 500 AD.[1] The foundation for Western civilization was laid by the Greeks and Romans and was extended and transformed with the emergence of Christianity. Late antiquity can be marked by the rise of Christianity from a small sect in Judea (a minor eastern province of Rome), slowly emerging as an influence during the later days of the Roman Empire, from AD 30 to around 500, combining the New Testament and patristic periods. The broader influence of Christianity on the world

1. Obviously, human history extends well back from this period, including primitive history and the history of Judaism. The early prehistorical period is more accurately called primitive history rather than classical and refers to cultures who did not write their histories. There are record-keeping cultures, such as the Egyptians, reaching back to c. 3200 BC. The Phoenicians, according to Jewish historian Josephus, "'made the largest use of writing,'" and may have been the first historians, although according to Michael Grant, it was the Greeks who learned to write from them. *The Ancient Historians*, 10. For reference to the Jews as the first historians, see Halpern, *The First Historians*.

began following Roman emperor Constantine's conversion to Christianity in 311, which resulted in the legalization of Christianity in 313 with the Edict of Milan. Constantine became emperor in 307 during the latter part of the decline of the empire and consolidated it one final time before his death in 337. The classical intellectual culture competed, coexisted, and was eventually adapted and transformed by the emerging Christian church during the first five centuries of the new era. Working through a variety of heresies (particularly Gnosticism), this new culture was significantly established by the time Rome first fell in 410.

The medieval period gradually arose after the empire fell in the west, and it extends to the late northern Renaissance (i.e., the Renaissance in Europe beyond Italy) during the fifteenth and early sixteenth centuries. Thus, the medieval period covers about one thousand years. During this period in the West, Christianity was extremely influential in shaping a new, fully integrated church, state, and social structure. After the fall of Rome, the Holy Roman Empire eventually emerged, an early beginning point often marked by the crowning of Charlemagne in AD 800.[2] The old "Roman" empire continued in the East as the Byzantine Empire until the fifteenth century, with its center in Constantinople (now Istanbul, Turkey). Christianity's influence on the culture continued to flourish in the East, just as in the West, until the rise of Islam in the seventh century AD. Gradually over the next three centuries, the Eastern Christian Church (Eastern Orthodoxy) became an island in a dominant Islamic empire, and in the twelfth century it expanded into Russia (Russian Orthodoxy). The Eastern Church and Islam learned to

---

2. The Holy Roman Empire lasted for a thousand years, from AD 800 to 1805. The final demise of the empire was Napoleon's defeat of Holy Roman Emperor Francis II on December 2, 1805, at the Battle of Austerlitz in Austria, also known as "The Battle of Three Emperors" (Tsar Alexander I of Russia, Francis II, and Napoleon). Though mostly remembered today for its association with Germany, "the Holy Roman Empire embodied the ideal that Europe was a single pacific Christian order upheld by the emperor as pre-eminent monarch and guardian of the papacy. More directly, it provided the political framework for what are now Germany, Austria, Switzerland, Liechtenstein, Belgium, Luxembourg, the Netherlands and the Czech Republic, as well as most of Italy and parts of Denmark, France and Poland." Wilson, "The Holy Roman Empire." The significance today of the Holy Roman Empire is, first, its relation to Hitler's "Third Reich" (the Holy Roman Empire was the First Reich—*reich* means "empire" in German); second, clarification about the Christian Crusades (the Crusades were the empire acting as a political empire in response to the expansionism of the Islamic Caliphate); and third, its comparison by some today to the federation of European states called the European Union (but there is little comparison). The Holy Roman Empire was severely affected by the rise of the nation-state and political, social, and economic changes that fractured and broke down the feudal loyalty system, due in no small part to the Protestant Reformation. On *Modus Vivendi*, see Thomas, "Early Muslim Relations with Christianity."

coexist (*Modus Vivendi*—a "way of living") in a form where they agreed to disagree.[3]

Throughout the medieval period in the West, the Christian church and its developing theology interacted with and shaped political and cultural life into an integrated, religiously based intellectual, sociopolitical, economic, and artistic cultural worldview.

What we think of as the medieval period is associated with the story of Western civilization, not the East. Geographically the Western world became demarcated west of the Adriatic Sea and north of the Italian boot along the Mediterranean Sea and up across Western Europe. The Eastern Church extended predominantly east of the Adriatic, along and east of the eastern Mediterranean[4] (i.e., Turkey, Syria, and Persia), the Holy Land, and back across to Egypt (home of the Coptic church) and North Africa.

Combined, the classical and medieval worlds lasted approximately 2,300 years, until around AD 1500. Together they form the foundation of Western civilization. Many of the seminal ideas, traditions, cultural habits, and habits of mind that constitute "civilization" as we know it today were born and shaped during this period. Unquestionably the most influential were the cultures and ideas of Greece, Rome, and Christianity.

In the ancient Western world, the roots of reason are found, interestingly, among the poets (e.g., Homer and Hesiod). After the epic poets came

3. A signal event portending Islamic expansionist aims occurred when the Rashidun Caliphate seized and eventually captured Jerusalem is 678. Aggressive conquest continued by the Islamist caliphate throughout the Middle East, North Africa, Spain, and all the way up to 150 miles from Paris. This was partially enabled by the vacuum left by the fall of Rome in the West, though with some intermittent resistance, e.g., when the Normans drove the Muslims out of southern Italy and Sicily shortly before the First Crusade. Five hundred years after the siege on Jerusalem, in 1096, the now reconstituted Holy Roman Empire pushed back against the expansion of the growing Islamic empire (the First Crusade). Crusades continued through the twelfth and thirteenth centuries. These crusades were a military response to aggression. For a current reassessment of the Crusades, see Stark, *God's Battalions*. Christianbook.com provides the following product description: "In *God's Battalions*, Rodney Stark argues that the medieval Crusades were not waged in order to gain land, steal money, or to win converts as popularly believed today. Instead, Stark suggests that the Crusades were foremost a military response to unwarranted aggression by expanding Turkish invaders. By looking at the history of the seven major Crusades from 1095 to 1291, Stark argues that the crusaders launched their campaign because of extensive Islamic provocation after centuries of repeated attempts to colonize the West."

4. Christianity did spread farther east. During this same late classical and early medieval period, Christian churches existed as far east as India. Significant Christian communities have long existed in Armenia, Syria, and west of Israel into Saudi Arabia. Scholars have long debated the Judeo-Christian influence on the *Koran*, from textual analysis and also from the geographical presence of Judaism and Christianity found in areas where Muhammad lived.

the philosophers, and they were also the first scientists. The pre-Socratic philosophers followed the epic poets in the West to begin Western philosophy. Early among these philosophers, but most particularly later in Socrates, Plato, and Aristotle, we see not only very sophisticated reason—the foundational reason of the Western tradition—but also the foundational idea of a transcendent reality that gives being to the ever-changing world and that upholds that changing world in its being. These form the bedrock of the Hellenistic world into which Christianity was born.

Most of early Christianity's interaction with the prevailing ideas and philosophies of the classical world was reacting to strange admixtures of these ideas by some who identified as Christian but weren't following the apostolic faith. These early interactions took the form of defenses against heretical teaching, led by church priests and bishops. Since some of the early Christian bishops had themselves converted to Christianity from pagan religions and philosophies, which many of them knew extremely well, as time went along, some of these bishops (e.g., Augustine) began to discern how some of the philosophies of the classical world could integrate with Christian teaching, though with appropriate transformation. St. Augustine interpreted Plato's theory of ideas or forms in light of Christian thinking, providing a metaphysical explanation to the Christian understanding of God's relation to the world. Christianity, in short, became the inheritor of the classical world and was also the preserver of it and its deep and rich intellectual tradition, albeit with the Christian gospel always being the measure against which all classical philosophies were assessed.

This continued after the collapse of the Roman Empire and came to its height between the eleventh and the fourteenth centuries. In the thirteenth century, the preeminent philosopher-theologian St. Thomas Aquinas developed the most thoroughly integrated synthesis between theology and philosophy and faith and reason in his *Summa Theologica*. Aquinas's thoughts and explanations, which rigorously synthesized Aristotle with Christian theology (though not uncritically), along with St. Augustine's earlier embrace of Plato and accounted for by Aquinas, underwrote much of what came to be the foundation of the Western philosophical tradition until the eighteenth century. Augustine's and Aquinas's ideas, which reflected those of the ancient world as transformed by God's revelation, shaped the way people in the Middle Ages experienced the world.

God was pervasive in the world of daily life, not because people were inherently superstitious but because God was in integral relation with his creation. The transcendent mysteries of life were made sense of in the light of very sophisticated rational reflections that were thoroughly integrated with the orthodox Christian faith and revelation as found in the Bible.

It was all but impossible not to believe in transcendence and God in the premodern world. Certainly, however, just because people believed in God doesn't mean they all knew God in an active and personal way, nor was everyone a Christian. But the prospect of fuller belief didn't begin with unbelief that must be overcome. Nascent belief could more easily be ignited into knowledge of and an active relationship with God, through the Spirit by his grace, enabled by the shaping power of the rituals of belief embedded in the culture.[5] The way the premodern world lived and experienced the world, and the way they thought about the world, provided an integrated, coherent way to interpret the world *and* the signals of transcendence and the echoes of the voice of God found in it.

The premodern world was not at all naive, simpleminded, or ignorant. While it can unquestionably be labeled an age of faith in comparison to the modern world, it should fairly be labeled the age of faith and reason. Indeed, the intellectual foundations that gave rise to the modern period and the practices of reason that birthed Western philosophy and science were laid and built upon during the classical and medieval periods, to become an impressive and sophisticated edifice. An extremely unlikely candidate— Christianity, born as a small sect within Judaism by an infamous figure whose life, death, and resurrection were even more unlikely and unexpect- ed—would rise to become the dominant religion in a crumbling and falling Roman Empire and would step into the gap after it fell to build a whole new Western world—a fully integrated intellectual, artistic, sociopolitical cul- ture, grounded by the moral, spiritual, and theological underpinnings of its inherent religious impulse. The Christian faith and the church became the center around which the whole medieval world revolved. As Samuel Stumpf says, in the Middle Ages "the sky hung low, suggesting a close bond between heaven and earth, and accordingly between philosophy and theology. . . . The whole cultural atmosphere was affected by the predominance of the church so that moral theory, political doctrine, the institutions of society such as family and work, the arts and literature, and much of science—all these bore the imprint of theology."[6] The conditions for interpreting the signals of transcendence and mysterious echoes in and throughout the pre- modern world as the presence and voice of God were very conducive. It was all but impossible not to do so, not because premodern people were gullible and particularly susceptible to superstition but because the world picture

---

5. On how this cultural shaping effect works, from an evangelical Christian point of view, see Smith, *Desiring the Kingdom*.

6. Stumpf, *Philosophy*, 215–16.

they lived in told them that's how the world is—the transcendent is in and can be seen through the concrete world of everyday life.

Charles Taylor sums up the medieval world that would change over time, through the passage to modernity:

> (1) The natural world they lived in, which had its place in the cosmos they imagined, testified to divine purpose and action, and not just in the obvious way which we can still understand and . . . appreciate today, that its order and design bespeaks creation, but also because the great events in the natural order, storms, droughts, floods, plagues, as well as years of exceptional fertility and flourishing, were seen as acts of God, as the now dead metaphor of our legal language still bears witness.
>
> (2) God was also implicated in the very existence of society (but not described as such—this is a modern term—either as a polis, kingdom, church, or whatever). A kingdom could only be conceived as grounded in something higher than mere human action in secular time. And beyond that, the life of the various associations which made up society, parishes, boroughs, guilds, and so on, were interwoven with ritual and worship. . . . One could not but encounter God everywhere.
>
> (3) People lived in an "enchanted" world. This is perhaps not the best expression; it seems to evoke light and fairies. But I am invoking it here as negation, [Max] Weber's expression "disenchantment" as a description of our modern condition. . . . The enchanted world in this sense is the world of spirits, demons, and moral forces which our ancestors lived in. . . . People who live in this kind of world don't necessarily believe in God, certainly not the God of Abraham, as the existence of countless "pagan" societies shows. But in the outlook of European peasants in 1500, beyond all the inevitable ambivalences, the Christian God was the ultimate guarantee that good would triumph or at least hold the plentiful forces of darkness at bay.
>
> Atheism comes close to being inconceivable in a world with these three forces. It just seems obvious that God is there, acting in the cosmos, founding and sustaining societies, acting as a bulwark against evil. . . . Part of the answer to my opening question . . . [is that in the modern shift] . . . these three features vanished.[7]

---

7. Taylor, *A Secular Age*, 25–26.

PASSAGE TO THE MODERN WORLD: HOW WE GAINED THE WORLD BUT LOST OUR SOUL

These features didn't vanish overnight. The slow-moving passage would change the state of being in the world, the way we experience the world. In the late Middle Ages the world was changing, laying the foundation for what would become the Enlightenment. As natural philosophy increasingly became a discrete discipline with the rise of observational and inductive experimental methods, contributed to by ontological nominalism,[8] natural science was slowly becoming separated from theology and the church. As the northern Renaissance birthed a new widespread humanism in convergence with a host of emerging socio-cultural, -political, and -religious events, new ways of experiencing the world were developing along with a new understanding of human flourishing. The Western world became increasingly less focused on the world beyond and questions of being and more focused on this world and human-centric concerns and science. These movements and others were laying the foundation for the passage to the new world. The church, so crucial for establishing a new order from the ruins of the Roman Empire and for laying the moral and intellectual foundations for Western civilization, including the foundation for modern science, was now being questioned. Then came the explosion that exacerbated these changes: the Protestant Reformation in the sixteenth century. Converging with these influences, the Holy Roman Empire was declining as nation-states were being born. Amid and contributing to these changes, turf wars and religious wars arose and became incessant. The integrated world of the Middle Ages was fragmenting.

Spurred by and as an outgrowth of these events, the Enlightenment began, and with it came a conflict between faith and reason. Views of what reason meant and what being rational is would change. This was partly due to the success of the new science and its emphasis on mathematics and a rapid and increasing shift to instrumental reason focused on controlling

8. Nominalism in the modern world of philosophy is an ambiguous term. It sometimes refers to those who reject metaphysical universals (e.g., beauty as a universal reality in the transcendent sphere versus a name given the commonalities shared by particular instances of beauty) and sometimes to those who reject abstract objects (non-spatiotemporal and causally inert objects, e.g., mathematical objects). The term *nominalism* itself means "in name only" versus "real." William of Ockham (c. 1287–1347) is most often cited as the father of nominalism. In contrast to St. Thomas Aquinas, and virtually all classical medieval philosophers before him, Ockham rejected the actual reality of metaphysical universals; he held that, while we speak of them and make use of them as if they are real, they are actually only names we give to such phenomena. It is Ockham's form of nominalism that is referenced in this essay. Nominalism had a huge impact on classical and medieval philosophy.

nature—this would birth the very practical Industrial Revolution.[9] The new views of reason were also driven in no small part by the desire to establish universally accepted, disinterested foundations for knowledge based on reason alone. If achieved, this new reason-based world would help adjudicate disputes, overcome superstition, and establish an independent court of appeal against perceived arbitrary and corrupt authority—including, as some (especially the Protestant Reformers) had come to believe, the church itself. The metaphysical questions of being and God's relation to creation which had been so dominant in the classical and medieval periods receded into the background. There came a horizontal this-world anthropocentric and individualistic shift, in philosophy, politics, religion, and science. This was enabled further as Isaac Newton's new mechanical image and Francis Bacon's law-driven jurisprudence metaphor slowly began to change the way people felt about the cosmos, and a reduced, less intrusive, and more distant understanding of "God" emerged. "Deism"[10] posited a creator of a law-driven universe who stepped back and let everything run on its own, having little to do with its day-to-day operation.

Just as the rise of the new science brought new observational and inductive experimental methods, new theories and methods in philosophy also arose: empiricism (e.g., Bacon, Locke, Newton, and Hume) and rationalism (e.g., Descartes, Spinoza, and Leibniz) and Kant's attempt at a reconciliation.

Bacon was less interested in the big questions, or truth as such, as much as he was interested in how knowledge could be used. "Knowledge is power," he proclaimed. For him, "science was a road to power."[11] Thomas

---

9. The shift to instrumental reason has had far-reaching effect. The first industrial revolution (c. 1740–1820) was followed by a second one in the nineteenth century (c. 1860/70–1920). Then some historians have overlapping or succeeding the second industrial revolution (but beginning in earnest in the mid-twentieth century) the technological revolution (also called scientific and telecommunications revolution). For the key ideas and impact of the technological revolution, see Ellul, *The Technological Society*; Postman, *Technopoly*; and Gay, *Way of the Modern World*, chapter 2, "The Irrelevance of God in a Technological Society," 79–129.

10. Deism, according to *Encyclopedia Britannica*, is "an unorthodox religious attitude that found expression among a group of English writers beginning with Edward Herbert (later 1st Baron Herbert of Cherbury) [1583–1648] in the first half of the 17th century and ending with Henry St. John, 1st Viscount Bolingbroke, in the middle of the 18th century." The term was first used in France and was endorsed by others there such as Voltaire. Thomas Hobbes, Charles Blount (earl of Shaftsbury), and Matthew Tindal are perhaps the most well-known deists in England. Thomas Jefferson is the most well-known American. Deism is the first foray into "natural religion" that emerged in the Enlightenment period.

11. Jones, *History of Western Philosophy*, 3:75.

Hobbes so completely adopted the new science's view of nature that he declared that only matter exists; "men's thoughts and desires are but the by-products of motions occurring in their cortices and caused by events in the physical environment."[12] Hobbes's radical notion created a reactionary effect, with the philosophers after him trying to reestablish the metaphysical realm he had jettisoned.

Descartes made his case, as a good scientist and mathematician, going back to what he knew for sure. The "father of modern philosophy" began the new modern tradition of rationalism. He said doubt is the beginning point, not because he didn't believe in God but because he wanted a rational way to confirm the reality of God, and all knowledge, with certainty. Standing between the old world, which started with questions of being and existence, and the new philosophy, which focused on how we know, Descartes asserted his famous *cogito ergo sum* ("I think therefore I am"). If we begin with doubt about everything except that "I think," we can confirm that God exists, he concluded, because we must exist in order to think; since we cannot establish our own existence, therefore God, who gives us and holds us in existence, must also exist. For Descartes, the foundation for knowledge is within us; all knowledge of the external world and transcendent reality emerges from within us. There must be two substances according to Descartes, the physical and the mental (or spiritual or soul). "Man, it would appear, is a material substance, for the movements of his body are a part of the physical universe and as such are completely predictable; but he is also a spiritual substance and can freely choose to follow (or neglect, as the case may be) God's commands."[13] Spinoza rejected the notion of two realms, physical and mental (spiritual); for him everything is one, and all of it is physical and spiritual (pantheism).

Whereas "Descartes, Spinoza, and Leibniz tended to emphasize the mathematical elements, to take mathematical certainty as their ideal, and formulate their criterion of truth and reality in terms of the principle of contradiction, . . . Locke . . . tended to rely on sense perception for obtaining knowledge about the world, to emphasize experimental verification."[14] He concluded there are "ideas of sensation and ideas of reflection."[15] Following after him, an almost pristine example of nominalism, Berkeley (a pious and very religious man) declared there is no independent material substance; it's only names we give things. But the things themselves, the individual

12. Ibid., 3:xviii.
13. Ibid.
14. Ibid., 3:240.
15. Ibid., 3:299.

things, depend absolutely on a mind holding them in their existence, God. God is the active mind that is the cause of all particular things. Beginning with the observable things in the world, we see demonstrated before us the reality of God. So Berkeley was a kind of empiricist, but as W. T. Jones says, a "lukewarm" one.[16]

With David Hume, following in the empiricist line (though without the piety of Locke or Berkeley), a new skepticism of all things transcendent and of God emerged. Delving deeply into Locke's assertion of ideas of sensation, Hume focused on human perception. He distinguished between impressions and ideas. But Hume, too, adopted the nominalist philosophy, declaring all ideas only names. Whereas Hobbes, Locke, and Berkeley were also nominalists, they each allowed for some connection point in the transcendent realm (and God) that work like universals. Hume held out no such prospects. He rejected the core idea of "substances," so important to all prior philosophers. He said there is no such thing. That does not mean he rejected the external world; he did not. But neither did he think it could be proven. "Hume's case against the philosophers consists merely in pressing home the consequences of the representative theory of perception."[17] Perception only gives us impressions of what they are immediately being impressed with. There is no guarantee our impressions are real since they are a function of our perceptions, which may not be accurate, and since each impression is unique. Since for Hume "all knowledge is knowledge of the consequences of names," nothing can be considered knowledge except something we assign a name to. What, then, accounts for belief in an external "real" world? Imagination, Hume says. This imagination, he says, is grounded in our mind's continued propensity to assemble our disparate experiences into a coherent whole; but, Hume would say, it must be recognized that this tendency is a psychological phenomenon, not logic.

So, where does this leave us with respect to a reality transcendent to the empirical world? Even more skeptical. If it's illogical to believe in things we experience impressions of, how much more should we be skeptical of things we cannot? Hume says, "Our ideas reach no farther than our experience. We have no experience of divine attributes and operations: I need not conclude the syllogism. You can draw the inference yourself."[18] Hume developed his skepticism of religion in his *Dialogues Concerning Natural Religion*, posthumously published in 1779, leaving open the possibility of faith

16. Ibid., 3:294.

17. Ibid., 3:311.

18. Hume, *Dialogues Concerning Natural Religion*, as cited in Jones, *History of Western Philosophy*, 3:326.

based on irrationality. This idea would be picked up and directly engaged by Kierkegaard in the nineteenth century.[19]

While almost all Enlightenment philosophers still believed in God, with the new, restricted rationalist and empiricist methods of reason, a new meaning of realism emerged—this concrete world—whereas in the premodern world what was real applied to things of this world and to the transcendent realm. The material world is real by reference to the transcendent, by analogy.[20] And though many philosophers in the Enlightenment period continued to hold to a transcendent reality, as we have seen, under the developing new Enlightenment philosophy, the notion of "real" increasingly softened when speaking of the transcendent dimension and hardened when speaking of concrete, this-world reality. It became more and more challenging to speak with confidence about the transcendent realm.

Hume's skepticism raised new questions about human cognition and the nature of human perception. The most famous philosopher of the Enlightenment, Immanuel Kant, was not satisfied with Hume's skepticism and set out to solve the problem—with what he came to call the Copernican Revolution in philosophy. Whereas Locke and Hume had emphasized the passive reception of empirical data in forming the contents of the mind, Kant turned things around. His big revolution was that the human mind shapes the world we live in. Kant separated reality for human beings into two spheres, the noumenal (things in themselves) and the phenomenal (world of experience). The noumenal world provides raw data, but what we experience of this is filtered and conditioned through the limited human knowing grid. We cannot actually experience things in themselves, and we shape what we experience by our minds. We can know those things that our human capacities enable us to shape by our a priori thoughts; yet, while Kant believed a world beyond what humans can know (the noumena) exists, he also believed we simply cannot know anything about it. So the physical world is real and we can know about it, yet only within the limits of how our own minds shape it. And while Kant believed there is a transcendent realm, and God, he was skeptical of knowing anything about it within the bounds of experiential, sensory knowledge. Kant claimed that belief in God is not a constitutive principle but a regulative one. That is,

19. It should be noted, however, that despite popular belief to the contrary, Kierkegaard was not an irrationalist, nor was he an antirealist, nor a relativist. See Evans, "Realism and Antirealism in Kierkegaard."

20. In Plato's case, a "more real" world. Regarding the "by analogy" qualification, see St. Thomas's *analogia entis*, Karl Barth's *analogia fides*, and more recently Kevin Vanhoozer's *analogia dramatis*.

we must believe in God "if our practical lives are to be rationally stable."[21] His philosophy of religion, found in his *Religion Within the Boundary of Bare [or Mere] Reason*, was intended to show this. Yet while the opposite of his intent, for many following after him it reduced religion to morality and became extremely influential on nineteenth century Protestant theological liberalism.[22] Kant's overall philosophical project eventually led down three paths in the late eighteenth, nineteenth, and twentieth centuries: absolute idealism (Hegel), strong rationalism and empiricism (including the logical positivist movement focused on what counts as meaningful knowledge), and postmodern antirealism and constructivism.

In the wake of the Enlightenment period, faith—in God or in anything transcendent or beyond material reality—became anything that didn't fit the new models of knowledge. Reason came to mean a narrowed set of practices that yields genuine knowledge, or justified true belief; and faith in God came to mean a belief that is not justifiable within the constraints of the new practices. Faith and reason became markedly separated. The reduced meaning of reason became culturally prevalent, as did a perception that a methodology for determining all things true about nature and all genuine knowledge had been attained.

Despite that a main goal of the Enlightenment project was to establish a universal, neutral, and disinterested practice of rationality—a kind of intellectual appeals court to adjudicate differences—this was never realized.[23]

21. Hare, "Karl Barth," 76. In deference to Kant's project to recover from Hume's skepticism, Hare indicates that Kant himself says we have "to deny knowledge *in order to* make room for faith" (76). Further, Hare's work and other recent Kant scholarship reveals that Kant has a much stronger "vertical" dimension than often thought, stressing the requirement of God in what he called the important work of "philosophical theology." Hare suggests a close and discriminating reading of Kant, but indicates that until the last twenty years of Kant scholarship, many have overlooked his strong requirement for God. See Hare, "Karl Barth," 81–90.

22. The trajectory of liberal Christianity tended to flatten the focus to horizontal, this-world moral and social concerns. Karl Barth would eventually react to this, having become a converted liberal, in the early twentieth century, stressing God as "wholly other." Regarding Kant and morality, despite his self-legislative theory of moral obligation, in his *Critique of Practical Reason* Kant indicated "moral obligation was linked to belief in God," by what he called a "postulate of practical reason." See Evans, *Natural Signs and Knowledge of God*, 126. For a response to the notion of religion within the boundary of bare reason, see Wolterstorff, *Reason within the Bounds of Religion*.

23. See MacIntyre, *Whose Justice? Which Rationality?*, 6: "It was a central aspiration of the Enlightenment, an aspiration the formulation of which was itself a great achievement, to provide for debate in the public realm standards and methods of rational justification by which alternative courses of action in every sphere of life could be adjudged just or unjust, rational or irrational, enlightened or unenlightened. So, it was hoped, reason would displace authority and tradition. Rational justification was to appeal to

Yet though it wasn't achieved, the urban myth is that it was, and the culture of doubt toward all things transcendent developed in its wake. With the Enlightenment emphasis on how we know, it came to be believed (if only for a season) that "statements about being [are] equivalent to statements about knowledge," such that if we cannot know something with certainty by using certain universally approved methods of knowing, it doesn't exist.[24] A practical, if not always actual, default to a closed-world, materialistic naturalism emerged about what reality is. This is a new faith position that cannot be any more grounded in the new form of rationality than the beliefs it rejects. This new intellectual culture did not put away faith; it just pushed its faith into the background. The problem is, trading the old for new intellectual models resulted in an impoverished explanatory scheme.

What we see at work here is what is often called the "accidents of history," the (mostly) unintended consequences that occur in the wake of the convergence of a series of disruptive events and responses to them. This is what the "Enlightenment project" was. A culture of doubt about (or about the ability to know anything about) all things transcendent slowly but surely arose in its wake. But the culture of doubt created is unwarranted. The same big questions and wonders that led the first epic poets and philosophers to pick up their pens still haunt. The answers given in the past are no less viable simply because we've stopped asking their questions. The passage to modernity was subtle but monumental.

---

principles undeniable by any rational person and therefore independent of all those social and cultural particularities which the Enlightenment thinkers took to be the mere accidental clothing of reason in particular times and places. And that rational justification could be nothing other than what the thinkers of the Enlightenment had said that it was came to be accepted, at least by the vast majority of educated people, in the post-Enlightenment cultural and social orders. Yet both the thinkers of the Enlightenment and their successors proved unable to agree as to what precisely those principles were which would be found undeniable by all rational persons." Commenting on MacIntyre on this point, Alister McGrath says, this was a very bold and optimistic proposal but "the quest for a universal foundation and criterion for knowledge faltered, stumbled and finally collapsed under the weight of a massive accumulation of counterevidence. It simply could not be done; the vision simply could not be achieved. MacIntyre's historical research into the outcomes of the Enlightenment project convinced him that its legacy was an ideal of rational justification which it proved impossible to attain in practice." McGrath, "Atheism and the Enlightenment." The Enlightenment modernist ideal of totally objective human knowledge and truth, which emerged into a hubristic cultural mood, must now be tempered and humbled, even by its own standards.

24. McGrath, *Scientific Theology*, 2:218.

ADDITIONAL RESOURCES

Abraham, William J. *Crossing the Threshold of Divine Revelation.* Grand Rapids: Eerdmans, 2005.

Allen, Diogenes. *Christian Belief in a Postmodern World.* Louisville: Westminster John Knox, 1989.

Allen, Diogenes, and Eric O. Springsted. *Philosophy for Understanding Theology.* Louisville: Westminster John Knox, 2007.

Bishop, Morris. *The Middle Ages.* New York: Houghton Mifflin, 2001.

Boersma, Hans. *Heavenly Participation: The Weaving of a Sacramental Tapestry.* Grand Rapids: Eerdmans, 2011.

———. *Nouvelle Théologie & Sacramental Ontology: A Return to Mystery.* Oxford: Oxford University Press, 2009.

Cross, Richard. *The Medieval Christian Philosophers: An Introduction.* New York: IB Tauris, 2014.

Dupré, Louis. *The Enlightenment and the Intellectual Foundations of Modern Culture.* New Haven: Yale University Press, 2004.

———. *Passage to Modernity: An Essay in the Hermeneutics of Nature and Culture.* New Haven: Yale University Press, 1993.

———. *Religion and the Rise of Modern Culture.* Notre Dame: University of Notre Dame Press, 2008.

Grant, Edward. *The Foundations of Modern Science in the Middle Ages: Their Religious, Institutional and Intellectual Contexts.* New York: Cambridge University Press, 1996.

———. *God and Reason in the Middle Ages.* Cambridge: Cambridge University Press, 2001.

———. *Science and Religion, 400 B.C. to A.D. 1550: From Aristotle to Copernicus.* Baltimore: Johns Hopkins University Press, 2004.

Guardini, Romano. *The End of the Modern World.* Wilmington, DE: ISI, 2001.

Jones, W. T. *A History of Western Philosophy.* 2nd ed. 5 vols. New York: Harcourt Brace Jovanovich, 1969–70.

MacIntyre, Alasdair. *Whose Justice? Which Rationality?* Notre Dame: University of Notre Dame Press, 1988.

Taylor, Charles. *A Secular Age.* Cambridge, MA: Belknap, 2007.

Appendix 2

Detailed Summary of the Biblical Story

I PROVIDE THIS APPENDIX for two reasons: to enable the biblical story to be heard as a single narrative, not merely as pieces and parts, as so often occurs today both outside and inside the Christian fold. As a coherent narrative we can discover our own stories reflected in it, and yet through it to see how our stories participate and are encompassed in God's story. As we embrace Jesus Christ we each become part of this story and this concrete historical story becomes our own story, and through it we see that we all participate in God's Grand Story.

There are many resources that are helpful in obtaining a broad view of the Christian story reflected in the Bible. A few examples include the paraphrases and translations by Walter Wangerin in his *The Book of God*, Eugene Peterson's *The Message*, and N. T. Wright's *The Kingdom New Testament: A Contemporary Translation*. A few book references helpful to this end include, in a more popular vein, Craig G. Bartholomew and Michael W. Goheen, *The Drama of Scripture: Finding Our Place in the Biblical Story* and *The True Story of the World: Finding Your Place in the Bible* and N. T. Wright's recent popular works, including particularly *Simply Jesus: A New Vision of Who He Was, What He Did, and Why He Matters*; in a more scholarly vein, Wright's inestimable Christian Origins and the Question of God series and Kevin J. Vanhoozer, *The Drama of Doctrine: A Canonical Linguistic Approach to Christian Doctrine*. For purposes of this summary, I lean heavily on Wright's *Simply Jesus*, along with other references cited along the way.

The Christian story is a five-act drama: Creation, Fall, Redemption—Part I & II, and Consummation.

CREATION: A WORK OF GOD AS AN EXPRESSION OF DIVINE LOVE

The Judeo-Christian story begins in Genesis 1 with God creating all things. God's creation is an expression of his divine love.

Because we live in modernity there remains a common default perception that there are conflicts between faith and science. But there are no necessary conflicts, even when it comes to the Judeo-Christian understanding of God's creation. There are differing approaches to interpreting the Genesis creation story, even among Christians, and sometimes these differences create the appearance of a conflict between faith and science. But this is not necessary. Indeed, I'm convinced that many of the interpretive differences are due to naturalistic closed-world scientism (a philosophical position) creating a sense of conflict, and then unnecessary reactions by some Christians. In both cases we often wind up forcing our modern questions, cosmology, and approaches to how to answer our top-of-mind concerns back upon the text. This invariably leads to perceived conflicts. Let's begin with some prefatory remarks.

In early Judaism creation is an ordering of reality, with no explicit thought about a punctiliar beginning. The Jewish creation narrative, like all Near Eastern creation narratives, was functional (an ordering) not material (how did the whole thing come about).[1] While retaining the principle of ordering, from very early in the new era, the Christian doctrine of creation was that God, himself outside of and beyond all created things, created the heavens and the earth (all things) *ex nihilo*, out of nothing.[2] The New Testament offered new insights about creation that contributed to this doctrine, e.g., John 1:3; Colossians 1:15–17, as did heresies in the early church (e.g., Gnosticism) that brought focus to it. Ex nihilo contrasted with the whole ancient and classical world and the modern (until the big bang theory[3]). Thus, in the Judeo-Christian story, nature is more than just nature, it is God's creation. The notion of creation tells us that the universe is not just a system but is a purposive work of God. And God said his creation was good.

1. See Walton, *Lost World of Genesis One*, 14–35.

2. See McGrath, *Fine-Tuned Universe*, 72–74. See further McGrath, *Scientific Theology*, 1:220, and May, *Creatio ex Nihilo*, and Copan, "Is Creatio ex Nihilo a Post-Biblical Invention?"

3. While the notion of a finite universe had been broached by some in the Middle Ages, including some Islamic and Christian scholars, and is reflected obliquely in Kepler, the scientific basis for the universe having a beginning didn't occur until the twentieth century. The first theoretical basis for a beginning (the big bang as it was later called) was proposed by Belgian Catholic priest and astronomer Mgr. Georges Lemaître in 1927.

Because there is so much energy and intensity in public debates over science and evolution and multiverses and the Christian story of Creation, we need to remember that it's less about *how* than about *that*, and how wonderful *that* really is. What we call creation or the cosmos is a gift of love, a pure, gracious gift. This gift is the expressive act of divine overflowing love within the one true Triune God: father, son, and spirit. In theological language, it is an overflowing of the perichoretic love within the triune God. What we know as the act and sustenance of creation is a product of God's love.

Second, to avoid becoming analytically confused over the creation narratives in Genesis, we must realize

"there [was] no concept of a 'natural' world in ancient Near Eastern thinking. The dichotomy between natural and supernatural is a relatively recent one. Deity pervaded the ancient world. Nothing happened independently of deity. The gods did not 'intervene' because that would assume that there was a world of events outside of them that they could step into and out of. . . . No 'natural' laws [as we think of them in the modern, scientific world] governed the cosmos; deity ran the cosmos or was inherently in it. There were no 'miracles' (in the sense of events deviating from that which was 'natural'), there were only signs of the deity's activity (sometimes favorable, sometimes not). The [modern] idea that deity got things running then just stood back or engage himself elsewhere (deism) would have been laughable in the ancient world because it was not even conceivable. . . . If God were to unplug himself in that way from the cosmos, we and everything else would simply cease to exist. There was nothing 'natural' [in the modern sense of independent] about the world in biblical theology, nor should there be in ours. This does not suggest that God micromanages the world, only that he is thoroughly involved in the operations and functions of the world."[4]

In fact most of the debate about origins and the perceived conflicts between Christianity and science that surround various readings of Genesis

4. Walton, *Lost World of Genesis One*, 18. The views expressed in this work by Walton are also shared by N. T. Wright. For a few brief comments by Wright on this topic, see "Genesis with N. T. Wright." For a more detailed exploration into the issues and comments on the interpretation of Genesis and the relation between science and the Bible from an evangelical Christian perspective, see BioLogos at http://biologos.org. For a summary of the various hermeneutical approaches to the interpretation of Genesis 1 and 2, as well as a broad summary of the religious basis of the intended purpose of the Genesis account of creation, see Deffinbaugh, "Creation of the Heavens."

1 are clarified by Old Testament professor John H. Walton as he explains how the most compelling reading is as a description not of cosmic origins per se but rather God's ordering of his creation to function as his theater of activity. That is, it is his "temple" in which he will abide and relate to and with his creation, especially his people.[5]

On the other hand, however, the Genesis account of creation was specifically countering the prevailing pagan ideas of god or the gods as either the creation itself or elements of it. To help understand what this means, listen to particle physicist and well-versed philosopher and lay theologian Stephen Barr addressing the meaning of the Genesis account in a talk about science and religion:

> Modern cosmology is [often] invoked to argue that the universe could have created itself from nothing by a quantum fluctuation. . . . The philosophical critique of religion is largely based on crude misunderstandings about traditional ideas about God and creation. Let me start with supernaturalism, the supernatural. Christianity and Judaism were not and are not based on supernaturalism, if you mean by that the rejection of the idea that there is a natural order. On the contrary, scholars tell us that the book of Genesis was written as an attack, as a polemic against the supernaturalism and superstition of ancient pagan religion. When Genesis said that God placed the sun and the moon in the heavens, in the firmament to be lamps to light the day and the night, it was attacking the pagan religions which worshiped the sun and moon as gods. When Genesis said that man is made in the image of God and was to exercise dominion over the animals, it was, well it was saying many things, but in part it was attacking the paganism in which human beings bowed down to animals or to gods made in the image of animals. In paganism the world was filled with supernatural forces populated by numerous deities—gods of the ocean, of the earth, of the forest, goddesses of sex and fertility and so forth. But Jews and Christians taught that there was just one God who was not to be sought, not to be looked for *in* nature, *within* nature, but who was outside of nature. And was not to be found within the phenomena and forces of nature, but who is the *author* of nature. In this way biblical religion helped strip the world of supernatural elements and to make the world into a natural world. And thus, helped to prepare the way indirectly for the emergence of science. The

5. Walton, *Lost World of Genesis One*, 18. See Walton's detailed exegetical argument in *The Lost World of Genesis One*, which is an illustration that a great deal of the debate about origins between Christians and scientists is unwarranted and unnecessary.

biblical religions, then, taught that there is a natural order which comes from God. And what characterizes this order, this natural order, and reflects the rationality of its creator, is precisely that it is orderly, harmonious, and lawful.[6]

To avoid any confusion, let me clarify and reconcile what Old Testament professor John Walton and what Stephen Barr have said. Walton is calling attention to the way people in the ancient Near Eastern world would understand the book of Genesis. This is crucial to interpret it correctly. When he says, "The gods didn't 'intervene'," there were no "'natural' laws," and "no 'miracles' (in the sense of events deviating from that which was 'natural')," he is pointing out that creation could not exist without God and, as we suggested in chapter 2, the whole of the created order is a wonder, an astonishment. God was and is and must be intimately related to the creation because for him not to be, nothing would hold together; indeed, nothing would exist. Barr acknowledges the same thing, but he is talking about how we interpret the book of Genesis from this side of modern science. When he says, "Christianity and Judaism were not and are not based on supernaturalism, if you mean by that the rejection of the idea that there is a natural order," he is not saying that the whole of creation is not supernatural; indeed, it must be for the same reason as just stated: because without God, who is not a part of the fabric of creation but the author of it, there would be nothing at all. Creation itself, the whole order of what we call nature, is supernatural. God created nature with orderliness and processes that work in a consistent, orderly way, what since Francis Bacon we call "laws." (Bacon borrowed from his jurisprudence experience to create a metaphor to describe how nature works; we now take this metaphor as literal.) Barr's point is that part of the objective of the author of Genesis is to counter the many pagan religions of the day who had made nature, or parts of it, gods. In so doing they were making nature itself or parts of nature supernatural. Neither of these ways of explaining creation to the modern mind is wrong. They are both right and not contradictory. God is the creator and can and does act within and through his creation in ways we now call "natural" (indeed most often he does) and in ways we call "miracles." We get confused when we try and understand or interpret Genesis as if it were written to modern scientists and also when we do so from within a modern closed or even semi-closed (Deistic) outlook—as if God is not involved in his creation, or is merely creation itself or parts of it, or cannot and does not engage with his creation even in special ways that we call miracles. When we approach the biblical

---

6. Barr, "Science and Religion." Transcription is my own.

description of creation in any of these ways, we are bound to misunderstand it and misuse it.

In the concrete details of the Christian story, Creation is that the Triune God, the ground of *all being* (all that we call existence), whose being is a constant "dance" of interpenetrating love, freely overflowed in an expression of his divine will, giving existence to all that is. While a free expression of the divine will, God's creation is not a *mere* mechanical act as we think of our own acts of creation. God's love cannot *not* overflow. It is not that he is constrained out of need as if inadequate in some way but purely out of the unboundedness of his love. All of what we know as existence is the beneficiary of this overflowing act. God's act and ordering of creation is unto an active and ongoing relation of love with his creation, especially with human beings who are created in his Image (his icons). Our reason for being is to be in *responsive love* with him. This responsive love is thus to be a reflection of his love in the world. As his *images,* we are vice-regents of the King in this world that is his abiding place, his temple, his kingdom.

How? The divine Logos (Word) is the instrument of and sustainer of all creation. That is, "Reason" itself, "Truth" itself, "Beauty" itself, "Goodness" itself, "Love" itself, overflowed in the only begotten son of the Father. This caused Creation. The Word of God is the firstborn of all creation. "In the beginning was the Word, and the Word was with God, and the Word was God. The same was in the beginning with God. All things were made by him; and without him was not anything made that was made. In him was life; and the life was the light of men" (John 1:1–4, KJV). He is the one in whom all things hold together, the one who in due time would demonstrate the full extent of divine love. The divine Logos, the Word of God, the second person of the Triune God, is the instrument of creation.[7] This is the mystery of Creation.

FALL: BUT WE WOULD NOT

However one chooses to look at it, something is wrong, awry. The cry of our hearts tells us so even if nothing else does. We're not like fish who do not bemoan the water that surrounds them. There's something not right, and we all know it. We push back against the way things are—we cry out

---

7. In Col 1:16, St. Paul refers to this understanding: "For by [or 'in,' as in NRSV] Him all things were created that are in heaven and that are on earth, visible and invisible, whether thrones or dominions or principalities or powers. All things were created through Him and for Him" (NKJV). The Greek construction here is either an instrumental of means, "by means of," or as the "agent," either way reflecting that the Logos is the instrument of the creation of all things—that is, everything that has existence.

for justice, for things to be put right. Some suggest a response of endurance or resignation (as in Hinduism) and others for the attainment of perpetual bliss in the face of it (as in Buddhism), but we sense there is more, that there is something wrong that must be put right. The Christian story says this sense is true and that there is an answer to our cries. Our discontentment is because the world is not as it was meant to be.[8] It's broken, and this broken-ness is due to sin. Like Goethe's Faust, we sold our souls to Mephistopheles, believing it to be a bargain. But in gaining the world, we lost our souls, and now all we know is death—but our hearts cry out for life. We who were to be God the King's primary reflection in this world as his vice-regents sought to be king ourselves. Our hubris resulted in a world of sin and death, one where instead of God's fully satisfying love being reflected and displayed in the world through our responsive love with him, the constancy of death we now know is our perpetual reach for life in serially unfulfilling distorted loves.

According to Genesis 1 and 2 human beings (adam, both a name and a description—humankind) were formed from the red clay dirt from the earth (adamah, which means red dirt) and God breathed into them his own life (breath connotes spirit), and they became living souls. He made hu-man beings, male and female together as a whole, in his own image (tselem in Hebrew, eikōn in Greek, icon in Latin) and likeness, and gave them a mission: be fruitful, multiply, and be the caretakers and cultivators (culture-makers) of the world. The scene in which human beings were originally set was a garden. It depicted a tranquil paradise where the world and human beings flourished naturally, as a byproduct of God's life—the source of all life. It was good, according to God, very good.

The core calling of humankind was to be God's icons, his images, in his creation. Throughout the centuries there have been a variety of

---

8. "By suffering violence rather than giving it out, Christ shows that love—not violence—is, in Tennyson's words, 'Creation's final law.'" Cavanaugh, "'Creation's Final Law,'" 15. See Cavanaugh's short article in which he explains how to read the Genesis ac-count of creation and the fall in contrast with the prevailing Babylonian creation myths (e.g., the Enuma Elish myth). In the Babylonian myth (and all other similar ones), the core idea is that the whole of creation is evil and violent, and that's just the way things are, or in other words there is no "fall" because the ontological reality of things is not good but at its core bad. Despite the similarities between Enuma Elish and the Genesis account, the core difference is in the ontology and eschatology found in Genesis. The core idea in the Genesis creation account is the opposite of all other creation myths. In Genesis creation is ontologically different than the classical philosophers in that first it is made by God who is not a part of the creation and secondly it is good; and, notwithstanding the Fall, eschatologically it shall be redeemed and brought to its full goodness—redemption and fulfillment wrought by Christ's love and fulfilled in and the through his love.

interpretations of the meaning of "image."[9] The varied descriptions fall into four major categories: substantive; functional; relational; and divine destiny. The substantive view emphasizes how human beings are representations of God in various ways, such as the ability to know and understand, human being's intellectual and reasoning capacity and to be rationally and morally formed. The functional view emphasizes human beings as God's representatives in his creation—a word picture commonly found in the ancient near east, where kings of a territory place icons, markers throughout their kingdom to indicate whose kingdom it is and something of who the king is. This is the sense of human beings as vice-regents of the king (noticeable in Psalm 8 and Romans 5). The relational view emphasizes the I-Thou relationship between human beings and God, and from that, human beings' relationship between one another. The divine destiny view emphasizes human beings' capacity and ultimate destiny (the *telos*) to be shaped and formed into what God is like (this reflects the doctrine of *theosis*, stressed in Eastern Christianity particularly but also taught in the Latin West; and even in some Evangelical Christian circles.[10]) Support for each of these dimensions of the *imago Dei* can be found in Scripture, in the Apostolic Fathers, and throughout church history.

The core calling and capacity of human beings given to us by having been created in God's image is a stamp upon us and in us. Whenever we deny the calling or misuse the native capacities given to us leaves us with a deep longing that we try to fill with an endless array of other things. This is precisely what happened in God's original garden. In Adam and Eve human beings were disobedient, seeking to be God rather than be his representatives. They did not fulfill their calling and, according to the law of sin and death God's judgment fell upon them and they and all after them and the whole world have been broken ever since. We lost the life of God sustained in us by his spirit, though not our soul, and therefore, as St. Paul says, "we are dead in our trespasses and sin." The fall of humanity into sin (*hamartia*, to fall short of the target) became a world of sin and death. Yet our souls still pant for the life of God.

In his *Confessions*, St. Augustine recounts from his own personal story what can easily be the story of each of our lives, differentiated only by the

9. For a detailed Orthodox, Catholic, Protestant ecumenical exposition of the *imago Dei*, see Howard, *Imago Dei*.

10. See the key verse 2 Pet 1:4. St. Irenaeus, bishop of Lyons (c. 130–202), in his *Against Heresies*, book 5, said that God "became what we are in order to make us what he is himself;" and "If the Word became a man, it was so men may become gods." Also see Clendenin, *Eastern Orthodox Christianity*; Bray, "Deification"; Williams, "Deification"; and Rakestraw, "Becoming Like God."

details. Augustine's confessions, and ours, are the inheritance of the confessions of Adam and Eve. Peter Brown in his introduction to a translation of Augustine's book says this: "The *Confessions* is a history of the schooling of the heart in love."[11]

Continuing with the metaphor of kings, kingdoms, and regents, knights and noblemen, whereas humans were to be the faithful representations and representatives of the King, they desired to become king themselves. Though the King could mandate "love" from his subjects, understanding that a false coercion of "love" is not real love at all, in freedom the King allowed his subjects to wander aimlessly, constantly remaking and redefining themselves under the delusion that they could be king. This wandering oftentimes led to squalor, like that of younger son in the New Testament Parable of the Prodigal Son (see Luke 15:11–32). But even in their prodigality and wandering, the subjects did not lose their longing for the true object of their love; they simply filled their longing with distorted loves. The subjects gave ultimate love to less than ultimate things, seeking ultimate fulfillment in things that the *King alone* could satisfy. On the first page of *Confessions,* Augustine cites what he learned the hard way, as did the prodigal son: We are "but a particle of Thy creation. Thou awakes us to delight in Thy praise; for Thou madest us for Thyself, and our heart is restless, until it repose in Thee."[12]

As on so many occasions in the Judeo-Christian story, it was in a garden that the wandering Augustine sees things aright. As again so often happens, it was out of the mouths of babes that he heard God speaking and crossed the threshold of belief. He heard a child singing and dancing over the hedge separating them. Distraught and in reflection, he said, "I was dying a death that would bring me life . . . I was frantic, overcome by violent anger with myself for not accepting [God's] will and entering into [God's] covenant. Yet in my bones I knew that this is what I ought to do." In a "deluge of tears," he would not, until he gave in.

> I was asking myself questions, weeping all the while with the most bitter sorrow in my heart, when all at once I heard the sing-song voice of a child in a nearby house. Whether it was the voice of a boy or a girl I cannot say, but again and again it repeated the refrain "Take it and read, take it and read". At this I looked up, thinking hard whether there was any kind of game in which children used to chant words like these, but I could not remember ever hearing them before. I stemmed my flood

11. Naugle, *Reordered Love,* 34.
12. Augustine, *Confessions,* 5.

of tears and stood up, telling myself that this could only be a divine command to open my book of Scripture and read the first passage on which my eyes should fall. For I had heard the story of Antony, and I remembered how he had happened to go into a church while the Gospel was being read and had taken it as a counsel addressed to himself when he heard the words *Go home and sell all that belongs to you. Give it to the poor, and so the treasure you have shall be in heaven; then come back and follow me.* By this divine pronouncement he had at once been converted to you.

So I hurried back into the place where Alypius was sitting, for when I stood up to move away I put down the book containing Paul's Epistles [which Alypius had been reading]. I seized it and opened it, and in silence I read the first passage on which my eyes fell: *Not in reveling and drunkenness, not in lust and wantonness, not in quarrels and rivalries. Rather, arm yourself with the Lord Jesus Christ; spend no more thought on nature and nature's appetites.* I had no wish to read more and no need to do so. For in an instant, as I came to the end of the sentence, it was as though the light of confidence flooded into my heart and all the darkness of doubt was displaced.[13]

Through simple concrete things including the voice of a child, the world of one man changed. Not so different from Blaise Pascal when, on the night of November 23, 1654, his life was changed forever.

The story of our lives as the progeny of Adam,[14] of sin and death, is a core narrative of our own stories embedded within the Grand Story. But, as Paul Harvey would say, then there is "the rest of the story."

13. Augustine's *Confessions*, cited in Wolterstorff, *Divine Discourse,* 4.

14. We haven't discussed the question of common ancestry or special creation of kinds or species, say plants, animals, and particularly humans. We have accepted, for the sake of argument, contemporary evolution theory because on its face it does not conflict with Christian theism, which at its root recognizes God as Creator. How he may have chosen to create has not been a focus of our discussion. When asserting the Grand Story and citing Adam as a key character in it, the question of common ancestry arises. There has been much discussion on this topic, and it is on this topic, in part, that questions of "creation science" and even to some extent intelligent design arise. I would simply point out two things with respect to the term *adam* as used in the Bible: 1. The term *adam* comes from the Hebrew *adamah*, which means "man" or "mankind" and signifies the red color of the ground, dust, nothingness. This term is used in Genesis, and it is into this *adamah* that God breaths life and the *adamah* becomes a living being (that is, not any longer mere lifeless red colored dust). 2. In the New Testament (e.g., Rom 5) and for the duration of Judeo-Christian history, Adam and Eve have been referred to as the first couple, the first human beings. But precisely how to interpret what this understanding means has varied widely throughout Christian history. That

REDEMPTION—PART I

Long before Augustine in the fifth century AD, there was Abraham, whose story is the beginning of the new story. One night as he watched over his flock from atop a hill in Mesopotamia, near present-day Baghdad, the life of this man was changed. God said to him, "Go from your country and your kindred and your father's house to the land that I will show you. I will make of you a great nation, and I will bless you, and make your name great, so that you will be a blessing. I will bless those who bless you, and the one who curses you I will curse; and in you all the families of the earth shall be blessed." (Gen 12:1–3, NRSV) This is the promise of Abraham; the Abrahamic Covenant. Abraham went, and God was with him.

As time went along, remembering God's promise, Abraham still had no heir. His wife, Sarah, was getting older and older, and it seemed she was barren, so Abraham, at Sarah's urging, took matters into his own hands. He slept with Sarah's servant Hagar, and she bore a son, Ishmael. But God had not forgotten his promise. Late in years, well beyond childbearing, miraculously Sarah conceived and bore a son, Isaac, Abraham's seed.

Isaac and his wife, Rebecca, would have two sons, Esau and Jacob. God's favor was on Jacob, and through the wiles of his mother, he inherited his brother's birthright and father's blessing, although he was the younger son. Jacob had twelve sons, who would become the namesakes of the twelve tribes of Israel (Reuben, Simeon, Levi, Judah, Dan, Naphtali, Gad, Asher, Issachar, Zebulun, Joseph, and Benjamin). But what about Israel?

One night Jacob encountered and struggled with God. In the outcome of the struggle God gave Jacob a new name, "Israel," which can mean "struggles with God" but also "surrenders to God" or "God rules or reigns." Such would become the character of Israel the people in relation to their God.

Through Isaac, Jacob, renamed Israel, carried the blessing as the seed of Abraham. God would make a people blessed to be a blessing to the whole world—a progeny as numerous as the stars in the sky.

---

said, the question of whether there was an actual "first couple" can become significant to theological understanding, especially when it comes to Original Sin. But that there was a "fall," and that it was human beings that precipitated the Fall and that it affected not only humans but all of creation is undisturbed by the question of common ancestry or special creation of human beings. Further, the science of common ancestry is not at all as black and white as is popularly thought. For a review of how this topic may be thought of in a serious way, see Plantinga, "When Faith and Reason Clash"; Plantinga, "On Rejecting the Theory of Common Ancestry"; Behe, *Darwin's Black Box*; McGrath, *Fine-Tuned Universe*; and Walton, *Lost World of Adam and Eve*. For a recent scientific analysis on human distinctiveness vis-à-vis language that indirectly addresses the question of common human ancestry, see Berwick and Chomsky, *Why Only Us*, and Stephen Barr's review of this book, "First Words."

As was customary in those days, Israel and his family would be no-
madic, moving from place to place in the land God had shown their forefather Abraham. Though they struggled against the travails of life, God was
with them and provided for them. They knew this land as their place, their
home.

During those years, as younger brothers will do, Jacob's son Joseph
irritated his older brothers. He told them of the vision God had shown him
of his family bowing before him. One day Joseph's brothers had had it. To
teach Joseph a lesson, they threw him down a well and then sold him into
slavery to a passing caravan. He was taken to Egypt as a slave. About two
years later Joseph was called to the Pharaoh's court to interpret a dream of
the king. By a profound reversal of fortune, Pharaoh put Joseph in charge
of all of Egypt. During this time, he stockpiled grain in Egypt to ride out
inevitable famine soon to strike the region. One day his older brothers came
to neighboring Egypt in order to buy grain to get their family through the
famine. Joseph recognized them right off, but they did not know him. This
brother whom they had sold into slavery was now the most powerful man in
all of Egypt, except for Pharaoh himself. Joseph forgave his brothers and had
them go home to bring their father and the whole family to Egypt.

The sojourn of Abraham's family into Egypt, beginning with Joseph
until the Exodus, was 430 years. During the lifetime of Joseph and for many
generations afterward, life for the Hebrew people was sustainable even if in
a foreign land. Over the course of time, however, a new Pharaoh arose to
the throne in Egypt, and the growth of the Hebrew people threatened the
king. Then Joseph's legacy, which had protected his people, did no more.
The Hebrew people were ruthlessly enslaved. Then came Moses and the
birth of the nation.

The story is a familiar one. Because the new Pharaoh was so threatened by the growth of the Hebrew people in his land, he put out a decree:
the midwives who were to help birth the children of the Hebrew women
were instead to kill all the male children. But the midwives, fearing God,
refused to do so, at least in some cases. The Hebrews continued to multiply,
and they became "very mighty." So again, Pharaoh put out another decree,
this time that all newborn male children should be cast into the Nile River
to die. During this time there was a male child born to a Hebrew couple
from the tribe of Levi. They hid him and cared for him for three months,
until they could no longer hide him. As all mothers do, the child's mother
looked for a way to care for him and to keep him from being killed, and
she placed him in small basket and floated it down the river near where
Pharaoh's daughter had come to bathe. The princess saw the basket and had

her servants retrieve it and the boy inside. Thus begins the story of Moses in Pharaoh's court.

Like Joseph many years before, Moses was graced with a similar reversal of fortune. Pharaoh's daughter, knowing the boy in the basket was the child of a Hebrew woman, nevertheless sought to protect him. She engaged a Hebrew woman to nurse the child, and in a great irony, it was Moses' own mother. When the child had grown up, he was known as Pharaoh's daughter's son, the grandson of the King. All of the accolades and power that attends such a position would be his. But a problem arose. One day when Moses was surveying the Hebrew slaves' work, he saw one of the slave drivers mercilessly beat one of the workers. Later, when he saw the slave driver alone and thought no one else was around, Moses beat and killed him. Someone *was* around, though. Another Hebrew man saw Moses. Word spread about the event and found its way to Pharaoh himself. In retribution Pharaoh sought to kill Moses, and Moses fled all the way to the desert in Midian.

There Moses met the family of Jethro, who needed help tending their flock of sheep. After some time, Moses fell in love with Jethro's daughter, Zipporah, and Jethro gave his daughter to Moses in marriage. Moses was living a completely different but contented life, and by all accounts this is where he thought he would live out the rest of his days. But God had different things in mind.

God appeared to Moses in a flame of fire "in the midst of a bush" and called out to him, and he charged Moses to return to Pharaoh's court and demand that he "let his people go." It is in this passage that we first come to know how God identifies himself, when after Moses asks whom shall I say sent me—what is God's name—and God says I AM THAT I AM. Here, very early in the story we see that while God's Grand story is not a story of human philosophy, God's very name tells us that he is the source of all being whose own being is contained within himself. This began the grand drama of the Exodus.

Moses returned to Egypt and gave Pharaoh God's message, and Pharaoh's refusal to heed God's word resulted in the ten plagues, the last of which was the plague of death on the firstborn sons, including Pharaoh's. God warned the Hebrews to place blood from a slain spotless lamb above and on the doorposts of their homes so that when the angel of death passed by, it would "pass over" their houses and spare their firstborn sons. This marked the beginning of the Hebrew feast of Passover, celebrated every spring. After this plague, Pharaoh let God's people go, thus beginning Israel's wilderness experience on the road to nationhood.

Shortly after their release from Egypt, God delivered them miraculously when backed up against the unconquerable Red Sea,[15] and the freed Hebrew slaves arrived back at the mountain where Moses had met God earlier in the burning bush. There Moses met again with God on the mountain, where he received the covenant of God sealed in the Ten Commandments, which the Hebrew people in turn agreed to follow. Then only a short time later while Moses was back on the mountain receiving instructions from God, the people below became impatient and crafted an idol god to lead them. When Moses returned, he was so overcome with anger that he destroyed the tablets on which the Law was written. What should have been a short journey to the Promised Land became forty years of confusion. The journey was hard. Along the way, the Hebrew people complained, saying it would have been better if they had never left Egypt. The constant vacillation between faithfulness and murmuring of the Israelites depicts the constant rhythm of satiation and discontentment in us all. Also along the way, according to instructions from God, the Israelites crafted the Tabernacle and the Ark of the Covenant, which they would carry with them as God's dwelling place among them, a foreshadowing of his more permanent Temple. The Tabernacle was God's place of residence, and deep inside in a separate room was the Most Holy Place—the Holy of Holies. It was here that the Ark sat. On the top of the Ark sat the Mercy Seat, where the blood of the slain spotless lamb would be sprinkled once a year on the Day of Atonement (Yom Kippur). This ensured God's forgiveness for sin. The Tabernacle and the Ark were carried along with the Hebrews during their forty years of wandering.

When Israel finally arrived in the Promised Land, a nation was born. The social and religious ordinances given in the Mosaic Law took full effect, with priests, elders, and judges as overseers to ensure a distinctive people of God and proper social order. Over time the people of Israel decided they did not want mere judges, but they wanted a king like the nations around them had. God agreed to give them a king. Saul, from the tribe of Benjamin, was named the first king of Israel. Things began well enough, but over time the idea of kingship went to Saul's head, and as often happens, his suspicions of disloyalty overcame him. Finally, after Saul lost his life in a battle with the Philistines, a new king arose, one who had battled the Philistines on behalf of Israel as a young boy: David, the shepherd boy who had killed the Philistine giant Goliath with a mere sling.

The Davidic kingdom would be the heyday of Israel, and to this period all the people of Israel would forever look back in hope. David was known

---

15. This event metaphorically depicts death and resurrection, being delivered by God's grace. It foreshadows the same depiction of being buried (baptized) with Christ in his death and in him raised to new life in Rom 6.

as "a man after [God's] own heart" (1 Sam 13:14, NRSV). David, the king of Israel and therefore a representative of Israel as a whole, was a picture of what Israel was to be writ large. But at the same time David was also a weak man, and thereby was a picture of Israel's inconsistency and unfaithfulness. David was stricken, as are we all, with the heart of his forefather Adam. He would have to confess his sin and pray for forgiveness, as we all must:

> Have mercy on me, O God,
> according to your steadfast love;
> according to your abundant mercy
> blot out my transgressions.
> Wash me thoroughly from my iniquity,
> and cleanse me from my sin.
>
> For I know my transgressions,
> and my sin is ever before me.
> Against you, you alone, have I sinned,
> and done what is evil in your sight,
> so that you are justified in your sentence
> and blameless when you pass judgment.
> Indeed, I was born guilty,
> a sinner when my mother conceived me. . . .
>
> Create in me a clean heart, O God,
> and put a new and right spirit within me.
> Do not cast me away from your presence,
> and do not take your holy spirit from me.
> Restore to me the joy of your salvation,
> and sustain in me a willing spirit.[16]

The period of King David and his son Solomon saw prosperity and unity for Israel. All twelve tribes of Jacob's sons were united in one kingdom. And during Solomon's reign, God's permanent residence was built—the Tabernacle became the Temple, known as Solomon's Temple. This Temple was the place of God's abode with his people. It represented God's covenant of marriage with his bride, Israel. (Solomon wrote the Song of Songs with this image in mind.) But the bride was unfaithful, and the family fractured.

---

16. Ps 51, NRSV.

After Solomon died, there was revolt under his son Rehoboam. Jeroboam, one of Solomon's officials, persuaded the ten northern tribes to separate and form the Northern Kingdom of Israel,[17] and Rehoboam led the two southern tribes of Judah and Benjamin to form the Southern Kingdom of Judah.[18] The southern tribes would reside in the capital city of Jerusalem. Fractured now, Israel was no longer one nation. It was during this Divided Kingdom period that the prophet Hosea again drew on the image of marriage: God was the faithful husband and Israel his unfaithful wife. Despite Israel's unfaithfulness, God was persistent in undying love. He pursued her despite chronic adultery, and he paid an extraordinary price to redeem her.

As separate nations, Israel and Judah each survived for relatively long periods but finally succumbed to foreign powers. The Northern Kingdom of Israel lasted about 200 years until it was overthrown by Assyria; the Southern Kingdom of Judah lasted around 350 years until it was overthrown and exiled by Babylon. The period of Judah's captivity in Babylon lasted about 70 years, after which they returned to the land of Judah and there was a time of renewal and the restoration of the Temple.

> It was around the time of the restoration of the Temple that Greek philosophy was born, and near the time of the birth of Alexander the Great in 356 B.C. that the ideas of Socrates, Plato, and Aristotle emerged and would establish the way the world and reality would be understood for 2,500 years, especially in the West. It was the influence of these Greek ideas and Greek culture (Hellenization) under the conquering reign of young Alexander the Great that would influence and underwrite much of the culture and world into which Jesus Christ was born, along with the many-faceted adaptations of original ideas that emerged with the rise of the Roman Republic beginning around 500 BC and the Empire, under Augustus, in 44 BC. While the Israelites were not philosophers in the Greek sense, the life and the world they lived in would increasingly rub shoulders with the influence of these thoughts.

17. The Northern Kingdom of Israel was comprised of the territories of the tribes of Zebulun, Simeon, Issachar, Asher, Naphtali, Dan, Reuben, Gad, and Manasseh and Ephraim (which together are referred to as the House of Joseph). The Southern Kingdom, called "Judah," was made up of Judah and Benjamin. All of the preceding were landowner tribes with territories. Levi was a non-landowner tribe. It served the priestly function for all of the tribes.

18. The Southern Kingdom covered some of the Simeon territorial area, so some suggest Simeon was a part of the Kingdom of Judah.

All during the period of the Kings there were faithful and unfaithful times for both kingdoms. To call the kings and their people back, God persistently spoke special messages to them through prophets. The messages were of impending doom if God's people didn't return their hearts and actions to God and of hope when things seemed unbearable. The prophets variously spoke of a time of renewal, when, as Nathan told King David, a new King would arrive and would make a new house "not made of stone and timber . . . but a 'house' in the sense of a family,"[19] and the Kingdom would be restored:

> When your days are fulfilled and you lie down with your ancestors, I will raise up your offspring after you, who shall come forth from your body, and I will establish his kingdom. He shall build a house for my name, and I will establish the throne of the kingdom forever, I will be a father to him, and he shall be a son to me.[20]

After the death of Alexander the Great (323 BC), and after Ptolemaic rule, the Seleucids ruled much of the eastern part of Alexander's Macedonian empire from Syria until the Maccabean revolt (c. 166 BC), led by Judas Maccabeus, freed the Judean province and established the Hasmonean dynasty. This revolt is commemorated in the celebration now known as Hanukkah, the festival of lights. Judas Maccabeus reestablished the Temple, and for a season there was again a measure of independence. It was during this period that synagogues arose as the primary place of worship within Judaism and that the strict reformers the Pharisees arose. But the excitement and optimism brought by Judas Maccabeus would not last. Occupation, exile, and oppression would again befall Judah as it came under the power of Rome. But hope remained.

Years later another leader arose momentarily renewing hope. In 36 BC Herod the Great, using politics and his influential power with Rome, became the ruler of Judea and expanded the Temple restored by the Maccabees. But Herod was no real friend to the Jews, despite being partially Jewish himself. And he was ruthless, always suspicious of anyone who would encroach upon his power.

Near the final years of Herod the Great's reign, there came word to him of a child born in Bethlehem, whom some were saying would become the King of the Jews. To protect his throne, Herod sent soldiers to kill all male children under the age of two in and around Bethlehem.

19. Wright, *Simply Jesus*, 43.
20. 2 Sam 7:12–14, NRSV.

Judea had now been ruled by foreign occupiers, exiles in their own land, for almost four hundred years. And it continued under the thumb of the most powerful and extensive force the world had ever known: the empire of Rome.

As it always is, life was hard for the weak under the oppression of the powerful. This was the plight of the Jewish people and had been for a long, long time. As they had during the many and varied periods of captivity, they now felt the daily weight of Rome on their lives. While their hopes had been raised briefly by Herod, he was really nothing but an instrument of Rome. Herod made life worse, not better. The people of Israel longed for the long-ago time when David was on the throne, when they could see that God was with them. Israel was lost in the fog, under the powerful and brutal hand of tyrants, not their loving, covenant God.

This is the story of the promise of Abraham, Isaac, and Jacob (Israel), the birth and inheritance of a nation, the princely, promised kingdom People of God. But it didn't feel this way. The days were dark.

"Inheritors of the Promise to Abraham"? The "Kingdom People of David"? Where was God their King?

REDEMPTION—PART II

> **Christ Born of Mary**—Matt 1:21–23, NKJV
>
> "And she will bring forth a Son, and you shall call His name JESUS, for He will save His people from their sins."
>
> So all this was done that it might be fulfilled which was spoken by the Lord through the prophet, saying: "Behold, the virgin shall be with child, and bear a Son, and they shall call His name Immanuel," which is translated, "God with us."

> **The Annunciation**—Luke 1:30–33, NKJV
>
> Then the angel said to her, "Do not be afraid, Mary, for you have found favor with God. And behold, you will conceive in your womb and bring forth a Son, and shall call His name Jesus. He will be great, and will be called the Son of the Highest; and the Lord God will give Him the throne of His father David. And He will reign over the house of Jacob forever, and of His kingdom there will be no end."

Christ Born of Mary—Luke 2:1–20, NKJV

And it came to pass in those days that a decree went out from Caesar Augustus that all the world should be registered. This census first took place while Quirinius was governing Syria. So all went to be registered, everyone to his own city.

Joseph also went up from Galilee, out of the city of Nazareth, into Judea, to the city of David, which is called Bethlehem, because he was of the house and lineage of David, to be registered with Mary, his betrothed wife, who was with child. So it was, that while they were there, the days were completed for her to be delivered. And she brought forth her firstborn Son, and wrapped Him in swaddling clothes, and laid Him in a manger, because there was no room for them in the inn.

Now there were in the same country shepherds living out in the fields, keeping watch over their flock by night. And behold, an angel of the Lord stood before them, and the glory of the Lord shone around them, and they were greatly afraid. Then the angel said to them, "Do not be afraid, for behold, I bring you good tidings of great joy which will be to all people. For there is born to you this day in the city of David a Savior, who is Christ the Lord. And this will be the sign to you: You will find a Babe wrapped in swaddling clothes, lying in a manger."

And suddenly there was with the angel a multitude of the heavenly host praising God and saying: "Glory to God in the highest, and on earth peace, goodwill toward men!"

So it was, when the angels had gone away from them into heaven, that the shepherds said to one another, "Let us now go to Bethlehem and see this thing that has come to pass, which the Lord has made known to us." And they came with haste and found Mary and Joseph, and the Babe lying in a manger. Now when they had seen Him, they made widely known the saying which was told them concerning this Child. And all those who heard it marveled at those things which were told them by the shepherds. But Mary kept all these things and pondered them in her heart. Then the shepherds returned, glorifying and praising God for all the things that they had heard and seen, as it was told them.

Dramatic and clear, the peasant boy named Jesus, born in a livestock stable in Bethlehem, was special. Indeed, there was nothing more special that had ever happened in Israel's history. As the prophet Isaiah had cryptically prophesied long ago, he was Immanuel, "God with us"! This little boy was the son of the Most High God, of King David's lineage, and would himself sit on David's throne. He would be named Jesus (*Jehoshua* in Hebrew, which means "Jehovah (YHWH) is Salvation"), because "He will save His people from their sins." "Do not be afraid," the angel says, "for behold, I bring you good tidings of great joy which will be to all people. For there is born to you this day in the city of David a Savior, who is Christ the Lord." To Jewish ears, this meant "the anointed one," the long-awaited Messiah. He is Messiah, the "Lord," a term familiar from the Greek translation of the Old Testament. Many of the Jews had hoped Judas Maccabeus was the one almost two hundred years before, but it turned out he wasn't. Neither was Herod. Was Jesus the one for whom they had waited for so long, for more than four hundred years? Would he restore David's throne and the glory days of Israel? Hopes were high. But how could it be? He was a peasant boy—how could a peasant boy become king in the face of the seemingly infinite power of Rome?

Was there something more afoot here, more than meets the eye? Indeed there was, but it would not be revealed quickly, nor would it be accepted easily. The story was different and bigger than anyone could have ever expected—indeed, more mysterious than anyone could have imagined!

The boy grew up under the tutelage and discipline of his mother, Mary, the one on whom God's special favor had rested, and he worked with his adoptive father, Joseph, who was a carpenter and stonemason. Nothing much is known about Jesus' childhood other than that even at the young age of twelve he seemed exceptional in his understanding of the Hebrew Bible and the traditions of the Jews. His cousin John was an eccentric and would later become a prophet, opening the way for Jesus' public teaching ministry. At age thirty Jesus began that ministry, beginning near his home town of Nazareth in Galilee and never traveling very far from his home area and never outside his own homelands of Judea and Samaria.

Jesus was Jewish through and through. Except for encounters with a few Samaritans and Romans, a Canaanite woman, perhaps some lepers who were foreigners, and a Libyan on the day of his death, Jesus' teaching ministry and message was focused on his people in Judea. This was considered a good thing by the establishment. Their new king must be from the inside, clean and pure from the contamination of the pagans on the outside. Everyone in Jesus' day hoped and expected someone someday would rise up, conquer their oppressors, and lead as David had led. But from the beginning,

Jesus' actions and messages didn't meet their expectations. Though he was from the right lineage—the line of David—from the very start what he said and did was controversial, especially to the Jewish establishment, the priests and rabbis and the strict teachers and interpreters of the Law of Moses, the Pharisees.

Though a rabbi himself, Jesus did and said things rabbis weren't supposed to say and do. He associated with outcasts, tax collectors, and the so-called dirty Samaritans (intermingled, intermarried, Hellenized Jews); touched sick lepers and healed them and others on the Sabbath Day (when work was forbidden); and even made claims no rabbi should—no Jew at all should. At the start of his public ministry, for example, Jesus went back to his home town of Nazareth, and, as New Testament Scholar N. T. Wright says, "On the sabbath day [he] goes to the synagogue—a place of worship, but also the communal 'gathering place' (that's what the word means), the place where people come together to discuss, to think things through, to study the law and to reflect on what it means. Jesus stands up to read from the prophet Isaiah and chooses another of the great passages about the coming new age, the release from slavery, the new Exodus, and restoration after exile, which formed the hope that sustained so much Jewish life of his day."[21] This is what he read.

> "The spirit of the Lord is upon me
> Because he has anointed me
> To tell the poor the good news.
> He has sent me to announce release to the prisoners
> And sight to the blind,
> To set the wounded victims free,
> To announce the year of God's special favor."
> He rolled up the scroll, gave it to the attendant, and sat down. All eyes in the synagogue were fixed on him.
> "Today," he began, "this scripture is fulfilled in your hearing."[22]

Wright comments further: "This is a message of forgiveness, all right, but it's not just forgiveness for individuals who are physically or emotionally

---

21. This and all of the quotations from Wright in this long paragraph on Jesus in in the synagogue in Nazareth are from *Simply Jesus*, 73–77, including quotations from the New Testament Scriptures. The New Testament translation in these quotations is by N. T. Wright from his *Kingdom New Testament*. All references to this translation in this paragraph and all succeeding quotations from this translation from *Simply Jesus* will be identified as "KNT."

22. Luke 4:16–21, KNT.

crippled as a result of their guilt, real or imagined. It's a kind of corporate forgiveness, tapping into the ancient Jewish hope of the 'jubilee,' the year when all debts would be forgiven, when slaves would be set free (Lev. 25). The jubilee is the sabbath of sabbaths. If, every seven years, there is a sabbatical year, in which the land lies fallow and people rest, the jubilee is the sabbatical of sabbaticals, seven times seven years, producing a great celebration of release, forgiveness, and rescue from all that has crippled human life. That's what Jesus was announcing." The crowd in the synagogue who heard Jesus would have known this passage all too well and understood it in the sense Wright describes. They would have been "eager to know how exactly [Jesus] supposed these great prophecies would be fulfilled." But in the way Jesus says it, it is obvious to his hearers he is saying they "*are* being fulfilled" as he speaks, and especially so in a way not as they expected. "Jesus declares that the people who will benefit from this great act of God will not, after all, be the people of Israel as they stand."

Jesus' message was not that the Year of Jubilee, the year of forgiveness and release from oppression, would be for the benefit of Israel alone; rather, it was that it would be for outsiders, too—for everyone! Wright continues:

> Startling though this is, it fits with everything else we know about Jesus' public teaching. "Love your enemies," he told his followers (Matt. 5:44), and he elaborated the point from a dozen different angles. Forgiveness is the heart of his message. . . . As we have just seen, when Jesus expanded on his own jubilee program (Luke 4:24–27), he explained that this wasn't about God simply forgiving Israel its debts and punishing its ancient or contemporary enemies, the pagan nations all around. Rather, this was a message that would be good news—for those pagan nations themselves! . . . Somehow the message of forgiveness is doing more than simply reassuring God's people that they will be all right after all. In fact, it's not really doing that at all—it's warning them that they may *not* be all right after all. Their God isn't simply coming to endorse their national ambitions. He's doing what he said he would, but it won't work out the way they thought it would.

At various times and in multiple ways, Jesus' actions and his message continued both to excite many (typically the poor and the outcast) and enrage others (typically the religious establishment). Especially one night. A Pharisee invited Jesus, who had developed quite a reputation, to dine with him and several of his pious establishment leader friends. Like all Jews, they wanted to see the coming of God's kingdom. But they had also grown suspicious of Jesus and his radical ways. This dinner would be their chance to interrogate him and see what he might say or do.

Jesus went to the Pharisee Simon's house for dinner, and a local woman of suspect reputation apparently heard Jesus was there and showed up. She brought an alabaster jar of ointment (an expensive gift especially for a woman of her apparent means), and standing behind Jesus the woman fell near his feet and began to cry wiping her tears on his feet with her hair as well as the ointment. Simon was taken aback, first perhaps because this unseemly situation had occurred in his house, but particularly because Jesus, supposedly a prophet, allowed this woman of bad reputation to attend him in this way. The Pharisee said to himself, "If this fellow really was a prophet he'd know what sort of woman this is who is touching him! She's a sinner!" Then, almost incongruously it seemed, Jesus proceeded to tell Simon a story that had a question at the end.

> "Once upon a time there was a money-lender who had two debtors. The first owed him five hundred dinars; the second a tenth of that. Neither of them could pay him, and he let them both off. So which of them will love him more?"
>
> "The one he let off the more, I suppose," replied Simon.
>
> "Quite right," said Jesus.
>
> Then turning to the woman, he said to Simon,
>
> "You see this woman? When I came into your house, you didn't give me water to wash my feet—but she has washed my feet with her tears, and wiped them with her hair. You didn't give me a kiss, but she hasn't stopped kissing my feet from the moment I came in. You didn't anoint my head with oil, but she has anointed my feet with ointment.
>
> "So the conclusion I draw is this: she must have been forgiven many sins! Her great love proves it! But if someone has been forgiven only a little, they will love only a little."

Then Jesus said something astonishing to the woman: "Your sins are forgiven." When this happened everyone at the dinner, most of all Simon, was stunned.

Any number of things could be commented on in this passage of Scripture, but I'll focus on the forgiveness declared to the woman. First, it is not unusual that sins could be forgiven in Judaism. It's that it had to be done by God, under certain rules, with prescribed processes, and in the Temple. Wright points out that what makes this unusual is

> *Jesus seems to be claiming that God is doing, up close and personal through him, something that you'd normally expect to happen in*

the Temple. And the Temple—the successor to the tabernacle in the desert—was . . . the place where heaven and earth met. It was the place where God lived. Or, more precisely, the place on earth where God's presence interacted with human, this worldly reality. The Temple was also the place where the high priest had supreme authority. Already we can see what we should have expected if it was indeed true that Jesus was going around telling people that a new government was taking over, that God was in charge from now on [e.g., his comments on previous occasions, 'The Kingdom of God is at Hand']. His healings, his celebrations, his forgiving of those in dire need of it—all these were the up-close-and-personal versions of the larger picture he knew his hearers would pick up on whenever he spoke of God becoming king. These actions and sayings were ramming home the point, dangerous though it was, that the present rulers were being called to account and were indeed being replaced. This was the time for God to take charge, to fix and mend things, to make everything right. Starting with you here, and this person there. Whether or not the self-appointed pressure groups approved.[23]

What we begin to see is that Jesus is indeed different than what the Jews had expected. Increasingly he upset the Jewish authorities by his sayings and doings. While he was claiming in word and deed that he was the long-awaited return of King David, the Messiah, the one who would save Israel from their plight, he was saying much more. He was declaring a Jubilee that extended not just to Israel but to all people. And more, he was making claims that were blasphemous, implying by his actions and declarations that indeed *he was himself the Temple; he was himself the place where God met the world. He himself was Immanuel, God with us*. Yes, he was the long-awaited King of the Jews, but more: the Majestic King of All, greater than Augustus Caesar, greater than all kings at all times. Greater even than the cosmic prince and power of sin holding the whole world captive in exile. *He is God the King!* And his Kingdom was descending, present and with us, now in his lifetime—by and in him. But how was yet to be unveiled.

Though full disclosure would not come yet, a glimpse into just how unexpected and extraordinary the full unveiling would be came one day when Jesus took his three closest disciples up on a high mountain, as recorded in Matt 17:1–8 (KNT), what would later be called "the Transfiguration":

> There he was transformed in front of them. His face shown like the sun, and his clothes became as white as light. Then, astonishingly, Moses and Elijah appeared to them. They were talking

23. Wright, *Simply Jesus*, 77–80.

with Jesus. . . . While he was still speaking, a bright cloud over-
shadowed them. "This is my dear son," said the voice, "and I'm
delighted with him. Pay attention to him." When the disciples
heard this, they fell on their faces and were scared out of their
wits. Jesus came up and touched them. "Get up," he said, "and
don't be afraid." When they raised their eyes, they saw nobody
except Jesus, all by himself.

Commenting on this scene, N. T. Wright calls our attention to "space,
time, and matter," or "temple, sabbath, and new creation." This transfiguration revealed, cryptically at the time, that in Jesus himself God would abide
with his people. Up until then God had abided with them in the Temple in
Jerusalem. Now he was standing before them. Whereas the Sabbath had
been a marker of God's rest at the completion of Creation in Genesis, to be
reflected upon by his people with the institution of Sabbath rest on Saturday, now in Jesus there would be a new Sabbath, the completion of God's
new creation—as would be reflected in Jesus' last words on the cross, "it is
finished (or completed)"; and that in the incarnation of God in Jesus Christ,
God was remaking his world, redeeming his creation. The intersection of
heaven and earth, previously restricted to the Holy of Holies, first in the
Tabernacle and then the Temple, was descending in Jesus; the Kingdom of
God was arriving. But the story was still unfolding.[24]

Jesus continued his ministry for three years, and the crowds grew.

For David's throne to be reestablished, there was expected a great conflagration—a battle to retake Judah from its enemies. Well, there was a battle
brewing, but again, not of the kind that was expected. And the authorities
themselves were pawns unawares in seeing that it came about. "When the
power of Rome and the betrayal of Israel's leaders meets the love of God, the
great whirlpool that results will bring about God's kingly victory, the victory
of the kingdom of God over the kingdoms of the world."[25]

As it became clearer and clearer to the Jewish establishment that Jesus
was blaspheming God with his declarations and unorthodox actions, things
got hotter and hotter in the kitchen of the authorities. And, of course, claims
to usurp Rome's absolute authority? If they found out, it would not be pretty.
Throughout the provinces, as daily life and commerce went about, it was
commonplace to stroll under the shadows of Roman crosses dotting the
landscape, holding on them the bodies of the treasonous enemies against
the all-powerful sovereignty of Rome. The perfect storm was brewing, and
the Jewish establishment powers of the chief priests, teachers of the Law,

24. See Wright, *Simply Jesus*, 131–50; specific references here, 142.
25. Ibid., 182.

and Pharisees held all the cards—and they played them. Though Jesus had healed the sick and done many good works and attracted a following especially among the poor and the outcast, the religious leaders would not let this charismatic and dangerous rabbi lead their people astray. They had to act—and quickly. A plot was hatched, and it would co-opt the power of their enemy, Rome.

In a clandestine move, the chief priests infiltrated the ranks of Jesus' closest followers and convinced Judas Iscariot to betray Jesus.

Everyone was preparing for the annual feast of Passover, remembering when, long ago, the death angel had passed-over them and God delivered the Israelites from bondage under Pharaoh in Egypt.

And the night came on which Jesus would be betrayed. Jesus and his followers gathered in the upper room for the Passover meal. The Passover was celebrated every year, and many people from around Jerusalem came into the city to celebrate it. While the Passover event marked the miraculous release of the Hebrew people from Egyptian captivity and the eventual establishment of the nation of Israel so many years ago, for Jesus and the disciples this night was special. For the disciples, the preceding events of the week had led them to believe Jesus would finally announce his messiahship and Judah's release from captivity and exile under the Roman hand to everyone. But as they gathered, Jesus did something strange. He took his robe off, picked up a basin of water, came over to Simon Peter and started to wash his feet. Startled that the messiah would even think about washing the dust from his feet reacted, saying, No! As if to say, if anyone will wash feet, I'll wash yours. But Jesus says to him, "One who has bathed does not need to wash, except for the feet, but is entirely clean. And you are clean, though not all of you." This was the plural "you," spoken not just to Simon but to the whole group, particularly Judas. For he knew who was to betray him; for this reason he said, "Not all of you are clean." Jesus knew what lay in Judas's heart and what he planned to do that night. There, at that moment, in the upper room, Jesus began pulling back the veil. He said, "servants are not greater than their master, nor are messengers greater than the one who sent them." But they did not understand. Then it got even stranger. After replacing his robe, he returned to the table and began to explain, initially by quoting part of a Scripture passage from Ps 41:9: "'The one who ate my bread has lifted his heel against me.'" Then Jesus said, "I tell you this now, before it occurs, so that when it does occur, you may believe that I am he. Very truly, I tell you, whoever receives one whom I send receives me; and whoever receives me receives him who sent me." Judas knew he knew. Jesus picked up a piece of bread, soaked it, and gave it to Judas, and said go and "do quickly what you are going to do." No one but Judas understood. To the remaining disciples Jesus said,

> Now the Son of Man has been glorified, and God has been glorified in him. If God has been glorified in him, God will also glorify him in himself and will glorify him at once. Little children, I am with you only a little longer. You will look for me; and as I said to the Jews so now I say to you, "Where I am going, you cannot come." I give you a new commandment, that you love one another. Just as I have loved you, you also should love one another. By this everyone will know that you are my disciples, if you have love for one another.[26]

Even on the night he was betrayed, Jesus started with a lesson, again with a dramatic twist. It is not position and authority that commands power; power is made perfect in weakness. The infinite power of God is displayed in his love. Here, on this night, we can see T. S. Eliot's constant reiteration of the "point." Everything in the whole of Israel's history and in the history of the world draws to this point. The Passover that led to the Exodus is a foreshadowing. The Passover meal that Jesus and his disciples were eating in the upper room is a foreshadowing. As each Passover meal is celebrated, it is an acknowledgement of God's love and grace. Each time the words of institution are spoken in the Eucharist celebration, "Then he took a loaf of bread, and when he had given thanks, he broke it and gave it to them, saying, 'This is my body, which is given for you. Do this in remembrance of me.' And he did the same with the cup after supper, saying, 'This cup that is poured out for you is the new covenant in my blood,'" and we partake, we experience the grace of God.[27] Indeed, every meal we partake is a shadow of this story. God's power is made perfect in his sacrificial love. The way God is seen in the world is in the reflection of this love.

But even on this intimate night, the veil hiding the full extent of God's love was not yet pulled back.

Seemingly orchestrated by Jesus himself, the concrete events of the bigger story were occurring:

- The last meal Jesus ate with his disciples was the Passover meal—with all the symbolic references to bread in the wilderness when the disgruntled Israelites bemoaned no meat, symbolized by the Manna stored in the Ark of the Covenant and how God cared for his people in

---

26. The story in the upper room and the quotes from Jesus are found in John 13:1–35, NRSV.

27. Luke 22:19–21, NRSV.

their forty years of wandering. The wine bespeaks the vine or vineyard found so frequently referenced in the Psalms, in Isaiah, and Hosea and even to the water Jesus turned into wine in his first miracle at the wedding in Cana.

- Judas's betrayal led to the arrest of Jesus in the Garden of Gethsemane, where he had been praying, harkening back to all the many events that have happened in gardens in the history of Israel, especially in the very beginning—in the Garden of Eden. The symbols are vast.

- The arrest led to a mock trial and quick conviction among the chief priests, and Jesus was sent to the Roman proconsul Pilate for judgment and sentencing, where the question of truth comes up. (Pilate asks Jesus, "What is truth?"[28]) The question of truth harkens back to an earlier exchange between Jesus and his disciples, when he said, "I am the way, the truth, and the life. No one comes to the Father except through me."[29] Who is? "I Am," shades of Moses' encounter with God in the burning bush. When Moses asks God, "Whom shall I say sends me to Pharaoh?" God responds, "Tell them 'I AM' sent you." (There is a whole series of "I AM" sayings of Jesus in the New Testament.)

- Though he found no fault in him, but wanting to ensure peace within his region of the empire, Pilate remembered the custom that someone should be released at Passover season. So he asked the chief priests and gathered people whom they wished him to release, a proven robber (Barabbas) or Jesus. Urged by the priests, the crowd selected Barabbas. Shades of the grace extended to all in the Mosaic sacrificial system, now played out in virtue of the substitutionary sacrifice of Jesus.

The die was now cast; Jesus' fate was sealed. He was headed to the cross. A tragedy? Without question! But perhaps, as Tolkien's coined term captures it, a eucatastrophe.[30] The apostle John records Jesus: "Now comes the judgment of this world! Now this world's ruler is going to be thrown out! And when I've been lifted up from the earth, I will draw all people to myself."[31] "Somehow, Jesus's forthcoming death will constitute his victory, God's victory, over 'this world's ruler,' who seems to be not merely

28. John 18:38, NKJV.

29. John 14:6, NKJV.

30. Again, this is a term coined by J. R. R. Tolkien which refers to the sudden turn of events at the end of a story which ensures that the protagonist does not meet some terrible, impending, and very plausible doom. See reference to this term in Tolkien, "On Fairy-Stories."

31. John 12:31–32, KNT. Wright, *Simply Jesus*, 182.

Caesar, but the power that stands behind Caesar and uses him for its dark, destructive purposes."[32] The great conflagration anticipated is at hand, but again in an unexpected way, against an unanticipated enemy, the one who had originally tempted Adam and Eve to strike out on their own. The battle was not against Rome but over sin and death itself.

Jesus was scourged and whipped and must carry his own cross up the hill outside the gates of Jerusalem, to the city garbage dump, called Golgotha—but because of later events Golgotha could perhaps better be called the Mercy Seat of the World.[33] There he is nailed to the cross, and after great agony, from the cross he says, "It is accomplished" or "It is completed." Notice in these words "the echo . . . of Genesis: at the end of the sixth day, God *completed* all the work that he had done. The point was not to rescue people *from* creation, but to rescue creation itself. With the death of Jesus, that work is complete. Now, and only now, and only in this way can the new creation come about."[34] The fulfillment of the foreshadowed Yom Kippur. Jesus died as his mother, "highly favored" by God, watched in her own agony, dying in her heart for her firstborn son.

Impossibly sad! All the high hopes for Israel that had gathered so quickly among so many were now dashed—again, just as in the days of Judas Maccabeus. What happened to this one who was to "reign over the house of Jacob forever," the one of whose "kingdom there will be no end"?[35]

But it was not over!

Arriving early in the morning on the third day, one of Jesus' close friends, Mary of Magdalene, had gone to the tomb where he had been buried to anoint his body with spices, according to Jewish custom. When she arrived, the stone covering the sepulcher had been rolled back. She looked in and saw that Jesus' body was not there, and she was afraid. She thought someone had come and stolen the body. And she went to get Peter, another of Jesus' closest followers. They looked back into the tomb and saw the grave clothes but that Jesus' body was gone; then, still outside the tomb, as Mary was crying, she saw two angels of God sitting in the tomb, and they asked why she was crying. And, of course, she responded that it was because someone had taken the body of her Lord. Then she turned, and someone next to her whom initially she thought to be a gardener, sought to comfort her in her grief. Thinking he must know something, she inquired, "Where have

32. Wright, *Simply Jesus*, 182.

33. Jesus is referred to as the Mercy Seat in Romans 3:25, and in Hebrews 10 he is described as the fulfillment of Yom Kippur, the Jewish Day of Atonement.

34. Wright, *Simply Jesus*, 184.

35. For a theological exploration into Holy Saturday, see Lewis, *Between the Cross and the Resurrection.*

you taken him?" And then Mary was overwhelmed at the realization that the gardener was no gardener at all but Jesus himself, alive! Overjoyed, she reached to hug him, but he stopped her, saying something no less strange than that he was alive—that he had not yet ascended to the Father.

Mary quickly told the others that she had seen Jesus and that he was alive. After all of the excitement that arose when they entered Jerusalem a week ago, then the wonderful but strange Passover dinner they'd had together the previous week and the crashing disappointment and heartache of Thursday night and Friday, Jesus' small band of close followers was stunned—almost catatonic. Now, this Sunday morning, after everything, to learn the body of their astonishing teacher of the last three years had been taken, they were overcome. Then Mary's news: he was not stretched out on the cold hard stone in a dark cavern; his body was not stolen where they would never find him, but he was standing upright in front of her, Alive![36]

This is the climactic end to the drama of God's redemption. Jesus is Abraham's seed: in Christ, "Israel" is fulfilled, a New Adam is born. God's reign has come on earth as it is in heaven. The whole Judeo-Christian story is rife with foreshadowing, types, and symbols. It is like a mythopoetic grand poem, as J. R. R. Tolkien said to C. S. Lewis—but the Grand Poem has become fact.

CONSUMMATION

We now live in the already-and-not-yet time of redemption accomplished and not yet fully realized. This is the time in which the love of God is being witnessed to, still in a glass, darkly, but with the clear light shining through,

---

36. For the scriptural account of the resurrection morning, see John 20:1–18. Because it is not my scope or focus, I will not address the critical issues surrounding the resurrection. I simply point to the detailed scholarly work by N. T. Wright, *The Resurrection of the Son of God*. For cursory reference, I mention here Wright's own brief comments in his popular work *Simply Jesus*: "I have argued in detail elsewhere [in *The Resurrection of the Son of God*] that the only possible explanation for the rise of Christianity and for its taking the shape that it did was that Jesus of Nazareth, three days after being very thoroughly dead (Roman executioners were professional killers and didn't let would-be rebel leaders slip out of their clutches), was found by his followers to be very thoroughly and very bodily alive again. His tomb was empty; had it not been, his followers would have believed they were seeing some kind of an apparition. Such things were well known in the ancient world, as in fact they are today. Equally, they really did see, touch, and share food with Jesus as a real, bodily presence; had they not, they would have concluded that an empty tomb meant that the grave had been robbed. Such things were better known in the ancient world than they are today. The combination of the empty tomb and the definite, solid appearances is far and away the best explanation for everything that happened subsequently" (192).

as the reign of God is lived out in the New Adam, the image of God restored in his creatures, which is the Body of Christ on Earth. This in-between reality remains frail and succumbs to the temptations of the old, sinful nature, persistently not living up to the reality of the love to which it is drawn and in which it will ultimately be fulfilled at the final coming.

This is the concrete, real, transcendent historical story of Creation, Fall, and Redemption. Considered as a poem, it's concrete, real, and full of images that both speak in themselves as concrete things and yet are windows onto an even bigger story, a cosmic story—the Grand Story of the Triune God. This story is the localized historical grand narrative of Abraham, Isaac, and Jacob (Israel), and yet it is also the even grander transcendent narrative of the Word of God, the instrument and the sustainer of the whole creation, the I AM who is the Father of Adam, Abraham, Isaac, Jacob, Moses, and David and who in his person is the fulfillment of Israel itself, the Second Fulfilled Adam—the one who in his person is what all human beings were always meant to be. As such, in him we are now the reflection of God the King in this world, his realm, his theater of reign. It is in this Grand Drama that all smaller stories find their place. It is in the central figure of this drama, Jesus Christ, that we find that "life exists, and identity"—in Him that we live and move and have our being—that "the powerful play goes on and [we] will contribute a verse."

In this story we see God's mythopoetic project, in the myth become fact. In this story we find our true identity and our true home—the one toward which our deepest longings yearn. Here, at the end of all our exploring, we will arrive where we started and know the place for the first time.

Summary of the Christian Story—God's Grand Story of the World

Eternity Past

His-Story

THE "POINT"
Incarnation, Life, Death, Resurrection, Ascension

The "Center"
Of World History

Eternity Future

Creation —— Adam —— Abraham —— Israel —— Prophets —— Early Church —— Fractured Church —— Consummation

The New Heavens
& New Earth

Bibliography

Abraham, William J. *Crossing the Threshold of Divine Revelation*. Grand Rapids: Eerdmans, 2005.

Allen, Diogenes. *Christian Belief in a Postmodern World*. Louisville: Westminster John Knox, 1989.

Allen, Diogenes, and Eric O. Springsted. *Philosophy for Understanding Theology*. Louisville: Westminster John Knox, 2007.

Aquinas, Thomas. *Summa Contra Gentiles*. Translated by Joseph Rickaby, SJ. London: Burns and Oates, 1905. http://www3.nd.edu/Departments/Maritain/etext/gc.htm.

———. *Summa Theologica*. Translated by the Fathers of the English Dominican Province. Cincinnati: Benzinger Brothers, 1947. http://www.sacred-texts.com/chr/aquinas/summa/index.htm.

Aristotle. *The Poetics of Aristotle*. Translated by S. H. Butcher. http://www.literatureproject.com/poetics/index.htm.

Armstrong, D. M. *Nominalism & Realism: Universals & Scientific Realism*. Vol. 1. Cambridge: Cambridge University Press, 2009.

———. *A Theory of Universals: Universals & Scientific Realism*, Vol. 2. Cambridge: Cambridge University Press, 2009.

———. *Universals: An Opinionated Introduction*. Boulder: Westview, 1989.

Arnell, Carla A. "On Beauty, Justice, and the Sublime in C. S. Lewis's *Till We Have Faces*." *Christianity and Literature* 52, no. 1 (Autumn 2002): 23–33.

Augustine. *The Confessions of Saint Augustine*. Franklin Center, PA: The Franklin Library, 1982.

Barr, Stephen M. "The Beginning of the Universe, Physics and God." YouTube video, 54:03, lecture posted January 7, 2017, by Theology, Philosophy and Science. https://www.youtube.com/watch?v=qe9SQiNRBKo.

———. "First Words." Review of *Why Only Us: Language and Evolution*, by Robert C. Berwick and Noam Chomsky. *First Things*. April 2017. https://www.firstthings.com/article/2017/04/first-words.

———. "Much Ado About 'Nothing': Stephen Hawking and the Self-Creating Universe." *First Things*. September 10, 2010. http://www.firstthings.com/

onthesquare/2010/09/much-ado-about-ldquonothingrdquo-stephen-hawking-and-the-self-creating-universe.

———. "Science and Religion: The Myth of Conflict." YouTube video, 1:31:55, lecture posted November 9, 2015, by Copernicus Center for Interdisciplinary Studies. https://www.youtube.com/watch?v=fwaHcSK9NGA.

Begbie, Jeremy S. *Resounding Truth: Christian Wisdom in the World of Music.* Grand Rapids: Baker Academic, 2007.

Behe, Michael. *Darwin's Black Box: The Biochemical Challenge to Evolution.* New York: Simon and Schuster, 1996.

Bellah, Robert N. *Religion in Human Evolution: From the Paleolithic to the Axial Age.* Boston: Harvard University Press, 2011.

Berger, Peter L. *A Rumor of Angels: Modern Society and the Rediscovery of the Supernatural.* Expanded ed. New York: Anchor, 1990.

———. *The Sacred Canopy: Elements of a Sociological Theory of Religion.* New York: Anchor, 1990.

Berger, Peter, Brigitte Berger, and Hansfried Kellner. *The Homeless Mind: Modernization and Consciousness.* New York: Vintage, 1974.

Berwick, Robert C., and Noam Chomsky. *Why Only Us: Language and Evolution.* Cambridge, MA: MIT Press, 2015.

Bishop, Morris. *The Middle Ages.* New York: Houghton Mifflin, 2001.

Boersma, Hans. *Heavenly Participation: The Weaving of a Sacramental Tapestry.* Grand Rapids: Eerdmans, 2011.

———. *Nouvelle Théologie & Sacramental Ontology: A Return to Mystery.* Oxford: Oxford University Press, 2009.

Bonaventure. *On the Reduction of the Arts to Theology: Translation with Introduction and Commentary.* Prepared by Zachary Hayes, OFM. Allegany, NY: The Franciscan Institute of St. Bonaventure University, 1996.

Bray, Gerald L. "Deification." In *New Dictionary of Theology*, edited by Sinclair B. Ferguson, David F. Wright, and J. I. Packer. Downers Grove, IL: IVP Academic, 1988.

Brians, Paul. "The Enlightenment." Accessed August 4, 2015. http://public.wsu.edu/~brians/hum_303/enlightenment.html (page discontinued).

Bristow, William. "Enlightenment." In *Stanford Encyclopedia of Philosophy.* August 20, 2010. http://plato.stanford.edu/entries/enlightenment/.

Brock, Rita Nakashima. "Caitlin Jenner, Rachel Dolezal and the American Politics of Identity." *Huffington Post.* June 15, 2015. http://www.huffingtonpost.com/rita-nakashima-brock-ph-d/caitlin-jenner-rachel-dol_b_7574522.html.

Cahill, Thomas. *The Gift of the Jews: How a Tribe of Nomads Changed the Way Everyone Thinks and Feels.* New York: Nan A. Talese / Anchor, 1998.

Campbell, Joseph, and Bill Moyers. *The Power of Myth.* Edited by Bettie Sue Flowers. New York: Doubleday, 1988.

Candler, Peter M. "Tolkien or Nietzsche: Philology and Nihilism." In *Tolkien Among the Moderns*, edited by Ralph C. Wood, 95–130. Notre Dame: University of Notre Dame Press, 2015.

Carpenter, Humphrey. *The Inklings: C. S. Lewis, J. R. R. Tolkien, Charles Williams and Their Friends.* Boston: Houghton Mifflin, 1979.

Carroll, Lewis. *Through the Looking-Glass (And What Alice Found There).* http://literature.org/authors/carroll-lewis/through-the-looking-glass/index.html.

Cavanaugh, William T. "'Creation's Final Law': Evolutionary Violence and the Fall." *Books & Culture*. July/August 2016. http://www.booksandculture.com/ articles/2016/julaug/creations-final-law.html.

Charry, Ellen T. *God and the Art of Happiness*. Grand Rapids: Eerdmans, 2010.

Chesterton, G. K. *What's Wrong with the World?* New York: Sheed & Ward, 1910.

Cicero, Marcus Tullius. *Ethical Writings I (On Moral Duties)*. Translated by Andrew P. Peabody. Boston: Little, Brown, 1887. http://oll.libertyfund.org/titles/542.

Clendenin, Daniel B. *Eastern Orthodox Christianity: A Western Perspective*. Grand Rapids: Baker, 1994.

Coleridge, Samuel Taylor. *Poems of Samuel Taylor Coleridge*. Norwalk: The Easton Press, 1967.

Colish, Marcia L. *Medieval Foundations of the Western Intellectual Tradition: 400–1400*. New Haven: Yale University Press, 1998.

Copan, Paul. "Is Creatio Ex Nihilo A Post-Biblical Invention? An Examination Of Gerhard May's Proposal." *Trinity Journal* 17, no. 1 (Spring 1996): 77–93. https:// earlychurch.org.uk/article_exnihilo_copan.html.

Cowan, Louise, and Os Guinness. *Invitation to the Classics: A Guide to Books You've Always Wanted to Read*. Grand Rapids: Baker, 1998.

Craig, William Lane. "Argument from Contingency." Reasonable Faith. Accessed June 28, 2017. http://www.reasonablefaith.org/defenders-1-podcast/transcript/s04-01.

———. "The *Kalam* Cosmological Argument." Reasonable Faith. Accessed June 28, 2017. http://www.reasonablefaith.org/popular-articles-the-kalam-cosmological-argument.

Cross, Richard. *The Medieval Christian Philosophers: An Introduction*. New York: IB Tauris, 2014.

Crouch, Andy. *Culture Making: Recovering Our Creative Calling*. Downers Grove, IL: InterVarsity, 2008.

———. "To Play and to Pray." Review of *Resounding Truth*, by Jeremy Begbie. Andy-Crouch.com. http://andy-crouch.com/articles/to_play_and_to_pray.

dal Covolo, Fr. Enrico. "The Encounter of Faith and Reason in the Fathers of the Church." *L'Osservatore Romano*. March 17, 1999. https://www.catholicculture.org/ culture/library/view.cfm?recnum=940.

Davies, Brian. *An Introduction to the Philosophy of Religion*. 3rd ed. New York: Oxford University Press, 2004.

Deffinbaugh, Bob. "The Creation of the Heavens and the Earth (Genesis 1:1—2:3)." Bible.org. May 10, 2004. https://bible.org/seriespage/2-creation-heavens-and-earth-genesis-11-23.

Dickens, Charles. *Hard Times*. New York: Penguin Classics, 1995.

Dupré, Louis. *The Enlightenment and the Intellectual Foundations of Modern Culture*. New Haven: Yale University Press, 2004.

———. *Passage to Modernity: An Essay in the Hermeneutics of Nature and Culture*. New Haven: Yale University Press, 1993.

———. *Religion and the Rise of Modern Culture*. Notre Dame: University of Notre Dame Press, 2008.

Durant, Will, and Ariel Durant. *The Story of Civilization: The Age of Reason Begins*. New York: Simon and Schuster, 1961.

Eliot, T. S. *Four Quartets*. New York: Houghton Mifflin Harcourt, 1971.

Ellul, Jacques. *The Technological Society*. Translated by John Wilkinson. New York: Vintage, 1964.

Esolen, Anthony. "Humor on the Move: In the Christian World, Comedy Is King." *Touchstone* 23, no. 3 (May/June 2010): 19–24.

Evans, C. Stephen. *Natural Signs and Knowledge of God*. New York: Oxford University Press, 2010.

———. "Realism and Antirealism in Kierkegaard's Concluding Unscientific Postscript." In *Kierkegaard on Faith and the Self: Collected Essays*, 29–46. Waco, TX: Baylor University Press, 2006.

———. *Why Christian Faith Still Makes Sense: A Response to Contemporary Challenges*. Grand Rapids: Baker Academic, 2015.

Feser, Edward. *Edward Feser* (blog). http://edwardfeser.blogspot.com/.

Firestein, Stuart. *Ignorance: How It Drives Science*. Oxford: Oxford University Press, 2012.

Gallup. "Marriage" (poll). Accessed June 10, 2016. http://www.gallup.com/poll/117328/Marriage.aspx.

Gardner, John. *On Moral Fiction*. New York: Basic, 1977.

Gay, Craig. *The Way of the Modern World: Or Why It's Tempting to Live as if God Doesn't Exist*. Grand Rapids: Eerdmans, 1998.

"Genesis with N. T. Wright." BioLogos. Accessed July 1, 2017. http://biologos.org/resources/audio-visual/nt-wright-on-genesis.

Gillespie, Michael Allen. *The Theological Origins of Modernity*. Chicago: University of Chicago Press, 2009.

Grant, Edward. *The Foundations of Modern Science in the Middle Ages: Their Religious, Institutional and Intellectual Contexts*. New York: Cambridge University Press, 1996.

———. *God and Reason in the Middle Ages*. Cambridge: Cambridge University Press, 2001.

———. *Science and Religion, 400 B.C. to A.D. 1550: From Aristotle to Copernicus*. Baltimore: Johns Hopkins University Press, 2004.

Grant, Michael. *The Ancient Historians*. New York: Barnes & Noble Books, 1970.

Gregory, Brad S. *The Unintended Reformation: How a Religious Revolution Secularized Society*. Cambridge, MA: Belknap, 2012.

Guardini, Romano. *The End of the Modern World*. Wilmington, DE: ISI, 2001.

Halpern, Baruch. *The First Historians: The Hebrew Bible and History*. University Park, PA: Pennsylvania State University Press, 1996.

Hare, John E. "Karl Barth, American Evangelicals, and Kant." In *Karl Barth and American Evangelicalism*, edited by Bruce L. McCormick and Clifford B. Anderson, 73–90. Grand Rapids: Eerdmans, 2011.

Hart, Addison H. "Evangelical Ressourcement." Review of *Ancient-Future Faith: Rethinking Evangelicalism for a Postmodern World*, by Robert E. Webber, and *Retrieving the Tradition and Renewing Evangelicalism: A Primer for Suspicious Protestants*, by D. H. Williams. *Touchstone* 14, no. 3 (April 2001). http://touchstonemag.com/archives/article.php?id=14-03-038-b.

Hart, David Bentley. *Atheist Delusions: The Christian Revolution and Its Fashionable Enemies*. New Haven: Yale University Press, 2009.

———. *The Beauty of the Infinite: The Aesthetics of Christian Truth*. Grand Rapids: Eerdmans, 2003.

————. *The Experience of God: Being, Consciousness, Bliss*. New Haven: Yale University Press, 2013.

Hawking, Stephen, and Leonard Mlodinow. *The Grand Design*. New York: Bantam, 2010.

Heidegger, Martin. *The Principle of Reason*. Translated by Reginald Lilly. Bloomington, IN: Indiana University Press, 1991.

"Heraclitus." In *The Cambridge Dictionary of Philosophy*. 2nd ed. New York: Cambridge University Press, 1999.

Heyes, Cressida. "Identity Politics." In *Stanford Encyclopedia of Philosophy* online. Last revised March 23, 2016. http://plato.stanford.edu/entries/identity-politics/.

Hofstadter, Albert, and Richard Kuhns, eds. *Philosophies of Art and Beauty: Selected Readings in Aesthetics from Plato to Heidegger*. Chicago: University of Chicago Press, 1976.

Holyer, Robert. "C. S. Lewis on the Epistemic Significance of Imagination," *Soundings* 74, no. 1–2 (Spring/Summer 1991). ISSN. 0038–1861.

Hopkins, Gerard Manley. *Poems and Prose of Gerard Manley Hopkins*. Norwalk: The Easton Press, 1995.

Howard, Thomas. *Chance or the Dance?: A Critique of Modern Secularism*. San Francisco: Ignatius, 2001.

————. *Dove Descending: A Journey into T. S. Eliot's Four Quartets*. San Francisco: Ignatius, 2006.

Howard, Thomas Albert, ed. *Imago Dei: Human Dignity in Ecumenical Perspective*. Washington, DC: The Catholic University of America Press, 2013.

Hülsz, Enrique. "Heraclitus on Logos: Language, Rationality and the Real." In *Doctrine and Doxography: Studies on Heraclitus and Pythagoras*, edited by David Sider and Dirk Obbink, 281–301. Berlin/Boston: De Gruyter, 2013.

Hume, David. *Dialogues Concerning Natural Religion*. Edited by N. Kemp Smith. Edinburgh: Nelson, 1947.

Jenkins, Philip. "Believing in the Global South." *First Things*. December 1, 2006. https://www.firstthings.com/article/2006/12/believing-in-the-global-south.

Jenson, Robert W. "How the World Lost Its Story." *First Things* 36 (October 1993): 19–24.

John Paul II. *Fides et Ratio*. Vatican: Libreria Editrice Vaticana, 1998. http://w2.vatican.va/content/john-paul-ii/en/encyclicals/documents/hf_jp-ii_enc_14091998_fides-et-ratio.html.

Jones, W. T. *A History of Western Philosophy*. 2nd ed. 5 vols. New York: Harcourt Brace Jovanovich, 1969–70.

Joyner, James. "God Did Not Create Universe: Stephen Hawking." *Outside the Beltway*. September 2, 2010. http://www.outsidethebeltway.com/god-did-not-create-universe-stephen-hawking/.

Kaku, Michio. "M-Theory: The Mother of All SuperStrings." Dr. Michio Kaku (blog). Accessed June 28, 2017. http://mkaku.org/home/articles/m-theory-the-mother-of-all-superstrings/.

Kierkegaard, Søren. *Philosophical Fragments*. Edited and translated by Howard V. Hong and Edna H. Hong. Princeton, NJ: Princeton University Press, 1985.

Kosiński, Jerzy. *Being There*. New York: Bantam, 1970.

Koyré, Alexander. *From the Closed World to the Infinite Universe*. Baltimore: Johns Hopkins University Press, 1957.

Kreeft, Peter. "20 Arguments for God's Existence." Strange Notions. Accessed June 28, 2017. http://strangenotions.com/god-exists/.

————. Heaven: The Heart's Deepest Longing. San Francisco: Ignatius, 1989.

Lewis, Alan E. Between the Cross and the Resurrection: A Theology of Holy Saturday. Grand Rapids: Eerdmans, 2001.

Lewis, C. S. The Abolition of Man: How Education Develops Man's Sense of Morality. New York: MacMillan, 1947.

————. "Bluspels and Flalansferes: A Semantic Nightmare." In Selected Literary Essays, edited by Walter Hooper, 251–65. Cambridge: Cambridge University Press, 1969.

————. The Discarded Image. Cambridge: Cambridge University Press, 1964.

————. The Great Divorce. New York: Macmillan, 1946.

————. "Is Theology Poetry?" In The Weight of Glory and Other Addresses, 116–40. New York: HarperOne, 2001.

————. The Lion, the Witch and the Wardrobe. New York: HarperCollins, 1978.

————. "Meditation in a Toolshed." In God in the Dock: Essays on Theology and Ethics, edited by Walter Hooper, 230–34. Grand Rapids: Eerdmans, 1970.

————. Mere Christianity. New York: Macmillan, 1979.

————. "Myth Became Fact." In God in the Dock: Essays on Theology and Ethics, edited by Walter Hooper, 54–60. Grand Rapids: Eerdmans, 1970.

————. Surprised By Joy. New York: Harcourt, Brace & World, 1955.

————. Till We Have Faces: A Myth Retold. New York: Harcourt, 1956.

————. "Transposition." In The Weight of Glory and Other Addresses, 91–115. New York: HarperOne, 2001.

————. "The Weight of Glory." In The Weight of Glory and Other Addresses, 25–46. New York: HarperOne, 2001.

Liddell, Henry George, and Robert Scott. A Lexicon: Liddell and Scott's Greek-English Lexicon. Oxford: Clarendon Press, 1972.

MacIntyre, Alasdair. Whose Justice? Which Rationality? Notre Dame: University of Notre Dame Press, 1988.

MacKinnon, Donald. Themes in Theology: The Three-Fold Cord. Edinburgh: T&T Clark, 1987.

Marsden, George M. The Twilight of the American Enlightenment: The 1950s and the Crisis of Liberal Belief. New York: Basic, 2014.

May, Gerhard. Creatio ex Nihilo: The Doctrine of "Creation out of Nothing" in Early Christian Thought. Edinburgh: T&T Clark, 1995.

McClay, Wilfred M. "Uncomfortable Unbelief." First Things. May 1, 2008. https://www.firstthings.com/article/2008/05/004-uncomfortable-unbelief.

McGrath, Alister. "Atheism and the Enlightenment: Leszek Kołakowski and the Intellectual Roots of the 'New Atheism.'" Paper presented at an international symposium to mark the eightieth birthday of Leszek Kołakowski, All Souls College, Oxford, October 2007.

————. C. S. Lewis—A Life: Eccentric Genius, Reluctant Prophet. Carol Stream, IL: Tyndale, 2013.

————. A Fine-Tuned Universe: The Quest for God in Science and Theology. Louisville: Westminster John Knox, 2009.

————. The Intellectual World of C. S. Lewis. Malden, MA: Wiley-Blackwell, 2014.

————. The Open Secret: A New Vision for Natural Theology. Malden, MA: Blackwell, 2008.

————. *A Scientific Theology*. 3 vols. Grand Rapids: Eerdmans, 2001–3.

McManus, Barbara F. "Outline of Aristotle's Theory of Tragedy in the Poetics." Accessed June 9, 2011. http://www2.cnr.edu/home/bmcmanus/poetics.html (page discontinued).

Milbank, John. *Theology and Social Theory: Beyond Secular Reason*. 2nd ed. Oxford: Blackwell, 2006.

Moreland, J. P., and William Lane Craig. *Philosophical Foundations for a Christian Worldview*. Downers Grove, IL: InterVarsity, 2003.

Myers, Ken. "The Lost Sense of Learning." Contours of Culture. *Touchstone* 26, no. 3 (May/June 2013). http://www.touchstonemag.com/archives/article.php?id=26–03-014-c.

Naugle, David K. *Reordered Love, Reordered Lives: Learning the Deep Meaning of Happiness*. Grand Rapids: Eerdmans, 2008.

————. *Worldview: The History of a Concept*. Grand Rapids: Eerdmans, 2002.

Nietzsche, Friedrich. *The Gay Science*. Edited by Walter Kaufmann. New York: Vintage, 1974.

————. *On the Genealogy of Morality*. Edited by Keith Ansell-Pearson. Translated by Carol Diethe. Cambridge: Cambridge University Press, 2006. http://www.cambridge.org/9780521871235.

————. *Thus Spoke Zarathustra: A Book for All and None*. Translated by Walter Kaufmann. New York: Modern Library, 1995.

————. *Untimely Meditations*. Edited by Daniel Breazeale. Translated by R. J. Hollingdale. Cambridge: Cambridge University Press, 2007.

Noll, Mark. *From Every Tribe and Nation: A Historian's Discovery of the Global Christian Story*. Grand Rapids: Baker, 2014.

Oden, Thomas C. *After Modernity, What?* Grand Rapids: Zondervan, 1990.

Patrick, James. "The Limits of Skepticism." *Text and Talk* (presentation). December 13, 2014, unpublished.

Pearce, Joseph. "J. R. R. Tolkien: Truth and Myth." Catholic Authors. Accessed July 1, 2017. http://catholicauthors.com/tolkien.html.

————. *Tolkien Man and Myth: A Literary Life*. London: HarperCollins, 1998.

Pearson, Keith Ansell, and Duncan Large, eds. *The Nietzsche Reader*. Malden, MA: Blackwell, 2006.

Peck, Roger. "C. S. Lewis and Tolkien on Myth and Knowledge." *Faith*. March 1, 2011. http://www.faith.org.uk/article/march-april-2011-cs-lewis-and-tolkien-on-myth-and-knowledge.

Peterson, Eugene. *Christ Plays in Ten Thousand Places: A Conversation in Spiritual Theology*. Grand Rapids: Eerdmans, 2005.

Pew Research Center. "Belief in God." *Religious Landscape Study*. Accessed June 28, 2017. http://www.pewforum.org/religious-landscape-study/belief-in-god/.

Plantinga, Alvin. *Does God Have a Nature?* Milwaukee: Marquette University Press, 1980.

————. "How to Be An Anti-Realist." *Proceedings and Addresses of the American Philosophical Association* 56, no. 1 (September 1982): 47–70. http://www.jstor.org/stable/3131293?seq=1#page_scan_tab_contents.

————. "On Rejecting the Theory of Common Ancestry: A Reply to Hasker." *Perspectives on Science and Christian Faith* 44 (December 1992): 258–63.

————. "When Faith and Reason Clash: Evolution and the Bible." *Christian Scholars Review* 21, no. 1 (September 1991): 8–33.

————. *Where the Conflict Really Lies: Science, Religion, and Naturalism.* Oxford: Oxford University Press, 2011.

Plato. *The Republic. Plato Selected Dialogues.* Translated by Benjamin Jowett. Franklin Center, PA: The Franklin Library, 1983.

"Poetry." In *The Lost Country: A Literary Journal of the Exiles* 3, no. 1 (Fall 2014): 1.

Postman, Neil. *Technopoly: The Surrender of Culture to Technology.* New York: Vintage, 1993.

Prager, Dennis. "Cahill's Gift." Review of *The Gifts of the Jews: How a Tribe of Desert Nomads Changed the Way Everyone Thinks and Feels,* by Thomas Cahill. *First Things* no. 87 (November 1998): 42–50. http://www.firstthings.com/article/2009/03/002-cahills-gift-33.

Pucker, Joe Jr. *The Apologetics of Joy.* Eugene, OR: Wipf & Stock, 2012.

Rakestraw, Robert V. "Becoming Like God: An Evangelical Doctrine of Theosis." *Journal of the Evangelical Theological Society* 40, no. 2 (June 1997): 257–269.

Rea, Michael. "Divine Hiddenness, Divine Silence." In *Philosophy of Religion: An Anthology,* 6th ed., edited by Louis Pojman and Michael Rea, 266–75. Boston: Wadsworth / Cengage, 2011.

Reichenbach, Bruce. "Cosmological Argument." In *Stanford Encyclopedia of Philosophy* online. Revised November 10, 2016. https://plato.stanford.edu/entries/cosmological-argument.

Reno, R. R., and Barbara McClay, eds. *Religion and the Social Sciences.* Eugene, OR: Cascade Books, 2015.

Sartwell, Chrispin. "The 'Postmodern' Intellectual Roots of Today's Campus Mobs." *Wall Street Journal.* March 24, 2017. https://www.wsj.com/articles/the-postmodern-intellectual-roots-of-todays-campus-mobs-1490394294.

Sauter, Gerhard. *The Question of Meaning: A Theological and Philosophical Orientation.* Translated and edited by Geoffrey W. Bromiley. Grand Rapids: Eerdmans, 1995.

Sayers, Dorothy. *The Mind of the Maker.* San Francisco: HarperSanFrancisco, 1979.

Schmemann, Alexander. *For the Life of the World: Sacraments and Orthodoxy.* Rev. ed. Yonkers, NY: St. Vladimir's Seminary Press, 1973.

Scruton, Roger. *The Face of God: The Gifford Lectures* 2010. New York: Continuum International, 2012.

————. *The Soul of the World.* Princeton, NJ: Princeton University Press, 2014.

"A Secular Age." Harvard University Press (website). Accessed June 28, 2017. http://www.hup.harvard.edu/catalog.php?isbn=9780674026766&content=reviews.

Smith, Christian. *Moral, Believing Animals: Human Personhood and Culture.* New York: Oxford University Press, 2003.

————. *What Is a Person: Rethinking Humanity, Social Life, and the Moral Good from the Person Up.* Chicago: University of Chicago Press, 2010.

Smith, Christian, and Melinda Lundquist Denton. *Soul Searching: The Religious and Spiritual Lives of American Teenagers.* Oxford: Oxford University Press, 2005.

Smith, Christian, and Patricia Snell. *Souls in Transition: The Religious and Spiritual Lives of Emerging Adults.* New York: Oxford University Press, 2009.

Smith, James K. A. *Desiring the Kingdom: Worship, Worldview, and Cultural Formation.* Grand Rapids: Baker, 2009.

———. *How (Not) to Be Secular: Reading Charles Taylor.* Grand Rapids: Eerdmans, 2014.

———. *Who's Afraid of Relativism?: Community, Contingency, and Creaturehood.* Grand Rapids: Baker, 2014.

Stark, Rodney. *Discovering God: The Origins of the Great Religions and the Evolution of Belief.* New York: HarperOne, 2007.

———. *God's Battalions: The Case for the Crusades.* New York: HarperOne, 2009.

Stumpf, Samuel Enoch. *Philosophy: History and Problems.* New York: McGraw-Hill, 1971.

Swinburne, Richard. *The Existence of God.* 2nd ed. New York: Oxford University Press, 2004.

———. *Is There a God?* Oxford: Oxford University Press, 1996.

Taylor, Charles. *A Secular Age.* Cambridge, MA: Belknap, 2007.

Taylor, Daniel. "Rest for the Weary." Review of *Dove Descending: A Journey into T.S. Eliot's Four Quartets,* by Thomas Howard. *Books and Culture.* January/February 2009. http://www.booksandculture.com/articles/2009/janfeb/15.41.html.

———. *Tell Me a Story: The Life-Shaping Power of Our Stories.* St. Paul, MN: Bog Walk, 2001.

Taylor, James S. *Poetic Knowledge: The Rediscovery of Education.* New York: State University of New York Press, 1998.

Thomas, David. "Early Muslim Relations with Christianity." *Anvil* 6, no. 1 (1989): 23–31.

Thoreau, Henry David. *Walden.* Boston: Houghton, Mifflin, and Co., 1906. www.walden.org/work/walden.

Tolkien, J. R. R. *The Lord of the Rings.* Collector's ed. Boston: Houghton Mifflin, 1987.

———. *Tolkien on Fairy-Stories.* Expanded ed. Edited by Verlyn Flieger and Douglas A. Anderson. New York: HarperCollins, 2014.

"T. S. Eliot—Biographical." Nobelprize.org. Accessed June 28, 2017. http://www.nobelprize.org/nobel_prizes/literature/laureates/1948/eliot-bio.html.

Turner, James. *Without God, Without Creed: The Origins of Unbelief in America.* Baltimore: Johns Hopkins University Press, 1985.

Vanhoozer, Kevin J. *The Drama of Doctrine: A Canonical Linguistic Approach to Doctrine.* Louisville: Westminster John Knox, 2005.

———. "In Bright Shadow: C. S. Lewis on the Imagination for Theology and Discipleship." YouTube video, 56:46, lecture posted October 21, 2013, by Desiring God. https://www.youtube.com/watch?v=nw2yDvX18q8.

———. *Remythologizing Theology: Divine Action, Passion.* New York: Cambridge University Press, 2010.

Vidal, Gore. "Gore Vidal on America." Interview by Studs Terkel (1961). The Story. August 16, 2013. http://www.thestory.org/stories/2013-08/gore-vidal-america.

von Balthasar, Hans Urs. *Love Alone Is Credible.* Translated by D. C. Schindler. San Francisco: Ignatius, 2004.

Walton, John. *The Lost World of Adam and Eve: Genesis 2—3 and the Human Origins Debate.* Downers Grove, IL: IVP Academic, 2015.

———. *The Lost World of Genesis One: Ancient Cosmology and the Origins Debate.* Downers Grove, IL: InterVarsity, 2009.

Ward, Michael. "C. S. Lewis on Reason and Imagination in Science and Religion." YouTube video, 1:37:36, lecture posted April 8, 2013, by Chesterton House. https://www.youtube.com/watch?v=WYgVNvIurpQ.

———. "The Good Serves the Better and Both the Best." In *Imaginative Apologetics*, edited by Andrew Davison, 59–78. Grand Rapids: Baker Academic, 2011.

———. "How Lewis Lit the Way to Better Apologetics." *Christianity Today.* October, 22, 2013. http://www.christianitytoday.com/ct/2013/november/cs-lewis-better-apologetics.html.

———. "'Looking along the Beam': Divine and Literary Hiddenness in C. S. Lewis's *The Voyage of the 'Dawn Treader.'*" In *C. S. Lewis and the Inklings: Discovering Hidden Truth*, edited by Salwa Khoddam, Mark Hall, and Jason Fisher, 10–32. Newcastle upon Tyne, UK: Cambridge Scholar's Publishing, 2012.

———. "Science and Religion in the Writings of C. S. Lewis." *Science & Christian Belief* 25, no. 1 (April 2013): 3–16.

Ware, Timothy. *The Orthodox Church.* New York: Penguin Books, 1997.

Webb, Stephen H. *The Divine Voice.* Eugene, OR: Wipf and Stock, 2004.

Whitman, Walt. "O Me! O Life!" In *Leaves of Grass.* http://whitmanarchive.org/published/LG/1881/poems/127.

Williams, Charles. *Outlines of Romantic Theology with Which Is Reprinted, Religion and Love in Dante: The Theology of Romantic Love.* Edited by Alice Mary Hadfield. Grand Rapids: Eerdmans, 1990.

Williams, Rowan. "Deification." In *The Westminster Dictionary of Christian Spirituality*, edited by Gordon S. Wakefield. Philadelphia: Westminster, 1983.

Wilson, Peter H. "The Holy Roman Empire." *History Today* 66, no. 4 (April 2016). http://www.historytoday.com/peter-h-wilson/holy-roman-empire.

Wolterstorff, Nicholas. *Art in Action: Toward a Christian Aesthetic.* Grand Rapids: Eerdmans, 1980.

———. *Divine Discourse: Philosophical Reflections on the Claim That God Speaks.* New York: Cambridge University Press, 1995.

———. *On Universals: An Essay on Ontology.* Chicago: University of Chicago Press, 1970.

———. *Reason within the Bounds of Religion.* Grand Rapids: Eerdmans, 1984.

Wood, James. "Reformed Sacramental Ontology." The Blog of James Wood. March 31, 2016. https://jamesrwood.com/2016/03/31/reformed-sacramental-ontology/.

Wood, Jay W. *Epistemology: Becoming Intellectually Virtuous.* Downers Grove, IL: InterVarsity, 1998.

Wood, Ralph C., ed. *Tolkien among the Moderns.* Notre Dame: University of Notre Dame Press, 2015.

Wood, Robert E. *Placing Aesthetics: Reflections on the Philosophic Tradition.* Athens, OH: Ohio University Press, 1999.

Wright, N. T. "Abandon Studying the Historical Jesus? No, We Need History." *Christianity Today.* April 9, 2010. http://www.christianitytoday.com/ct/2010/april/16.27.html.

———. *The Kingdom New Testament: A Contemporary Translation.* New York: HarperOne, 2011.

———. *The Resurrection of the Son of God.* Minneapolis: Fortress, 2003.

———. *Simply Jesus: A New Vision of Who He Was, What He Did, and Why He Matters.* New York: HarperOne, 2013.

Yeats, W. B. *The Poems*. Edited by Richard J. Finneran. Rev. ed. New York: Macmillan, 1989.

Zachhuber, Johannes. "Christology after Chalcedon and the Transformation of the Philosophical Tradition: Reflections on a Neglected Topic." In *The Ways of Byzantine Philosophy*, edited by Mikonja Knežević, 89–110. Alhambra, CA: Sebastian Press, 2015.

Made in the USA
Lexington, KY
26 September 2017